THE FORMS OF THE OLD TESTAMENT LITERATURE

*Now available

D0927426

EXODUS 1–18

GEORGE W. COATS

The Forms of the Old Testament Literature
VOLUME IIA
Rolf P. Knierim and Gene M. Tucker, editors

WILLIAM B. EERDMANS PUBLISHING COMPANY
GRAND RAPIDS, MICHIGAN / CAMBRIDGE, U.K.

© 1999 Wm. B. Eerdmans Publishing Co.
255 Jefferson Ave. S.E., Grand Rapids, Michigan 49503 /
P. O. Box 163, Cambridge CB3 9BA U.K.

Printed in the United States of America

05 04 03 02 01 00 99   7 6 5 4 3 2 1

Library of Congress Cataloging-in-Publication Data

Coats, George W.
Exodus 1–18 / George W. Coats.
p.   cm.   — (The forms of the Old Testament literature; v. 2A)
Includes bibliographical references.
ISBN 0-8028-0592-2 (pbk.: alk. paper)
1. Bible. O.T. Exodus I–XVIII — Criticism, Form.
I. Title.   II. Series.
BS1245.2.C58   1999
222′.12066 — dc21   98-37772
                                                            CIP

CONTENTS

ABBREVIATIONS AND SYMBOLS

I. MISCELLANEOUS ABBREVIATIONS AND SYMBOLS

cf.	compare
ch(s).	chapter(s)
Diss.	Dissertation
Dtr	Deuteronomistic source
E	Elohistic source
ed.	editor(s), edited by; edition
e.g.	for example
Eng.	English
esp.	especially
et al.	*et alii* (and others)
Fest.	*Festschrift*
f(f).	following verse(s), page(s), line(s)
Intro.	Introduction
J	Yahwistic source
JE	combined Yahwistic and Elohistic source
LXX	Septuagint
m.	masculine
MT	Masoretic Text
n.	note
OT	Old Testament
P	Priestly source
P$_s$	supplemental (secondary) Priestly source
pl.	plural
Rje	Redactor of the combined Yahwistic and Elohistic source
rev. ed.	revised edition
s.	singular
Sam Pent	Samaritan Pentateuch
tr.	translator(s), translated by
v(v).	verse(s)

vol.	volume
Vulg	Vulgate
→	cross reference to another section of the commentary
//	parallel

II. PUBLICATIONS

ABD	*Anchor Bible Dictionary*
AETh	Abhandlungen zur evangelischen Theologie
AGSU	Arbeiten zur Geschichte des Spätjudentums und Urchristentums
AJSL	*American Journal of Semitic Languages and Literature*
ArOr	*Archiv orientální*
ATANT	Abhandlungen zur Theologie des Alten und Neuen Testaments
BGBE	Beiträge zur Geschichte der biblischen Exegese
Bib	*Biblica*
BibLeb	*Bibel und Leben*
BK	*Bibel und Kirche*
BKAT	Biblischer Kommentar: Altes Testament
BN	*Biblische Notizen*
BT	*The Bible Translator*
BZ	*Biblische Zeitschrift*
BZAW	Beihefte zur *Zeitschrift für die alttestamentliche Wissenschaft*
CBQ	*Catholic Biblical Quarterly*
ConBOT	Coniectanea biblica, Old Testament
COT	Commentar op het Oude Testament
ErFor	Erträge der Forschung
EstBib	*Estudios Bíblicos*
ETL	*Ephemerides theologicae lovanienses*
ETR	*Etudes Théologiques et Religieuses*
ETS	Erfurter theologische Studien
EvT	*Evangelische Theologie*
ExpTim	*Expository Times*
FAT	Forschungen zum Alten Testament
FB	Forschung zur Bibel
FOTL	Forms of the Old Testament Literature
FRLANT	Forschungen zur Religion und Literatur des Alten und Neuen Testaments
HAR	*Hebrew Annual Review*
HBT	*Horizons in Biblical Theology*
HeyJ	*Heythrop Journal*
HS	*Hebrew Studies*
HUCA	*Hebrew Union College Annual*
Int	*Interpretation*

JBL	Journal of Biblical Literature
JNSL	Journal of Northwest Semitic Languages
JQR	Jewish Quarterly Review
JR	Journal of Religion
JSOT	Journal for the Study of the Old Testament
JSOTSup	Journal for the Study of the Old Testament Supplement Series
JTC	Journal for Theology and the Church
JTS	Journal of Theological Studies
Jud	Judaism
KD	Kerygma und Dogma
LTQ	Lexington Theological Quarterly
NCBC	New Century Bible Commentary
NRSV	New Revised Standard Version
OBO	Orbis biblicus et orientalis
OTL	Old Testament Library
OTS	Oudtestamentische Studiën
OTSSA/ OTWSA	Old Testament Society of South Africa/Ou-Testementiese Werkgemeenskap in Suid-Afrika
PJ	Palästina-Jahrbuch
RB	Revue biblique
ResQ	Restoration Quarterly
RevExp	Review and Expositor
SBLSP	Society of Biblical Literature Seminar Papers
SBLSS	Society of Biblical Literature Semeia Studies
SBM	Stuttgarter biblische Monographien
SBS	Stuttgarter Bibelstudien
SBT	Studies in Biblical Theology
SJT	Scottish Journal of Theology
SNTSMS	Society for New Testament Studies Monograph Series
ST	Studia theologica
StudBib	Studia Biblica
ThA	Theologische Arbeiten
TLZ	Theologische Literaturzeitung
TBü	Theologische Bücherei
TynBul	Tyndale Bulletin
TZ	Theologische Zeitschrift
USQR	Union Seminary Quarterly Review
UUÅ	Uppsala universitetsårsskrift
VT	Vetus Testamentum
VTSup	Vetus Testamentum Supplements
WMANT	Wissenschaftliche Monographien zum Alten und Neuen Testament
YNER	Yale Near Eastern Researches
ZAW	Zeitschrift für die alttestamentliche Wissenschaft
ZDMG	Zeitschrift der deutschen morgenländischen Gesellschaft
ZDPV	Zeitschrift des deutschen Palästina-Vereins
ZTK	Zeitschrift für Theologie und Kirche

Editors' Updated Foreword

The editors' foreword to this volume of the FOTL series does not repeat the essentially standardized forewords in volumes I, IX, X, XI, XIII, XIV, XVI, XIX, and XX published thus far. While the guidelines for the series expressed in those volumes remain unchanged and can be reviewed in them, three particular matters deserve to be addressed here. One concerns the much delayed appearance in the present volume of Professor George W. Coats's work on Exodus 1–18. The second, occasioned by this delay, concerns the continuing particular contribution of the FOTL series to exegetical work, especially in relation to other recent Old Testament commentaries. The third matter concerns the announcement of new contributors to the series.

First, the unusually long delay between the preparation of Professor Coats's commentary and its publication must be acknowledged. The delay is the result of the inability of both Coats and the Claremont office of coeditor Knierim to complete their respective parts earlier in the process. Professor Coats submitted a first draft in June 1972, a revised second draft in June 1977, and a revised third draft in October 1984. He did not delay the completion of his initial assignment. Indeed, the drafts of his part of the originally planned FOTL volume II, combining Coats's and Knierim's work on the book of Exodus, was far ahead of Knierim's part. For that reason, and because Coats's part is a sizable volume of its own, the publisher agreed to the publication of volume IIA, on Exodus 1–18, by Coats, followed by volume IIB, on Exodus 19–40, by Knierim.

Nevertheless, Coats's drafts never contained the total extent of his assignment and were never ready for normal editorial work. Coats cannot be faulted for the limitations of his drafts. His name is internationally known as an author of many excellent scholarly works, including the typescript of this commentary. Less well known is the condition under which he had to work. According to his own words, at age seventeen he suffered a fractured skull, which resulted in perpetual physical impairment that could be kept under control only through a series of periodic surgeries whose effectiveness decreased as the decades passed on. This condition not only forced him into premature retirement from teaching and scholarship, but also caused, long before his retirement, an increasing inability, only gradually realized by his collaborators, to respond to a history of appeals for completing his assignment. Not until the current time could Knierim and his Claremont staff afford to complete this volume for Coats in addition to editing what he had submitted.

Since it is the editorial policy of FOTL not to interfere with the substance of a contributor's typescript, Coats's work has been edited but not rewritten. In order to provide the reader with additional information, however, the following items refer to parts of the specific editorial agenda on Coats's original typescript:

1. References to the English Bible are based on the *New Revised Standard Version (NRSV)*.
2. Where advisable, an editorial remark added to Coats's text is introduced by the word ANNOTATION.
3. In most of his bibliographies, additional bibliographical information about more recent publications relevant for form-critical interpretation is introduced by the word ADDENDUM.
4. Very detailed subdivisions of verses in the presented structures follow the system of accents in the *Biblia Hebraica Stuttgartensis (BHS)*.
5. On occasion, the narrative formulae, when introducing speeches, are specifically accounted for structurally because they represent essential elements of the structures of the texts (e.g., Exod 5:1–6:1; 7:7–10:29). These formulae, by and large not in Coats's own typescript, ought in further studies, especially of *narrative* texts, to be accounted for in all texts.
6. The Glossary of Genres and Formulae, editorially provided in toto, includes, after introductory explanations, refinements of some previously offered genre definitions and the replacement of Coats's TALE, already used in FOTL I, by STORY.

Second, the appearance of the present volume offers the opportunity to highlight aspects of the ongoing contribution of the FOTL series to exegetical work. This contribution can be exemplified by comparing FOTL with some of the other commentaries that have appeared in recent decades. Coats's Exodus commentary is a case in point. Its focus is strikingly different not only from all past commentaries but also from the most recent ones by B. S. Childs (fully available to Coats), W. H. Schmidt (available to Coats in the earliest stage of Schmidt's work), and J. I. Durham (not available to Coats). Although these commentaries include or refer to form-critical work, the difference is clearly seen in the way form criticism is applied.

On Structure. Because it is fundamental to the approach, the exhibition and explanation of the structure of the texts is most important in FOTL. Nowhere has the controlled exegesis of the structure of each text unit the same importance as in the FOTL series. Whereas Coats executes this task for each text unit, no one else does the same.

Attention to a text's own structure as the initial exegetical step can also be demonstrated elsewhere (e.g., in the Word Biblical Commentary and adopted directly from work for FOTL in J. E. Hartley's commentary on Leviticus). Childs and Schmidt — genuinely at home in form criticism — regularly discuss structures or patterns of texts. But they do so more generally and certainly not at all by presenting the specifically reconstructed structure of each text unit. Durham's commentary includes in the discussion of each text unit a section called "Form/Structure/Setting," but one has difficulty distinguishing the meaning of the first two of these terms, as well as getting a clear idea about what is meant by "setting."

Schmidt's commentary is original in the sense that it represents the exegete's differentiating encounter with the text directly and as closely as possible. The originality of Childs's commentary lies elsewhere. When we come to the attempt to discover how a text unit consists of progressively narrowing layers of subdivisions in the order of a whole unit, the originality of the structures — at least basically presented by Coats as in the other volumes of FOTL — and the originality of the consistent, truly scholarly effort to discover these structures are distinctive in the history of exegetical work.

For remarks on the commentary by N. M. Sarna, see the ANNOTATION to Chapter 1A.

The presentation of a text's structure points to the systematic thought in any text, be it narrative, legal, poetic, prophetic, or any other kind. Ideally, presentation of the structure exhibits both the cohesion of all parts in the surface of a text unit and their inexplicit conceptual coherence generative for and also operative in that surface. Such exhibition is basically different from the mere juxtaposition of parts. Compared to it, discussions of texts under headings such as "(table of) contents" or "outline" may or may not involve serious analysis of structure.

With regard to large literary corpora — entire biblical books such as Exodus, or on major subdivisions such as Exodus 1–18 and Exodus 19–40 — the commentaries treat matters of "structure" very differently. For example, Childs's table of contents for the book of Exodus lists twenty-four parts (pp. vii-viii), eight of which cover the unit Exodus 1:1–13:16. For Coats, 1:1–13:16 is one major part of Exodus, whereas the first major part for Schmidt is 1:1–15:21 (p. 1). Durham, who coincides with Coats on 1:1–13:16 for his first part, differs from Coats on Exodus 13:17–Deuteronomy 34:12(!) but also from Childs's sixteen subdivisions for Exodus 13:17–40:30 by having only two subdivisions, 13:17–18:27 and 19:1–40:38. He also differs from Schmidt at least in as much as his second subdivision starts with 13:17 compared to Schmidt's starting at 15:22. The list of differences as well as agreements in the publications is endless, and cause for all sorts of reflection.

One must assume that the subdivisions of large corpora and their individual units presented by these and all commentators are meant to be part of exegetical work and to reflect considered, scholarly defensible judgments rather than arbitrary subdivisions made capriciously for the sake of convenience. It is evident, then, that the analysis of structure demands not only its own distinct place in the method and a much more conscious and controlled effort in the application of exegesis, but a higher degree of training and experience than has generally been the case for everyone involved in the reading of the Bible. The results of this work published in FOTL cannot claim to be everywhere right. But more than other commentaries, the work done in it carries this task forward.

On Genre. The kind of analysis of structure aimed at in FOTL must be distinguished from other kinds such as that done either in anthropological structuralism, in rhetorical criticism, or in style criticism. The analysis of structure in this series seeks to discover the genres and their societal settings in which the texts are imbedded and without which they are not sufficiently understood. Structuralist, rhetorical, and stylistic "structure" are, or may be, employed within genres, but are not constitutive for them. Although a text belongs to a genre, its genre as such is not yet revealed through its specific structure, i.e., through the text's individuality. The signals for the genre of a text consist of those features of structure in it that point to typical forms of oral or written expression and communication in societal settings. They are found in more than one text.

Nevertheless, the access to the discussion of genre via the texts' individual structure has at least two purposes. Methodologically, it demonstrates that the determination of genre remains tied to the structures of texts rather than becoming disconnected from them. Substantively, it accounts for the fact that the variability of the individual texts within the relative stability of their genres is as real as the stability of genres that pervades the variability of their texts. The interpenetration of individuality and genre in each text reflects the indissoluble connectedness, balance, and interplay of both the societal and individual aspects in human reality. Texts, like all human expressions, reflect both the typical patterns of society and the differences of individuals. For special explanations on narrative genres, see the Introductory Explanations to the Glossary.

On Setting. The contributors to FOTL are committed to identifying, wherever reasonable, the societal settings of the genres, the settings either of oral expressions in typical situations or of typical conditions for the authors of literary works. The setting of many genres changed as societal structures changed, both in the course of ancient Israel's history and as genres were adapted to diverse settings. These changes and diversifications are part of the study of the history of the transmission of the traditions. Only in the study of that history is it meaningful to ask about the time of a genre and its setting. But in this context an expression such as "historical setting" is unfortunate. Besides being ambiguous, it sometimes refers to a particular historical situation rather than to a typical societal condition. It is better to distinguish between "societal setting" and "historical situation."

Last but not least, the form-critical aspect of the original connection of genres and their settings and of the texts themselves, with their sociohistorical realities, must be maintained especially in light of interpretative developments in which this aspect is set aside — if not denied its legitimacy altogether — in favor of the focus on literature as literature. To be sure, once established, texts have a life of their own as literature. But even that life is engaged in the societal settings and historical situations of the readers, rewriters, translators, and interpreters of the text.

Since the biblical literature would never have come into existence without the people who produced the texts, the conditions for these productions belong inseparably to the reality of the texts themselves. Those conditions are as important for understanding the biblical literature as are the conditions for their ongoing rewriting and translations as well as the conditions of modern readers. There is no literature separated from human conditions, including those in which it was produced and transmitted, and those in which it is read and interpreted.

On Structure, Genre, Setting, and Function and Intention. The specific and often detailed focus in FOTL on these aspects of the texts may appear technical, but every kind of exegesis is in one way or another technical, requiring the development of particular skills of interpretation. The series is designed, however, to guide its readers in the serious study of the texts themselves. The volumes in the series are not intended to replace that study. Those who have practiced the approach, especially in educational settings for students, rabbis, ministers, priests, and laypersons, have seen how the analysis can open up the understanding of the Bible.

To some, the predominantly sociohistorical focus in form criticism and in FOTL may appear to be at the expense of the essentially theological nature of the texts. But although these commentaries may at times not be explicit in highlighting the "faith" in the texts or the texts' theology, their approach points to the outreach of that faith and its theology into all spheres of not only Israel's but also of human reality. Many if not most genres were international and certainly not specifically cultic. The glossaries in the volumes provide comprehensive pictures of the depth of Israel's religion in all of life and of the many dimensions of human reality. The rich and diverse discourse in the Bible, elucidated in important ways by form criticism, reveals the believing community's awareness of the footsteps of the deity in this world, not only in the specific settings of Israel's worship and for the "believers" but in all settings of human life and for all humans.

Third, we would like to announce new contributors to the FOTL series:

Leviticus	Rodney R. Hutton Trinity Lutheran Seminary Columbus, Ohio
Joshua	Robert L. Hubbard, Jr. North Park Theological Seminary Chicago, Illinois
Jeremiah	Richard W. Weis New Brunswick Theological Seminary New Brunswick, New Jersey
Hosea, Micah	Ehud Ben Zvi University of Alberta Edmonton, Alberta, Canada

Editors' Updated Foreword

Again, the editors are deeply grateful to the Institute for Antiquity and Christianity at Claremont and to Claremont Graduate School for the availability of their various facilities. Moreover, they are indebted beyond words to Ms. Mignon R. Jacobs and Mr. David B. Palmer, senior Old Testament Ph.D. candidates at Claremont Graduate School and research associates in the FOTL project. Without their very competent and extensive assistance, substantively as well as technically, the editorial work on this volume could not have been completed at this time.

August 1996   ROLF P. KNIERIM
                                                   GENE M. TUCKER

EXODUS AND MOSES
TRADITIONS

Chapter 1

THE FRAMEWORKS

Chapter 1A
THE EXODUS SAGA, Exod 1:1–13:16

Bibliography

H. Cazelles, "Rédactions et Traditions dans l'Exode," in *Studien zum Pentateuch* (ed. G. Braulik, et al.; Vienna: Herder, 1977) 37-58; B. S. Childs, *The Book of Exodus: A Critical, Theological Commentary* (OTL; Philadelphia: Westminster, 1974); idem, "Deuteronomic Formulae of the Exodus Traditions," in *Hebräische Wortforschung* (*Fest.* W. Baumgartner; ed. G. W. Anderson, et al.; VTSup 14; Leiden: Brill, 1967) 30-39; G. W. Coats, "Moses in Midian," *JBL* 92 (1973) 3-10; idem, "A Structural Transition in Exodus," *VT* 22 (1972) 129-42; D. Daube, *The Exodus Pattern in the Bible* (All Souls Studies 2; London: Faber and Faber, 1963); T. B. Dozeman, *God at War: A Study of Power in the Exodus Tradition* (New York and Oxford: Oxford Univ. Press, 1996); I. Engnell, "The Exodus from Egypt," in *A Rigid Scrutiny: Critical Essays on the Old Testament* (tr. and ed. J. T. Willis; Nashville: Vanderbilt Univ. Press, 1969) 197-206; G. Fohrer, *Überlieferung und Geschichte des Exodus* (BZAW 91; Berlin: Töpelmann, 1964); W. Fuss, *Die deuteronomistische Pentateuchredaktion in Exodus 3–17* (BZAW 126; Berlin: de Gruyter, 1972); M. Greenberg, *Understanding Exodus* (Heritage of Biblical Israel 2/1; New York: Behrman House, 1969); H. Gressmann, *Mose und seine Zeit: Ein Kommentar zu den Mose-Sagen* (FRLANT 18; Göttingen: Vandenhoeck & Ruprecht, 1913); W. Gross, "Die Herausführungsformel — Zum Verhältnis von Formel und Syntax," *ZAW* 86 (1974) 425-52; H. Hubert, "The Exodus, Sinai, and the Credo," *CBQ* 27 (1965) 101-13; W. Johnstone, "The Exodus as Process," *ExpTim* 91 (1979-80) 358-63; K. Koch, "Die Hebräer vom Auszug aus Ägypten bis zum Grossreich Davids," *VT* 19 (1969) 37-81; H. J. Kraus, "Das Thema 'Exodus,'" *EvT* 31 (1971) 608-23; A. Lacocque, *Le devenir de Dieu: Commentaire biblique* (Paris: Editions universitaires, 1967); F. Langlamet, "Die deuteronomistische Pentateuchredaktion in Exodus 3–17," *RB* 80 (1973) 3-17; S. E. Loewenstamm, *The Tradition of the Exodus in Its Development* (Jerusalem: Magnes, 1965); B. O. Long, *The Problem of Etiological Narrative in the Old Testament* (BZAW 108; Berlin: Töpelmann, 1968); H. Lubsczyk, *Der Auszug*

3

Israels aus Ägypten: Seine Theologische Bedeutung in Prophetischer und Priester-licher Überlieferung (ETS 11; Leipzig: St. Benno, 1963); A. Malamat, "The Danite Migration and the Pan-Israelite Exodus-Conquest: A Biblical Narrative Pattern," *Bib* 51 (1970) 1-16; S. Mowinckel, "Die vermeintliche 'Passahlegende' Ex 1–15 in Bezug auf die Frage: Literarkritik und Traditionskritik," *ST* 5 (1951) 66-88; M. Noth, *Exodus: A Commentary* (tr. J. S. Bowden; OTL; Philadelphia: Westminster, 1962); J. Plastaras, *The God of Exodus* (Milwaukee: Bruce, 1966); G. von Rad, "Beobachtungen an der Moseerzählung Exodus 1–14," *EvT* 31 (1971) 579-88; H. Schmid, *Mose: Überlieferung und Geschichte* (BZAW 110; Berlin: Töpelmann, 1968); W. H. Schmidt, *Exodus* (BKAT 2; Neukirchen-Vluyn: Neukirchener, 1974-88); H. Seebass, *Mose und Aaron; Sinai und Gottesberg* (AETh 2; Bonn: H. Bouvier, 1962); P. Weimar, "Hoffnung auf Zukunft: Studien zur Tradition und Redaktion des priesterschriftlichen Exodus-Berichts in Ex 1–12" (Diss., Freiburg, 1971); idem, *Untersuchung zur priesterschriftlichen Exodusgeschichte* (FB 9; Würzburg: Echter, 1973); J. Wijngaards, "הוציא and העלה: A Twofold Approach to the Exodus," *VT* 15 (1965) 91-102; idem, *The Dramatization of Salvific History in the Deuteronomic Schools* (OTS 16; Leiden: Brill, 1969).

ADDENDUM. E. Blum, *Die Komposition der Vätergeschichte* (WMANT 57; Neukirchen-Vluyn: Neukirchener, 1984); idem, *Studien zur Komposition des Penta-teuch* (BZAW 189; Berlin and New York: de Gruyter, 1990); S. Boorer, *The Promise of the Land as Oath: A Key to the Formation of the Pentateuch* (New York: de Gruyter, 1992); J. J. Burden, ed., *Exodus 1–15: Text and Context* (Proceedings OTSSA/OTWSA 29 [1986]; Pretoria: Old Testament Society of South Africa, 1987); G. W. Coats, *Moses: Heroic Man, Man of God* (JSOTSup 57; Sheffield: Sheffield Academic Press, 1988); J. S. Croatto, "Exodo 1–15: Algunas claves literarias y teológicas para entender el Pentateuco," *EstBib* (1994) 167-94; G. I. Davies, "The Wilderness Itineraries and the Composition of the Pentateuch," *VT* 33 (1983) 1-13; J. I. Durham, *Exodus* (WBC; Waco: Word, 1987); T. E. Fretheim, *Exodus* (Interpretation; Louisville: John Knox, 1991); C. Houtman, *Exodus* (2 vols.; COT; Kampen: Kok, 1986-89); J. P. Hyatt, *Exodus* (NCBC; Grand Rapids: Eerdmans, 1981); B. Jacob, *The Second Book of the Bible: Exodus* (tr. Walter Jacob; Hoboken: KTAV, 1992); W. Johnstone, "The Deuteronomistic Cycle of 'Signs' and 'Wonders' in Exodus 1–13," in *Understanding Poets and Prophets: Essays in Honor of George Wishart Anderson* (JSOTSup 152; ed. A. Graeme Auld; Sheffield: JSOT Press, 1993); R. P. Knierim, "The Composition of the Penta-teuch," SBLSP 24 (1985) 393-415; S. McEvenue, "The Speaker(s) in Ex 1–15," in *Biblische Theologie und gesellschaftlicher Wandel: Für Norbert Lohfink* (ed. George Braulik, et al.; Freiburg: Herder, 1993); P. D. Miscall, "Biblical Narrative and Catego-ries of the Fantastic," *Semeia* 60 (1992) 39-51; W. Resenhöfft, *Die Quellenberichte im Josef-Sinai-Komplex (Gen 37 bis Ex 24 mit 32–34)* (Bern: Lang, 1983); N. M. Sarna, "Exodus, Book of," ABD (New York: Doubleday, 1992), 2:689-700; idem, *Exodus* (Jewish Publication Society Torah Commentary; New York: Jewish Publication Soci-ety, 1991); W. H. Schmidt, *Exodus, Sinai, und Mose* (ErFor 191; Darmstadt: Wissen-schaftliche Buchgesellschaft, 1983); J. Van Seters, *The Life of Moses: The Yahwist as Historian in Exodus–Numbers* (Louisville: Westminster/John Knox, 1994).

Structure

Structure in the narrative of the exodus traditions builds around one dominant motif: The Egyptians oppress the Israelites with hard labor. The theme opens with a transition from the patriarchal traditions and an exposition for the exodus narration (Exod 1:1-14). The point of tension developed from the exposition is not resolved until the traditions report Israel's departure from the oppression of Egyptian bondage (12:1-51). That span of tension defines the extent of the exodus theme (so Coats, "Transition").

The most striking characteristic of structure in the final stage of the exodus narrative is the duplication of the VOCATION ACCOUNT. The Moses stories in 1:15–2:22 and the reports of commission executed in 4:27-31 and 5:1–6:1 adhere more closely to the account in 3:1–4:18. The major break in the narrative appears in ch. 6, with 6:2–7:6 regressing in the line of narration to repeat the vocation account. The exposition, 1:1-14, introduces narrative motifs intrinsic for both units. The sign cycle in 7:7–10:29, along with its appendix in 11:1–12:36, completes the plot for both. It is thus clear that the focal points of structure for the final stage of this material lie in the two vocation accounts.

Structure in the P version of the exodus traditions is:

I.	Transition	1:1-7, 13-14
II.	Vocation account (Moses and Aaron)	6:2–7:6
III.	Execution of vocation commission	7:7–10:27; 11:9-10; 12:1-28
	A. Sign cycle	7:7–10:27; 11:9-10
	1. Exposition	7:7
	2. Cycle	7:8–10:27

5

For P the span of tension between the exposition, with its theme of oppression under Egyptian labor, and resolution of the tension in release from the oppression constitutes the chain of unity for the exodus narration. The exposition functions as a transition from the patriarchal theme to the exodus theme by summarizing the end of the patriarchal cycles (1:1-7), then opening the exodus narration with the oppression crisis (1:13-14). The vocation account, 6:2–7:6, connects immediately to the oppression motif in 1:13-14. It constitutes God's response to the oppressive service Israel endures (cf. 6:5-6). Through Moses and Aaron, God promises the people not only that he will deliver them from their bondage, but that he will also make them his own possession. The vocation tradition is not complete at the formal break between vv. 6 and 7 in ch. 7, however. Moses has been commissioned with more than a message for the people. He is also to go to the pharaoh in order to bring the people out of the land of Egypt.

The P version of the sign cycle in 7:7–10:27 and 11:9-10 is the execution for the commission in the VOCATION ACCOUNT. For P, the sign cycle ends in failure. Despite the repeated chain of signs presented before the pharaoh, the pharaoh refuses to let Israel go. But at just this point, P makes an important point in his theology clear: the failure of the signs was by design (cf. 11:9-10). There was no negotiation between Moses and the pharaoh, only a series of signs to demonstrate the majesty of Israel's God. To be sure, the process of negotiation lies immediately behind the surface of P's account. But the negotiation signs do not convince the pharaoh to release Israel. For P, negotiation motifs are not crucial. To the contrary, the exodus occurred only by properly executing the Passover ordinance (12:1-28, 43-51), and that execution does not presuppose further contact between Moses and the pharaoh. The exodus is totally a cultic event.

P follows the conclusion to the exodus narration in 12:27b-28 with a summary of the exodus theme, 12:37-42 (cf. Coats, "Transition"). The next theme of traditions for P begins with a new exposition, a notice of God's leadership through the wilderness (13:17-19). Between these two points of transition in the structure of P lies a distinct formulation of Passover ordinance, 12:43-49, and a repetition of the exodus conclusion, 12:50-51 (cf. the verbal agreement between vv. 28 and 50). The new conclusion serves to bind the ordinance in 12:43-49 into the exodus theme. Repeating the conclusion suggests that the ordinance is a secondary development in the Passover tradition (→

12:43-51). Nevertheless, P again indicates that the exodus event itself, presented in vv. 50-51, occurs by proper execution of the Passover ordinance. Isolation in a transition seam seems even more pronounced for the ordinance in 13:1-2 and the Dtr section in 13:3-16.

Structure in J appears in the following outline:

I. Exposition   1:8-12
II. Stories about Moses   1:15–2:22
    A. Adoption legend   1:15–2:10
    B. Marriage story   2:11-22
III. Moses vocation account   2:23–4:23
    A. Transition   2:23-25
    B. Narration of the Moses-Aaron vocation tradition   3:1–4:18
    C. Transition   4:19-23
IV. Etiology for circumcision ritual   4:24-26
V. Execution of vocation commission accounts   4:27–6:1; 7:7–12:36*
    A. Report to elders   4:27-31
    B. Negotiations with the pharaoh   5:1–6:1
    C. Sign cycle   7:7–10:29*
    D. Passover sign   11:1-8; 12:29-36
        1. Narration of the Passover sign   11:1-8
        2. Conclusion to the exodus traditions   12:29-36

This structure is more complex than the one in P, suggesting that J preserves the tradition at a stage much closer to its oral transmission. The narration opens with a statement of the major theme, Egypt's oppression against Israel through unreasonable servitude. Transition from the patriarchal cycle is not developed as a structural element, although J highlights the difference between the old days when the relationship with the Egyptians was good and subsequent hard days simply by reporting that the new king over Egypt did not know Joseph.

Contrary to P, J does not move immediately to a Moses (→) vocation account. Between the exposition and the vocation account stand two distinct but related stories about Moses' personal life. The midwives tradition in 1:15-21 and the story of child exposure in 1:22–2:10 presuppose the oppression theme. But the exposition does not continue organically into a story of exposure and death for the Israelite children (cf. Schmidt, BKAT, 20). Moreover, the marriage story also has a loose contact with its context. The introduction in 2:11-15a presupposes the oppression of the slaves, as well as the ADOPTION LEGEND. Moses is presented as an aristocrat, distinct from the Hebrew slaves, yet very much aware of the Egyptian oppression. The loose connection between these stories and the larger context suggests the combination of thematic elements at a stage close to the oral transmission of the tradition.

The Moses vocation account for J follows the two stories. But structural problems continue to appear. The vocation account has been cemented into its present position as part of a complex of traditions about Moses in Midian by two transitions, 2:23-25 and 4:19-23. The relationship between the vocation tradition and its apparent Midianite setting is thus tenuous (cf. Coats, "Moses in Midian"). In P the vocation tradition appears immediately before the plague cycle, set in Egypt. The commissioned leaders can carry out the commission immediately. For the JE VOCATION ACCOUNT, with its structural position among traditions about Moses in Midian, the leaders must move from Midian back to Egypt in order to execute their commission. The movement is accomplished (1) by the transition in 4:19-23, and (2) by the position of the circumcision ETIOLOGY in 4:24-26. (Since the events in the ETIOLOGY occur at an inn for travelers [cf. Gen 42:27], its position contributes to the image of a trip from Midian to Egypt.) The summary describing execution of the commission to the Israelite elders, Exod 4:27-31, is thus cut away from the primary unit and placed after the structural transition. Its position in a redactional seam creates an impression that it does not belong to the primary level of the Moses tradition (cf. below on Exod 4:27-31). But the basic problem of the position in the organization of the series is not Aaron's role, as it is in the internal structure of the vocation unit, but the Midianite point of departure. The transition in 4:19-23 thus does not mean that the vocation account has been inserted into a new position in the overall organization of the exodus traditions. It functions only as a transition from the secondary setting for the vocation account in Midian to the primary setting for the exodus traditions in Egypt.

The organizational problem reflected by these units of tradition can be understood if one recognizes two different schemes of structure in J. The scheme dominated by the vocation account presents the thematic organization of the exodus traditions centered in the oppression motif. The two stories about Moses look beyond the exodus theme to contacts with stories about Moses in the wilderness (cf. Exod 18). The point of unity here derives from heroic motifs about Moses himself; indeed, it suggests that the thematic structure in the Pentateuch, particularly the exodus and wilderness themes, has been combined with a heroic pattern centered on Moses. (That structure would account readily for the absence of conquest as a theme structure in the Pentateuch since the Pentateuch breaks off with the death of Moses.)

The relationship between the summary of the execution of Moses' commission in Exod 4:27-31 and the STORY of negotiations with the pharaoh in 5:1-6:1 should not be easily broken. The two units are joined simply by a temporal particle, wĕ'aḥar, "afterward." They are distinct, but structurally they fit close together. Both function as accounts for the execution of the vocation commission in 3:1-4:18 (for problems in the history of the vocation tradition, → 3:1-4:18). Moreover, the juxtaposition of the VOCATION ACCOUNT in 3:1-4:18 and these units of commission execution parallels the relationship in P between the vocation account and the sign cycle. The sign cycle is itself a combination of P and J and thus constitutes a continuation of the commission execution, at least for J, from 4:27-31 and 5:1-6:1 (on tradition history in these traditions, → 5:1-6:1).

The sign cycle has a problematic ending in J. The Passover does not appear to be an original part of the series, and the conclusion to the exodus theme it represents may be a secondary reinterpretation of the exodus event itself (→ 11:1-12:36). Moreover, some expansions in the narrative may be

8

associated with Elohistic elements or even more directly with a Deuteronomistic expansion (→ 13:1-16). Whether the expansions generally reflect a Deuteronomistic redaction of this material cannot be clearly determined as yet (but see Fuss). The Deuteronomistic ending in 13:3-16 does not, however, obscure one point. The conclusion to the exodus theme as a whole can be found in 12:29-36. Israel leaves Egypt, if not as the direct result of the pharaoh's dismissal, at least with spoil as proof of their victorious struggle against their oppressors (12:35-36).

Thus, for J as for P, the exodus traditions are presented under the structural patterns of a Moses VOCATION ACCOUNT. Complaint motifs play a role (cf. 2:23-25), but structure in the traditions as a whole does not derive from complaint ritual (against Plastaras). To the contrary, each source develops the exodus narration, with its climax in escape or release from oppressive bondage as an elaboration of the vocation commission and its execution. Moreover, tradition history of the exodus narrative suggests that contrary to both patriarchal traditions and wilderness traditions, this theme did not develop from a number of originally independent narratives. Independent narratives can be seen here (ch. 2), but the exodus narrative develops from one or two basic traditions. Furthermore, the exodus traditions seem to have undergone a distinct process of transmission. Narration here is far more polished, more theologically sophisticated, than in the wilderness or patriarchal themes.

Genre

In the final stage of the text, the theme of the exodus narrative is part of the theme of the larger Moses saga and of the theme of → The Pentateuch/ Hexateuch. Cf. FOTL I. This stage is a composition of two distinct narratives, J and P, each with its own set of genre indicators.

The Priestly narrative about the exodus concludes with a cultic text, an ORDINANCE for the Passover, and casts the exodus event itself as an execution of the ordinance. It is the exodus-Passover legend. Yet designation of the text as a legend for a cultic drama of the Passover does not seem to be convincing. There is no indication that the entire text was read as part of a worship celebration, much less divided into parts as the script for a Passover drama (against Fohrer). Nor does the arrangement of the text reflect the liturgy of a (→) complaint rite (against Plastaras, who suggests that the plagues, Passover night, and the miracle at the sea have been bracketed between parts of a complaint liturgy). Rather, suggestions within the scope of the Priestly text itself indicate that the exodus-Passover legend was used as part of a catechesis (cf. Exod 12:26-27a). An important aspect of its use as a catechesis would be its transmission, not simply from priest to catechumen, but from father to son.

In J the exodus narrative belongs to national tradition, transmitted from father to son over the course of many generations. It is thus closely tied to the thematic structure of the Hexateuch (→ The Pentateuch/Hexateuch, FOTL I). Moreover, the structural pattern suggests that the tradition is characterized as a vocation-execution account. Behind J may have been a national (→) saga reporting the efforts of unnamed representatives to win freedom for the Hebrew slaves. Yet, at the present stage, it is dominated by the interests of the Moses HEROIC SAGA (→ The Pentateuch/Hexateuch, FOTL I). The relationship between the two poles constitutes a unique element in J (→ the Yahwist, FOTL I, 21-24).

The genre of the exodus narrative is determined by the focus of this narrative on the exodus tradition in its own right, notwithstanding the fact that it is part of, and pervaded by, the larger Moses saga and the total Pentateuch/Hexateuch history.

The motif of the exodus tradition has in its history received unfoldings in various aspects and generic characteristics. These unfoldings, or their results, are for Exodus 1–13 especially discernible in J and P. Nevertheless, the variations are controlled by the traditional motif and the characteristics of its oral and literary narrative tradition that focus on this motif. These characteristics point to the genre of SAGA. Since the exodus saga is combined with the Moses saga, the combination, insofar as it focuses on the exodus itself, amounts to the saga of Israel's exodus from oppression under the leadership of its hero, Moses.

Setting

The final stage of the exodus narrative reflects the redactional activity that brought J and P together into one single narration. In P the exodus narrative has a cultic setting. But the cultic character of this narrative develops as much contact with the family as it does with the sanctuary. In J, one setting is the family. Earlier stages of tradition behind J seem to draw on traditions basically at home in family circles. Yet particularly here one must not draw setting too sharply. (For exceptions to this general statement, → the individual texts.)

Intention

The exodus traditions function as an explanation to younger generations that their history unfolded under the control of their God. The saga thus provides a national or religious context for younger generations to develop a sense of identity. At the latest stage, the J and P exodus narratives have been combined. Reasons for preserving the two versions are not clear. I cannot discover any greater significance in the structure of the final stage in the exodus narration than a careful and artistic combination of two distinct and relatively complete versions of the exodus traditions. With one exception, all significant characteristics of structure, as well as genre, setting, and intention (beyond careful preservation of the two accounts in a single narration), belong primarily to one of the two versions. The one exception is in 11:1-10 (→ 11:1-10 for details).

In P the intention is fully religious: the exodus saga functions as a catechism. In J the intention is not quite so clearly tied to a cultic process. But even here the religious aspect is clear. The father explains to his son that God acted on his behalf by bringing the ancestors out of Egypt. The narrations also entertain. Israel can enjoy hearing how God ridiculed the Egyptians in the series of signs. But they also teach by providing a context of history for the new generation to find its identity.

ANNOTATION. Although some publications do not refer to form criticism, they clearly use elements that are germane to this method. The commentary by N. M. Sarna is a case in point.

Sarna addresses the question of what is generally called composition, or structure, of the narrative by speaking about its "special literary mold" (p. xiv): in view of "the richness and variety of the subject matter," immediately revealed in the table of contents of his commentary (p. ix), criteria such as "geographic location" (Egypt — the way — Sinai) or chronology, let alone other unmentioned aspects, are not valid indicators of this mold (p. xii). Instead, and in virtual opposition to a long exegetical, especially literary-critical but also form-critical tradition up to the most recent studies, Sarna says that "a close examination of the constituent elements of the Book of Exodus determines at once that we do not have a comprehensive, sequential narrative, only an episodic account" (p. xii).

Sarna's emphasis on the episodes, the individual units, and their demarcation by him in his table of contents are certainly, and inevitably, a relevant compositional aspect, quite apart from different demarcations. But it remains implausible that the "narrative" (s.) should not be sequential because it is episodic, not comprehensively telling all and everything.

Are the episodes not strung together as at least a chain of events, basically seen sequentially rather than placed randomly and unconnectedly? Does the one theme of the book, stated by Sarna, play a role in connecting the episodes, regardless how else one defines it and its concept? Would the study of the structure of each individual episode provide evidence not only for its own integrity but also for the connectedness of all, stylistically, thematically, and conceptually? Are the geographical aspects, of Egypt — the way in the desert — and of Sinai, not significant territorial aspects in the composition and meaning of the narrative, as Exod 19:4 knows? Indeed, are the theme and concept or idea of the entire book, even of its place in the entire Pentateuch, not the reasons for the selection of all its episodes in the first place, and for their placement in context and even their individual shape as well?

Sarna clearly draws the necessary distinction between the narrative and the question of the historical background of the exodus event itself (p. xiv). Would this distinction, and Sarna's focus on the narrative, not lead to the obvious questions about the history of successive, at least different, narrators or writers, and at least about the societal setting of the author of the whole, the question of setting, if one accounts for one author only?

The book is not historiography but historiosophy (p. xiii). The latter term suggests a particular genre of history writing: Wisdom about history, even if in the form of episodes about that history. Is historiosophy a unique genre, or is it only a unique kind of wisdom in the ancient genre of history writing?

Inevitably, Sarna's approach touches on several aspects in the total form-critical method. This approach, and its results, can only gain from a more fully adapted usage of that method.

For more recent studies within the range of Coats's Chapters 1A and 1B, the following annotations to the previous bibliographical ADDENDUM point generally to the different directions of these studies, to their greater or lesser contact with form criticism or their different direction altogether. Of relevance for form criticism are the studies by Davies (direct discussion of Coats's work), Knierim, and Van Seters, but also those by Blum (on the *Vätergeschichte* and the Pentateuch), Boorer, Burden, and Coats himself for their focus on composition and concept. For Croatto, Exodus 1–15 is both the climax of and the key to understanding the Pentateuch. Fretheim and Hyatt discuss contextuality, divisions, and transitions. Source-critical discussion is advanced by Johnstone and Resenhöfft, whereas McEvenue and Miscall focus on structure in terms of modern literary and rhetorical criticism. Generally important are the commentaries, monographs, and articles by Houtman, Jacob, Sarna, and — as it progresses — W. H. Schmidt.

Chapter 1B
THE MOSES SAGA, Exod 1:15–Deut 34:12

Bibliography

W. F. Albright, "Moses in Historical and Theological Perspective," in *Magnalia Dei: The Mighty Acts of God* (*Fest.* G. E. Wright; ed. F. M. Cross, W. E. Lemke, and P. D. Miller; Garden City: Doubleday, 1976) 120-31; E. Auerbach, *Moses* (Amsterdam: G. J. A. Ruys, 1953); C. Barth, "Mose, Knecht Gottes," in ΠΑΡΡΗΣΙΑ (*Fest.* K. Barth; Zurich: EVZ, 1966) 68-81; F. Baumgärtel, "Der Tod des Religionsstifters," *KD* 9 (1963) 223-33; M. Buber, *Moses* (Oxford: East and West Library, 1946); P. Buis, "Les conflits entre Moise et Israel dans Exode et Nombres," *VT* 28 (1978) 257-70; J. B. Burns, "The Mythology of Death in the Old Testament," *SJT* 26 (1973) 327-40; T. C. Butler, "An Anti-Moses Tradition," *JSOT* 12 (1979) 9-15; E. Campbell, "Moses and the Foundations of Israel," *Int* 29 (1975) 141-54; G. W. Coats, "Legendary Motifs in the Moses Death Reports," rep76-87 *CBQ* 39 (1977) 34-44; idem, *Moses: Heroic Man, Man of God* (JSOTSup 57; Sheffield: JSOT Press, 1988); L. Dunlop, "The Intercession of Moses: A Study of the Pentateuchal Traditions" (Diss., Rome, 1970); J. Dus, "Mose oder Josua? Zum Problem des Stifters der israelitischen Religion," *ArOr* 39 (1971) 16-45; J. K. Eakins, "Moses," *RevExp* 74 (1977) 461-71; O. Eissfeldt, "Mose," in *Kleine Schriften* (6 vols.; ed. R. Sellheim and F. Maass; Tübingen: Mohr, 1962-79) 3:240-55; H. Gressmann, *Mose und seine Zeit: Ein Kommentar zu den Mose-Sagen* (FRLANT 18; Göttingen: Vandenhoeck & Ruprecht, 1913); H. Gross, "Der Glaube an Mose nach Exodus (4.14.19)," in *Wort — Gebot — Glaube: Beiträge zur Theologie des Alten Testaments* (*Fest.* W. Eichrodt; ed. H. J. Stoebe, J. J. Stamm, and E. Jenni; ATANT 59; Zurich: Zwingli, 1970) 57-66; S. Herrmann, "Mose," *EvT* 28 (1968) 301-28; J. Jensen, "What Happened to Moses?" *CBQ* 32 (1970) 404-17; A. S. Kapelrud, "How Tradition Failed Moses," *JBL* 76 (1957) 242; C. A. Keller, "Von Stand und Aufgabe der

Moseforschung," *TZ* 13 (1957) 430-41; K. Koch, "Der Tod des Religionsstifters," *KD* 8 (1962) 100-23; T. J. Meek, "Moses and the Levites," *AJSL* 56 (1939) 113-20; J. Muilenburg, "The 'Office' of the Prophet in Ancient Israel," in *The Bible in Modern Scholarship* (ed. J. P. Hyatt; Nashville: Abingdon, 1965) 74-97; M. M. Mulhall, "Aaron and Moses: Their Relationship in the Oldest Sources of the Pentateuch" (Diss., Catholic University, 1973); R. W. Neff, "Saga," in *Saga, Legend, Tale, Novella, Fable: Narrative Forms in the Old Testament* (ed. G. W. Coats; JSOTSup 34; Sheffield: JSOT, 1984), 17-32; J. Nohrnberg, "Moses," in *Images of Man and God: Old Testament Short Stories in Literary Focus* (ed. B. O. Long; Sheffield: Almond, 1984) 35-57; M. Noth, *A History of Pentateuchal Traditions* (tr. B. W. Anderson; Englewood Cliffs: Prentice-Hall, 1972); E. Osswald, *Das Bild des Mose in der kritischen alttestamentlichen Wissenschaft seit Julius Wellhausen* (ThA 18; Berlin: Evangelische Verlagsanstalt, 1962); L. Perlitt, "Mose als Prophet," *EvT* 31 (1971) 588-608; G. von Rad, *Moses* (World Christian Books 32; New York: Association Press, 1960); R. Rendtorff, "Mose als Religionsstifter?" in *Gesammelte Studien zum Alten Testament* (Munich: Kaiser, 1975) 152-71; H. H. Rowley, "Moses and Monotheism," in *From Moses to Qumran* (New York: Association Press, 1963) 35-63; J. Schildenberger, "Moses als Idealgestalt eines Armen Jahwes," in *La rencontre de Dieu: Mémorial Albert Gelin* (Bibliothèque de la Faculté catholique de theologie de Lyon 8; Le Puy: Xavier Marus, 1961) 71-84; H. Schmid, *Mose: Überlieferung und Geschichte* (BZAW 110; Berlin: Töpelmann, 1968); idem, "Der Stand der Moseforschung," *Judaica* 21 (1965) 194-221; H. Schmidt, "Mose und der Dekalog," in *ΕΨΞΑΡΙΣΤΗΡΙΟΝ: Studien zur Religion und Literatur des Alten und Neuen Testaments* (Fest. H. Gunkel; ed. H. Schmidt; FRLANT 36; Göttingen: Vandenhoeck & Ruprecht, 1923) 78-119; J. M. Schmidt, "Aaron und Mose: Ein Beitrag zur Überlieferungsgeschichte des Pentateuchs" (Diss., Hamburg, 1963); F. Schnutenhaus, "Die Entstehung der Mosetraditionen" (Diss., Heidelberg, 1958); J. Schreiner, "Moses, Der 'Mann Gottes,'." *BibLeb* 8 (1967) 94-109; S. Schwertner "Erwägungen zu Moses Tod und Grab in Dtn 34 5.6," *ZAW* 84 (1972) 25-46; H. Seebass, *Mose und Aaron, Sinai und Gottesberg* (AETh 2; Bonn: H. Bouvier, 1962); R. Smend, *Das Mosebild von Heinrich Ewald bis Martin Noth* (BGBE 3; Tübingen: Mohr, 1959); P. Volz, *Mose und sein Werk* (2nd ed.; Tübingen: Mohr, 1932); G. Widengren, "What Do We Know about Moses?" in *Proclamation and Presence: Old Testament Essays in Honor of G. H. Davies* (ed. J. I. Durham and J. R. Porter; Richmond: John Knox, 1970) 21-47; F. V. Winet, *The Mosaic Tradition* (Toronto: Univ. of Toronto Press, 1949).

ADDENDUM. For added bibliographical information see the **ADDENDUM** in Chapter 1A.

Structure

I. Moses stories	Exod 1:15–2:22
A. Moses adoption legend	1:15–2:10
B. Moses marriage story	2:11-22
II. Moses vocation account	Exod 2:23–12:36
A. Call	2:23–4:23
B. Execution of call	4:24–6:1

A narrative structure designed to present Moses as the hero of his people complements the overarching structure of the Pentateuch built around the mighty acts of God. The exodus, wilderness, and Sinai themes describe these narratives from one direction. But the Moses saga moves in a complementary direction as well and thereby achieves a richer affirmation about God and his creation.

An initial sign of the competing structures is the disjunction between the exodus exposition, Exod 1:1-14, and the report of an Egyptian pogrom against Israelite children, a lead into the Moses BIRTH-ADOPTION STORY (→ 1:15–2:10). Successive stories present the image of Moses, and one can most adequately describe that image in terms of the traditional hero. Thus the birth occurs under unusual and dire circumstances. The young man defends his people and, as a consequence, is forced to flee. In his refuge he again defends innocent and helpless people. By his deed he wins status in a new household, as well as a bride.

The following vocation account plays a dual role in the complementary structures. Its importance for the exodus theme is clear. In addition, however, it also sets the stage for Moses' particular vocation, a vocation that one cannot describe adequately as prophet, as judge, or even as covenant mediator. Moses' vocation unravels on a stage set for a people's hero. Typical pieces in that literary portfolio include the repeated reluctance to accept the role and the signs used to identify the authentic player in the role. Moreover, the signs in 7:7–12:36 appear as proper execution of the call. The hero appears for his people before their traditional enemy. With repeated signs he claims the authority of his commissioner and thus the authority of his commission. That the repeated signs end in failure does not upset the heroic figure. To the contrary, his heroic stature enables him to win by cunning what he could not win by open negotiations. Indeed, the very heroic stature that enhances him before his people enhances him before his enemy (cf. 11:3b).

14

The signs continue in the wilderness, and with their display the heroic figure provides, through the authority of his commissioner, for the needs of his followers. This point is clear in Moses' defense of his people before their enemies (→ 17:8-16). It is no less present in his efforts to provide food and water (cf. Num 11:10-14). It is perhaps most sharply present in his defense of his people before God (→ Exodus 32–34). The pattern concludes appropriately with a report of the hero's death (→ Deuteronomy 34). In addition to the episodes that carry the events in Moses' heroic leadership, legends such as Exod 17:8-16 and Numbers 12 establish a reverence for the hero (cf. also Exod 14:31). Expansions (cf. Numbers 12) suggest that negative response was also his lot. I must note here, however, that conquest traditions (cf. Numbers 20–21, 22–25) seem consciously to reject any implications of connections with Moses. The details for distributing the land (cf. Numbers 26–36) make some contact in that direction, but the contact is peripheral and unimportant. The Moses traditions basically reject contact with the conquest theme.

The two patterns typical for the wilderness theme (→ The Framework, Chapter 3) also affect the Moses structure. The one pattern concerned to show Yahweh's aid reveals the intrinsic contribution of Moses to the picture. The other shows rebellion against his leadership. In both cases a central feature for the narrative is the leadership of the heroic figure.

ANNOTATION. Above (pp. 5, 13f.), the units identified for Exod 2:23–12:36 are, except for 4:24-26, identical. But their places in the signalized structures differ. The reason for these differences Coats apparently sees in his different understanding of the compositions of the "Moses Saga" (s.) in the entire Pentateuch and the exodus traditions of which the "Moses Stories" (pl.) are a part. The comparison of the two structures deserves further study.

In P the structure is as follows:

I. Moses vocation account	Exod 6:2–12:36*
A. Call	6:2–7:6
B. Execution	7:7–12:36*
II. Mighty deeds, enemy, and hunger	Exodus 14 (also J), 16
III. Sinai	Exod 24:15–31:17;
	34:29–Num 10:28
IV. Mighty deeds, enemy, and thirst	Numbers 13–14 (also J),
	15 (also in ch. 16 [*NRSV* 16:1-35]),
	17–19 (*NRSV* 16:36–19:22), 20 (also J)
V. Conquest traditions	Num 25:6–27:23; 28–31; 33–36
VI. Legend about Moses' successor	Num 27:12-23

P depicts the Moses traditions no longer in terms of the heroic but rather with the heroic Moses receding behind the presentation of God's mighty acts. The point can be illustrated in the remains of the Moses death report, Num 27:12-23, now transformed into the legend of the election and installation of Moses' successor, Joshua. Not only does the unit use none of the heroic elements present in Deuteronomy 34, not only does it report simply the necessity for Moses' death without flourish, but it depicts the reason for the death as Moses' sin. There is no vicarious quality, no heroic stature — only the necessity of death.

In J the structure is as follows:

I.	Moses stories	Exod 1:15–2:22
II.	Moses vocation	Exod 2:23–6:1; 7:7–12:36
III.	Heroic deeds	Exodus 14 (also P), 15, 17
IV.	Judicial and military organization	Exod 18:1-27
V.	Sinai	Exod 19:1–24:14; 32:1–34:28
VI.	Heroic deeds	Num 10:29–12:16; 13:17–14:45
		(also P); 16:1–17:15 (*NRSV* 16:1-50); 20:1–25:5
VII.	Conquest traditions	Numbers 32
VIII.	Death report (Moses)	Deut 34:1-12

The structure of the final text is thus derived in large measure from J (see the comments above). It is, moreover, most strongly in J that the heroic stamp for the Moses traditions appears.

Insofar as form-critical methodology is concerned, no evidence can be found that Moses was originally attached to only one theme in the total structure of Israel's confession. It is not possible to limit the Moses traditions to the exodus or Sinai. Neither is it possible to defend a thesis that the primary Moses tradition is the death report (contrast Noth, *Traditions,* 173-74). To the contrary, the Moses traditions from birth to death belong together and deny any possibility for limiting the Moses figure to one theme unit.

Genre

The Moses narrative appears in the final form of the text, and especially in J, as a HEROIC SAGA. For details see Coats, *Moses Tradition;* Neff.

Setting

The Moses saga reflects the entertainment quality of Israel's life that doubles as a resource for preserving moral and popular historical narratives. The Moses saga does not belong to an office or institution, but to the storyteller, the entertainer. The so-called singer of tales gives a key insight into the context for preserving such narrative material.

Intention

The Moses saga depicts the key contributions of the heroic figure in order to effect the moral fiber of the people (cf. 14:31). To believe in Moses is to believe in Yahweh — and vice versa.

Bibliography

G. W. Coats, *The Moses Tradition* (JSOTSup 161; Sheffield: Sheffield Academic Press, 1993); R. W. Neff, "Saga," in *Saga, Legend, Tale, Novella, Fable: Narrative Forms in Old Testament Literature* (ed. G. W. Coats; JSOTSup 35; Sheffield: JSOT Press, 1985), 17-32.

ANNOTATION. The following detailed macrostructures of P and J not provided by Coats were reconstructed from his typescript and are presented here for further study and interpretation.

Macrostructure of P

I. Transition	Exod 1:1-7, 13-14
A. Summary conclusion for preceding traditions	1-6
1. Name list	1-5
2. Death report	6
B. Leitmotif for following traditions	7, 13-14
1. Motivations for oppression	7
2. Oppression and results	13-14
II. Vocation account (Moses and Aaron)	Exod 6:2–7:6
A. Speech	2-8
1. Introduction: God to Moses	2a-bα
2. Commission to speak	2bβ-8
B. Execution of the message commission	9
C. Vocation dialogue	10-12
1. Speech: commission for action	10-11
2. Speech: objection	12
D. Narration: recapitulation of the commission of Moses and Aaron	13
E. Genealogy	14-25
1. Superscription	14a
2. List	14b-25
F. Recapitulation of the vocation of Moses and Aaron	26-30
1. Speech: commission recapitulation	26
2. Execution of commission	27
3. Speech: commission recapitulation	28-29
4. Speech: objection recapitulation	30
G. Reassurance speech (vocation dialogue resumed)	7:1-5
1. Narrative introduction	1aα
2. Speech	1aβ-5
H. Execution of commission	6
III. Execution of vocation commission	Exod 7:7–10:27; 11:9-10; 12:1-28
A. Sign cycle	7:7–10:29; 11:9-10
1. Exposition	7:7

Macrostructure of J

Chapter 2

THE INDIVIDUAL UNITS

EXPOSITION: TRANSITION TO
THE EXODUS TRADITIONS, 1:1-14

Structure

Two principal elements constitute this unit: I, a summary of preceding traditions, in this case only a part of the Jacob traditions; and II, an exposition in summary form of the theme for the following traditions.

The NAME LIST in I.A is problematic. Its introduction defines the names in the list: "These are the names of the sons of Israel who came to Egypt with Jacob." The number in v. 5a should mark the conclusion, the total offspring represented by the list. In the present form of the text, Joseph stands outside the list (v. 5b). But the number in v. 5a includes Joseph and his children (cf. Gen 46:8-27). The names in the list follow a traditional order: sons of Leah,

21

sons of Rachel, followed by the sons of Bilhah and Zilpah, the two handmaidens. (For the same order see Gen 35:22-26.) Lists of the sons of Jacob show a range of variations in order for the four principal groups and even in the order for some names within a single group. Levi can be dropped from the Leah group, with Manasseh and Ephraim replacing Joseph in the Rachel group (cf. Num 13:8-11). Joseph or his sons, however, maintain a consistent place in the structure of the list, with the exception of this text (so Childs, *Exodus*, 2; Schmidt, BKAT, 26-28). The reason for the break in order here is clear: since Joseph and his sons were already in Egypt, they could not be listed with the sons who entered Egypt with Jacob. The name Joseph thus stands outside the formal structure of the list but nevertheless belongs to the traditions summarized by the list. The traditional list has thus been adapted for its function in this particular place (→ Gen 46:8-27).

The DEATH REPORT, I.B, marks the end of all the patriarchal traditions by noting the death not only of Joseph and his brothers but of the entire generation (cf. Judg 2:8-10).

Element II.A introduces the principal participants for the exodus traditions. In contrast to the relatively small group of people represented by the *běnê-yiśrā'ēl*, the "sons of Israel," in vv. 1-5, the same expression in v. 7, the "sons of Israel," should be considered the whole people, significantly expanded and threatening the security of Egypt (so Schmidt, BKAT, 29-30). Element II.B introduces the antagonists. The king of Egypt is given no exact identity; Israel's opposition remains simply the pharaoh or the king of Egypt throughout the exodus traditions, even though one pharaoh dies and a new one comes to the throne (cf. 2:23). The major structural element in II.B, a SPEECH (see Schmidt, BKAT, 23, for the significance of speech as a structural device), contrasts sharply with the impersonal report in II.A. The speech is an EXHORTATION for a policy of oppression against Israel. II.C reports the consequences of the policy: Israel thrives, increasing the threat against Egypt and its corresponding demand for more severe oppression. The motif of increase is thus a complement to the basic theme of the longer narrative. Yet it plays no independent role apart from its complementary position and functions primarily as a means of transition from patriarchs to exodus. It is a product of the redaction that brought patriarchs and exodus together (cf. Schmidt, BKAT, 47).

Redundancy in the structure of the exposition suggests a multiplicity of sources and confirms source analysis from stylistic grounds: Vv. 8-12 belong to J, while vv. 7, 13-14 derive from P (on secondary elements in P see Schmidt, BKAT, 16). Vv. 1-6 should also be considered P.

The P transition reflects the following structure:

I. Summary conclusion for preceding traditions — 1:1-6
   A. Name list — 1-5
   B. Death report — 6
II. Leitmotif for following traditions — 7, 13-14
   A. Motivation for oppression — 7
   B. Oppression and results — 13-14

The structure for the final form of the transition thus derives basically from the transition in P. The first part parallels the Joseph story as a summary of the preceding narratives. The second part focuses on the oppression motif without reference to the corresponding threat to Israelite sons (see Schmidt, BKAT, 42). Continuation for the P tradition, developing out of this specification of motif, lies in 6:2–7:6.

Structure in the J transition is as follows:

I.	Exposition of character: the chief antagonist	1:8
II.	Speech	9-10
	A. Introduction: king of Egypt to his people	9
	B. Exhortation to oppress Israel	10
III.	Execution of instructions (exhortation)	11-12
	A. Report of oppression with specification of work	11
	B. Results	12

The final form of the text preserves the J section as part of element II. For J there is no distinct structural element for a summary conclusion to the patriarchal theme, although the definition of an antagonist in v. 8 implies a conclusion: since the new king over Egypt did not know Joseph, the period characterized by good relationships between the Egyptians and the Israelites must be over. Nevertheless, rather than a distinct structural conclusion for the patriarchal traditions, J simply introduces the oppression theme for the following exodus traditions (→ The Joseph Story, FOTL I, 263ff.).

The transition should be considered a foundation not primarily for the Moses tales in Exod 1:14–2:10 and 2:11-22 but for the principal collection of exodus traditions in subsequent chapters. Its clearest continuation lies in 2:23-25 and 3:1–4:18, with significant points of contact in ch. 5 and the sign cycle in 7:7–10:29*.

Genre

The two principal elements of structure in this text appear consistently in TRANSITIONS (Gen 25:12-20; 35:22b-37:4; Exod 2:23-25; 4:19-23; Judg 2:8-10). Characteristic vocabulary for transitions include in v. 6, *wayyāmot,* "he died" and in v. 8, *wayyāqom,* "he arose" (so Vriezen). The subject of the second verb is normally identified as the successor to the subject of the first (cf. Judg 2:8-10). Since here the pharaoh (v. 8) cannot be the successor to Joseph (v. 6), the unity that can be defined by these verbs breaks down. Joseph's successor (v. 7) is the people of Israel (against Vriezen).

The TRANSITION is a literary device, a collection of motifs or distinct units as summaries of traditions. A NAME LIST is a common device in such collections (cf. Gen 35:22b-37:4), although other devices can be used (cf. Exod 2:23-25). The NAME LIST itself is a distinct genre. It should not be confused with a (→) genealogy, although the two have much in common. Normally introduced by a stereotyped refrain, expanded to define the particular character of the names in the list, and concluded by a similar refrain (cf. Num 13:4 and 16), the LIST reflects organizational functions (cf. 1:1-16; 13:4-16; 34:16-29). Specific concern to stipulate the number of people represented by the names in the list is characteristic for the genre. Thus the CENSUS LIST in 1:17-54 reflects the twelve-tribe organization of Israel, but the numbers reflect the total male population available from each tribe for military service (→ Gen 46:8-27).

The same twofold transition pattern appears in P. The J counterpart comprises only a report of an event and its results, Exod 1:8-12 (see Childs, *Exodus,* 7). Since it functions as an introduction of a controlling theme in the following collection of traditions, however, it should be more narrowly defined as an exposition for the exodus tradition (so Coats, "Transition"; Schmidt, BKAT, 32). It may be called a SUMMARY STORY OR REPORT.

Setting

TRANSITIONS generally, and this unit particularly, derive from a redactional context. At its latest stage, this unit reflects the structural seams in the final form of the Pentateuch (see Schmidt, BKAT, 7). Since traditions had already been organized into an extensive collection, the process here involves the combination of completed collections rather than an original organization of material. The P transition belongs to a literary process of organization for significantly large collections of tradition. It is not yet clear, however, to what extent P constructs tradition still relatively independent into an organized collection despite organizational schemes already present in his sources. J also sets his exposition for the exodus theme at just this point in the narrative. Whether J was first responsible for the organization of traditions into the extensive theme suggested by this transition unit is not yet clear (see Schmidt, BKAT, 31). The J exposition thus belongs to a redactional setting; it is a sign of organizational activity in Yahwistic traditions along the lines of thematic elements.

The NAME LIST is borrowed for the task of literary organization from social institutions. A basic institutional setting for the list is the military (cf. Num 1:1-16) and this suggests that the twelve-tribe organization of Israel has a military character (see Schmidt, BKAT, 27).

Intention

This unit provides a structural transition between the patriarchal traditions of Genesis and the following exodus traditions by summarizing major segments or motifs from each of the two themes. The P transition accomplishes this function by summarizing one facet of the Jacob traditions, Jacob's move to Egypt, and thus duplicating the structural role of the Joseph story for the organization of the Pentateuch. It then highlights major motif elements from the coming exodus collection (cf. Coats, "Transition"). J accomplishes this function only by highlighting the Egyptian oppression as the major exposition of

24

the exodus theme. The NAME LIST functions as a device for summarizing that part of the Jacob traditions that moved Israel's fathers from Canaan to Egypt (cf. Gen 46:8-27).

Bibliography

R. Borchert, "Stil und Aufbau der priesterschriftlichen Erzählung" (Diss., Heidelberg, 1957); G. W. Coats, "A Structural Transition in Exodus," *VT* 22 (1972) 129-42; M. Fishbane, "Exodus 1–4: The Prologue to the Exodus Cycle," in *Text and Texture: Close Readings of Selected Biblical Texts* (New York: Schocken, 1979) 63-76; C. Isbell, "The Structure of Exodus 1:1-14," in *Art and Meaning: Rhetoric in Biblical Literature* (ed. D. J. A. Clines, D. M. Gunn, and A. J. Hauser; JSOTSup 19; Sheffield: JSOT Press, 1982) 37-61; K. Rupprecht, "עלה מן הארץ" (Ex 1[10] Hos 2[2]) 'sich des Landes bemächtigen'?" *ZAW* 82 (1970) 442-47; T. C. Vriezen, "Exodusstudien. Exodus I," *VT* 17 (1967) 334-53; D. W. Wicke, "The Literary Structure of Exodus 1:2–2:10," *JSOT* 24 (1982) 99-107.

ADDENDUM. B. Gosse, "Transitions rédactionnelles de l'historie des clans à l'historie des peuples en Ex 1,7; 2,24b," *EstBib* 51 (1993) 163-70; J. Siebert-Hommes, "Die Geburtsgeschichte des Mose innerhalb des Erzählzusammenhangs von Exodus 1 und 2," *VT* 42 (1992) 398-404.

MOSES ADOPTION LEGEND, 1:15–2:10

Structure

I. Exposition   1:15-22
  A. Report of conflict between king of Egypt and midwives   15-21
    1. Speech: instructions to execute Israelite sons   15-16
    2. Response to instructions   17
    3. Dispute   18-19
      a. Accusation: king of Egypt to midwives   18
      b. Response: midwives to king of Egypt   19
    4. Conclusion   20-21
  B. Speech: instructions to execute Israelite *sons*   22
II. Crisis: report of threat to a particular Israelite (Levite) son   2:1-4
  A. Marriage   1
  B. Conception, birth, concealment, and disposal of a son   2-4
III. Resolution of the threat: adoption legend   2:5-10
  A. Discovery by the pharaoh's daughter   5-6
  B. Business negotiation (wet-nurse motif)   7-8
    1. Dialogue about wet nurse   7-8a
    2. Conclusion of negotiation   8b
  C. Wet-nurse contract   9

Tradition about a threat to the lives of Israelite sons (1:15-22) is not simply an extension of the oppression motif from 1:8-12 (so Childs, "Birth," 117). Yet the adoption narrative in its present form presupposes 1:8-12. Execution of male children is a drastic alternative for a problem unaffected by increased oppression. The Moses adoption narrative thus relates tenuously with the independent introduction of the Egyptian oppression motif. Its major point of contact, however, moves beyond the boundaries of the exodus theme to the larger context for Moses traditions (→ The Pentateuch/Hexateuch, FOTL I).

The adoption narrative comprises a basic core of tradition in 2:1-10 (II and III) plus an exposition (I) for that core, 1:15-22 (contrast Schmidt, BKAT, 62). The exposition has two parts: I.A, vv. 15-21, introduces the motif of a threat to Israelite sons. Report of a conflict between the king and midwives attending Israelite women reaches a climax in vv. 20-21, with a threat to the midwives resolved to the midwives' advantage (on the literary unity of this section see Schmidt, BKAT, 18-19). After this point the midwives play no further role in the narrative. In the present form of the text, vv. 15-21 do not stand as an independent narrative. They function structurally as a link between Egyptian oppression (1:8-12) and the birth-adoption tradition (2:1-10). The threat to Israelite sons sets the stage for the material in 2:1-10, while the midwives' response ties to the material in 1:8-12. The midwives successfully foil the king's plan to execute the children, and the Israelites multiply (see Schmidt, BKAT, 19). Element I.B, v. 22, picks up the threat by renewing the pharaoh's policy for executing Israelite sons and provides an exposition for the major crisis developed by the narrative in 2:1-10 (so Schmidt, BKAT, 20).

Element II builds the crisis to its peak: A son is born. Rhetorical play on the noun "son" (*bēn,* 1:16, 22; 2:2, 10), the noun "boy" (*yeled,* 1:17, 18; 2:3, 6, 7, 8, 9, 10), and various forms of the verb "to give birth" (*yālad,* 1:15, 16, 17, 18, 19, 20, 21, 22; 2:2, 10) bind elements I and II (1:15-22 and 2:1-4) together into an artistic whole. Since I.B shows the threat to Israelite sons to be immediate, a report of a marriage in the tribe of Levi with an immediate birth of a son sharpens the crisis. The crisis reaches its peak when the mother places her son in an ark in the river with a sister to observe his fate, and the pharaoh's daughter discovers him.

Element III then resolves the crisis. In v. 6 the princess' SOLILOQUY is introduced with a note about the child's fate. Then in vv. 7-8 a denouement appears in a dialogue between the princess and the sister. The child will be placed in the care of a wet nurse. V. 9a reports that a wet nurse, ironically the child's own mother, was instructed to care for the child over a prescribed period of time for a prescribed wage. But only after proper execution of the wet nurse's instructions (v. 9b) does the climax finally appear (v. 10). One Israelite son escapes the pharaoh's purge by becoming the adopted son of the pharaoh's daughter.

The narrative cannot be divided into different sources but belongs totally to J, or JE (so Childs, "Birth," 119). Yet the tradition in J shows evidence of growth at an oral level. In the present form of the tradition, element I functions as a bond between the Moses story and the oppression exposition. But earlier forms might be reconstructed. The basis for reconstructing a story with motivation for the pharaoh's decree in a missing prophecy (so Gressmann, 8) is thin (see Schmidt, BKAT, 57). It is more convincing to hypothesize that the tradition about a conflict between the king of Egypt and the midwives, I.A, had a life of its own before it was appropriated for this position in the exodus-Moses collection of traditions (cf. Schmidt, BKAT, 22). At least a distinct line of tradition could be defined in the midwives' conflict since I.B can provide sufficient basis for the exposure motif in element II as well as a connection with the oppression policy of 1:8-12. Whether this was indeed the case cannot yet be clearly determined. If it were the case, then the two traditions would have been combined at an early stage of oral transmission, or perhaps they were combined as a part of the redaction that brought Elohistic material into the Yahwistic narrative (so Schmidt, BKAT, 22; → The Yahwist, FOTL I, 21-24).

Genre

A narrative LEGEND (see Schmidt, BKAT, 23, 61), the Moses story cannot be aligned simply with (→) birth stories such as Genesis 16 and 18. The story, particularly in element III, follows a sequential pattern similar to one found in a series of bilingual Sumerian-Akkadian texts called *ana ittišu:* a child is found, recognized as a foundling, delivered to a wet nurse for a set wage, weaned, returned to his owner, and finally adopted (so Childs, "Birth," 111-14). The *ana ittišu* texts also suggest that following the adoption, a new son would be given a name, thus providing a parallel for the ETIOLOGY in 2:10b. Since the *ana ittišu* texts belong to a genre of legal documents rather than narrative (→) story, we can at most speak of influence from legal sources (so Childs, "Birth"). But the pattern suggests that the entire narrative should be considered an ADOPTION LEGEND rather than simply a (→) birth story.

The sudden introduction of a sister in v. 4 and the equally sudden exit of the same character after v. 8 should be seen as part of the artistic style of such stories: a new character appears to fulfill a distinct function and, once the function is fulfilled, drops away. The sister is dropped from the narrative after the wet nurse is summoned, just as the midwives are dropped after the penultimate climax in 1:20-21. At any given point in the narrative, principal characters number no more than four. Moreover, the climax of the story does not bring the narration to a sudden halt, but rather allows the action to fade slowly. The child is out of danger. But his future is not altogether certain.

An important parallel for the ADOPTION LEGEND, the *Legend of Sargon,* includes a report of conception, birth, and exposure of a foundling — significantly by leaving the unwanted child in a basket of reeds in a river — then discovery of the child, adoption, rearing, and the child's subsequent rise to a position of power. The Sargon narrative has no naming element, no reference to a wet nurse or to a general policy of the state for exposing children. Nevertheless, the pattern, clearly focused on adoption, corresponds to the Moses legend.

The ETIOLOGY in v. 10b represents an essential element in the unit. The adoptive parent gives the child a name (contrast Long, 57; so Schmidt, BKAT, 54-55). But it is not to be considered the primary core of tradition, stimulating the growth of the narrative. This is not an etiological story (so Childs, "Birth"; Long, 57; Schmidt, BKAT, 53; against a tentative proposal by Noth, *Exodus,* 26).

Formulae and distinct genre elements include: 1:18, an ACCUSATION from a preofficial stage of legal suit, with 1:19 a formal RESPONSE to the accusation (see Schmidt, BKAT, 44). Combination of the two elements compose a DISPUTE. 2:9a reflects the pattern of a formal LABOR CONTRACT for a wet nurse (cf. Childs, "Birth"). V. 10a is a FORMULA FOR ADOPTION (Childs, "Birth"). V. 10b is an ETIOLOGICAL FORMULA.

Setting

Typical motifs and a particular perspective for presenting material show contact with wisdom motifs (so Childs, "Birth," 119-22). The observation does not suggest, however, that the story derives from an institution dominated by the wise man. It points more readily to the people, perhaps the family structure, as the locus for preserving the tradition (see Schmidt, BKAT, 63). More precise definition of setting for the ADOPTION LEGEND as one of the various genres of a HEROIC SAGA is still incomplete. Its position as a narrative combined with the midwives tradition and grafted into the oppression theme reflects the structural combinations characteristic for Exodus as a larger context. It is part of the Moses traditions as well as part of the oppression theme. Whether it was originally an independent legend is not yet clear (see Schmidt, BKAT, 62-63) but is unlikely (→ The Pentateuch/Hexateuch, FOTL I).

Intention

Presupposing an established role for Moses in subsequent Exodus traditions, the LEGEND in its present stage focuses on Moses' adoption by a member of the Egyptian court and intends to describe the ironical failure of the pharaoh's extreme oppression. At least one secondary intention, perhaps more prominent at an oral stage in the history of the tradition, would be to explain that the legendary hero of the Israelites, known by tradition as the son of an Egyptian princess and labeled with an Egyptian name, was in fact an Israelite foundling, deserted by his parents under pressure from the pharaoh after they had taken precautions for his protection and future. The LEGEND introduces the name,

Moses, and the child who bears it as an Israelite whose fate cannot yet be clearly seen (see Schmidt, BKAT, 58).

Bibliography

H. J. Boecker, *Redeformen des Rechtslebens im Alten Testament* (WMANT 14; Neukirchen-Vluyn: Neukirchener, 1964); B. S. Childs, "The Birth of Moses," *JBL* 84 (1965) 109-22; J. Fichtner, "Die etymologische Ätiologie in den Namengebungen der geschichtlichen Bücher des Alten Testaments," *VT* 6 (1956) 372-96; M. Fishbane, "Exodus 1–4: The Prologue to the Exodus Cycle," in *Text and Texture: Close Readings of Selected Biblical Texts* (New York: Schocken, 1979) 63-76; H. Gressmann, *Mose und seine Zeit: Ein Kommentar zu den Mose-Sagen* (FRLANT 18; Göttingen: Vandenhoeck & Ruprecht, 1913); S. Herrmann, "Mose," *EvT* 28 (1968) 301-28; B. O. Long, *The Problem of Etiological Narrative in the Old Testament* (BZAW 108; Berlin: Töpelmann, 1968); S. E. Loewenstamm, "Die Geburtsgeschichte Moses," in *Studies in Jewish Religious and Intellectual History* (*Fest.* A. Altmann; ed. S. Stein and R. Loewe; University, Ala.: Univ. of Alabama Press, 1979) 195-213; D. B. Redford, "The Literary Motif of the Exposed Child," *Numen* 14 (1967) 209-28; D. W. Wicke, "The Literary Structure of Exodus 1:2–2:10," *JSOT* 24 (1982) 99-107.

ADDENDUM. G. F. Davies, *Israel in Egypt: Reading Exodus 1–2* (JSOTSup 135; Sheffield: JSOT Press, 1992); J. Siebert-Hommes, "Die Geburtsgeschichte des Mose innerhalb des Erzählzusammenhangs von Exodus 1 und 2," *VT* 42 (1992) 398-404; P. Weimar, *Die Berufung des Moses: Literarwissenschaftliche Analyse von Exodus 2,23–5,5* (OBO 32; Göttingen: Vandenhoeck & Ruprecht, 1980); I. Willi-Plein, "Ort und literarische Funktion der Geburtsgeschichte des Mose," *VT* 41 (1991) 110-18.

ANNOTATION. Emphasizing the birth rather than the adoption, the studies by Davies, Siebert-Hommes, and Willi-Plein are carried out in the mold of the study of literature.

MOSES MARRIAGE STORY, 2:11-22

Structure

The structure of this unit is similar to the structure of the ADOPTION LEGEND, 1:15–2:10. The initial element exposes the circumstances anticipating the major crisis of the narrative (element II); yet it binds the unit with the preceding adoption text. It presupposes Moses' life in the Egyptian court as an adopted Hebrew (cf. 2:1-10) as well as the general theme of oppression (cf. 1:11). Finally the crisis it introduces is resolved in element III.

Element I develops two clearly defined acts in identical structure. Following an initial exposition of circumstances, the narrative describes a conflict followed by Moses' intervention. I.A.3, Moses' intervention in the first act, carries the weight of the conflict report. I.B then narrates a second conflict. I.B.3, the second intervention, appears as a dialogue between the Hebrews involved in the conflict and Moses. The results in this case are disastrous rather than redemptive. It is clear, however, that the same basic structure appears in both I.A and I.B.

Element II begins with a statement of crisis (II.A), necessitating a change of scene and introduction of new characters. It is nevertheless bound into close unity with element I by repetition of the basic structure developed in I.A and I.B. Following the initial exposition of circumstances and new characters, the text narrates a conflict and Moses' intervention. In each case the intervention pattern suggests that the narration can be understood as an element in the heroic traditions about Moses. Moses defends the oppressed Hebrew, then a Hebrew oppressed by another Hebrew, and finally oppressed women of a different land.

In element III a DIALOGUE between the new characters, daughters of a priest of Midian and their father, replaces the dominant narration structure of the other parts in this element and prepares for the resolution of the crisis. Because the father is impressed with the heroic intervention, Moses finds a (relatively permanent) sanctuary from the pharaoh who seeks his life. Significantly, the structure of element III focuses on Moses' relationship with the priest despite the conclusion with Moses' marriage to one of the priest's daughters.

The story cannot be divided successfully among various literary sources. The entire unit belongs to one source (contrast Noth, *Exodus,* 34-35). Identity of the source is difficult to determine. It is perhaps J, although a firm conclusion seems impossible. Earlier stages of the tradition can be hypothesized behind elements II and III, a marriage tradition depicting Moses as a hero who wins the attention of a potential father-in-law and then a bride for himself (cf. Coats, "Moses in Midian").

This STORY serves in its present position as a transition from Moses in Egypt to Moses in Midian and lays the groundwork for the account of Moses' vocation, Exod 3:1–4:18. If the text served only that function, we would have to conclude that the marriage tradition does not represent a seed of tradition that could produce an independent narrative. The primary tradition for this unit would then be defined as the account of Moses' first encounter with God on the mountain of God (so Noth, *Exodus,* 30). Earlier stages of tradition, however, point to the independent status of the marriage tradition. The narrative is not simply dependent on the following text unit but has a distinct structure and genre of its own (cf. Coats, "Moses in Midian"). Its contact with the Moses (→) vocation account is tenuous (cf. The Exodus Saga, Chapter 1A). Even the contact with the opening pastoral scene is vague; there is no clear evidence that Moses is herding flocks as fulfillment of the bridal agreement (contrast Plautz, 304). The implication of this conclusion is that the admittedly very old element of tradition about Moses' marriage has been expanded in order to build a bridge from the adoption tradition to the vocation account. The expansion subordinated the marriage characteristics of the tradition to the crisis faced by Moses in the pharaoh's court and the call to challenge the Egyptian oppression.

Genre

This unit can be understood as a STORY in a larger HEROIC SAGA. It is brief, limited in complexity of plot and number of characters, and it ends not in a dramatic reduction of tension but in a fading tension (see Schmidt, BKAT, 23). Above all, the plot focuses on marriage as a principal event in the life of a hero, although it points to structural contact outside its own limits. It can thus be understood as an element in the larger context of Moses narratives (→ 1:15–2:10).

Structural patterns, closely parallel to the narratives of Genesis 24 and 29, suggest that this unit, at least vv. 15b-22, should be more specifically categorized as a MARRIAGE STORY. Three elements are crucial: (1) an introduction, with the location for action typically at a well and typically an excuse for introductory contact between the principal characters; (2) dialogue between father and daughters about events at the well, ending in instructions for the daughters to invite the man into their home; (3) marriage report, with notation of sons

31

born to the couple (cf. Genesis 24 and 29). Moreover, both here and in the parallels the narrative focuses on the relationship between the bridegroom and his father-in-law.

The structure of this story does not permit a conclusion that the genre should be defined as an (→) etiology for the name of Moses' son, despite the concluding ETIOLOGICAL FORMULA and Gershom's position as the ancestor for a priestly clan subsequently active in Israel (cf. Long). The genre emphasizes not the son of the marriage but the father-in-law.

Formulae in the text include ACCUSATION-RESPONSE from a preofficial (→) lawsuit, categorized together as DISPUTATION (vv. 13b-14a, 18b-20; → 1:15-21), and an ETYMOLOGICAL ETIOLOGY (v. 22b; → 2:10). V. 11a is a formula used to introduce a narrative (cf. 2:23; Judg 19:1).

Setting

As part of J, this STORY shares in the literary structure of the whole (→ The Yahwist, FOTL I, 21-24). At a popular level, a MARRIAGE STORY would have been spread among the general population, especially among families who delighted in popular folk stories. A more precise definition of setting for the genre has not yet appeared. This STORY connects with a distinct tradition about the originally unnamed Midianite priest who is Moses' father-in-law and suggests that the narrative may have been preserved in the legal-military organization in Israel that traced its origin to Moses and Jethro (→ Exodus 18). The expansion of the story, the stage of the tradition that connects it to the larger complex of Moses stories, would not be denied to the same setting noted for the expansion of the (→) adoption legend. Significantly, Moses' impulsive flight from Egypt would be foreign to a wisdom ideal. The setting here would be the activity associated with the combination of heroic Moses and thematic emphasis on Yahweh's deeds (→ The Exodus Saga, Chapter 1A).

Intention

The final form of the text reports Moses' escape from the pharaoh by finding sanctuary with the priest of Midian and provides a transition from traditions set in Egypt to a Midianite setting, with an opening for the VOCATION ACCOUNT in 3:1–4:18. In addition it joins the adoption TALE in presenting a foil to the pharaoh's plans that threaten to dispose of Moses. Earlier levels of the tradition, focusing not on Moses' relationship with Zipporah, the wife, or Gershom, the son, but on the originally unnamed father-in-law, grow out of a basic tradition about Moses and his father-in-law (Gunneweg). But the tradition establishes the relationship through Moses' heroic deeds. Its function would be to show how the relationship between Moses and the priest of Midian began.

Bibliography

B. S. Childs, "The Birth of Moses," *JBL* 85 (1965) 109-22; G. W. Coats, "Moses in Midian," *JBL* 92 (1973) 3-10; H. J. Gunneweg, "Mose in Midian," *ZTK* 61 (1965) 1-9; B. O. Long, *The Problem of Etiological Narrative in the Old Testament* (BZAW 108; Berlin: Töpelmann, 1968); W. Plautz, "Die Form der Eheschliessung im Alten Testament," *ZAW* 76 (1964) 298-318.

TRANSITION, 2:23-25

Structure

I. Conclusion of the preceding tradition (death report)	23aα
II. Anticipation of following traditions (complaint report)	23aβ-25
A. Complaint	23aβ-b
B. Promise for response	24-25

Element I marks a conclusion to the narrative in 2:11-22 by observing that the threat forcing Moses' flight from Egypt no longer exists. Significantly, the final part of element I is a DEATH REPORT (cf. 1:6). Element II sets the stage for the VOCATION ACCOUNT in 3:1–4:18 by reporting Israel's cry and the corresponding response from God. Cf. the similarity between vv. 24-25 and 3:7.

This unit is tightly constructed, showing no evidence of earlier levels in its history. It thus derives from only one source, in all probability J.

Genre

The unit is not an oral genre but a compilation of material to serve as a redactional transition. Influence from a classical (→) complaint ritual may be reflected in element II, particularly in Israel's cry *(zĕ῾āqâ)* and God's favorable response (thus Plastaras). But the element is not itself a lamentation ritual. It is a report of an event employed as one of two elements in a larger whole (→ 1:8-12). It may be called a SUMMARY STORY OR REPORT.

The formula "It was in those many days . . ." characteristically functions as the INTRODUCTION of a new narrative unit (cf. 2:11; Judg 19:1; 1 Sam 28:1).

Setting and Intention

A transition derives from a redactional setting, from a circle of editors-artists responsible for constructing smaller units of tradition into larger complexes. Its intention corresponds to its setting: to bind units of tradition, originally having no natural connection, or at best a rough one, into larger wholes. This example of transition provides a bridge between the Moses in Midian tradition and the (→) vocation account (→ The Exodus Saga, Chapter 1A).

The formula in v. 23 does not necessarily belong to a redactional setting but may reflect an oral setting as well, a typical introduction for a narrative (cf. Judg 19:1). Its function is thus simply to open a narrative unit.

MOSES-AARON VOCATION ACCOUNT, 3:1–4:18

Structure

I. Exposition	3:1-6
A. Introduction	1
B. Theophany	2-3
1. Natural phenomena	2
2. Moses' soliloquy	3
C. Dialogue	4-6a
1. Call to attention	4
2. Speech instructions	5
3. Self-revelation formula	6a
D. Narration of Moses' response	6b
II. Vocation dialogue	3:7–4:17
A. Commission speech	7-10
1. Promise for exodus and conquest	7-8
2. Commission	9-10
B. Moses' objection: self-abasement formula	11
C. Reassurance speech	12
1. Assistance formula	12aα
2. Sign	12aβ-b
D. Leading question	13
E. Reassurance speeches	14-22
1. "I am who I am"	14a
2. Instructions for message	14b
a. Message commission formula	14bα
b. Message (cryptic sentence)	14bβ
3. Instructions speech	15-22
a. For message	15
1) Message commission formula	15aα
2) Name	15aβ-b
b. For message	16-22
1) Message commission formula	16a
2) Message	16b-22
a) Promise for exodus and conquest	16b-17
b) Instructions for Israel's action	18
c) Expected response	19
d) Promise for exodus	20-22

The present form of the Moses VOCATION ACCOUNT comprises three basic elements: I, Exposition, 3:1-6; II, VOCATION DIALOGUE, 3:7–4:17; and III, Conclusion, 4:18. In its latest stage the VOCATION ACCOUNT ties into the narrative about Moses in Midian (2:11-22). It presupposes the introduction of the oppression motif (1:8-14), but shows no reflection of an Egyptian pogrom (1:15-22). Moreover it anticipates subsequent narratives about the exodus (5:1–6:1 and 7:7–10:29). Yet the transition in 2:11-22 is not a primary part of the unit (see Childs, *Exodus,* 51; Richter, 74). The conclusion in 4:18 rounds off the narrative context for Moses in Midian, preparing for the shift in scene back to Egypt. (For a different definition of the end of the unit see Childs, *Exodus,* 52.)

Element I introduces the unit. Its relationship with element II, however, is loose (so Richter, 85). After a brief exposition in v. 1, introducing the principal character with his occupation and the place, vv. 2-3 describe a theophany. The weight of the unit, however, does not appear in the description. Rather, vv. 2-3 set the stage for dialogue between Moses and the deity who introduces himself in the theophany. The SPEECH in v. 5 announces necessary precautions for anyone who would stand on holy ground. With a new speech introduction, v. 6a employs a SELF-REVELATION FORMULA and establishes a connection with the patriarchal tradition. The God who introduces himself to Moses is the God of the fathers. V. 6b then notes Moses' response. No explicit reaction to the theophany in vv. 2-3 or the instructions for proper entrance to holy ground in v. 4 are spelled out. The messenger and the burning bush are dropped completely, leaving only the self-revelation as a bridge to element II.

Element II develops almost entirely without narration of events, employing instead an exchange of speeches between Moses and God. That dialogue follows a recognizable pattern of repetition. The constituent parts are: (1) commission, (2) objection, and (3) reassurance (so Habel; see also Richter, 97; Plastaras, 77).

The COMMISSION can be seen most clearly in 3:7-10, construed as a divine speech setting out instructions for a basic task. Vv. 15-22 hide a duplication of the commission in a speech structured as reassurance for an objection to the earlier commission. In contrast to the first commission, to be carried out directly with the pharaoh, the second commission sends Moses initially to the elders of Israel, and only then with the elders to assist him is he to go to the pharaoh. The problem of duplication in the commission is, however, basically traditio-historical, not a combination of sources. (Vv. 14-15, a response to Moses' objection in the first commission, presuppose that Moses is sent to the elders of Israel.)

The objection is generally brief, but repeated at least four (3:11; 4:1, 10, 13), perhaps five (3:13) times. Various stylistic devices and formulas appear. The most common is bî 'ădōnāy, "Oh, my Lord" (4:10, 13; cf. Judg 6:13, 15). A SELF-ABASEMENT FORMULA (Exod 3:11) also appears here. V. 13 is not precisely an objection to the commission, but rather a leading question opening to the cryptic saying of v. 14. It functions nevertheless as an objection in the structure of the whole, a delay in the move toward final dispatch of the commissioned leader.

Reassurance, a regular response to the objection (3:12; 4:2-9, 11-12, 14-17, and perhaps 3:14-22), can be constructed around one or both of two subelements: a promise from God for his presence, and a sign confirming his presence (against Habel, who considers the sign a distinct element). In 4:2-9 reassurance is composed only of sign, in 4:11-12 only of promise. The two can, however, appear together (cf. 3:12; 4:14-17) and seem to function structurally as a single element. Both are constituents for the commission itself, suggesting that reassurance should be seen as an extension to the initial commission (cf. Judges 6).

This point would be particularly clear if the antecedent for the demonstrative pronoun "this," zeh, in 3:12a could be taken as the promise for presence. V. 12b however, makes such a conclusion difficult (see Childs, Exodus, 56-59). Perhaps the sign should be seen here as the theophanic burning bush, a confirmation of Moses' authority (so Childs, "Deuteronomic Formulae").

The structural unity between v. 12 and the following verses may illumine the question still further. Vv. 14-22 carry three distinct movements of reassurance. V. 14a is the cryptic sentence, "I am who I am." V. 14b appropriates the verbal construction from v. 14a as a name for the commissioning deity. The final speech, vv. 15-22, introduces the name Yahweh and completes the commission with a promise for the exodus and instructions for realizing the promise. Moreover, the cryptic sentence in v. 14a can be understood as a wordplay on the ASSISTANCE FORMULA of v. 12, particularly since the formula in v. 12 employs the same verbal construction, "I am," *'ehĕyeh,* even though syntactically the construction is redundant. The play suggests that the name Yahweh is in itself a promise for divine presence. Would it be possible, then, to suggest that the sign of v. 12 is the name, introduced so distinctively in vv. 13-22? (For the most penetrating analysis of this structure, cf. Richter, 85-99; similarly, Habel.)

Structural doublets suggest that two distinct sources have been combined. (Cf. vv. 7-8 and 16-20 as a single commission, especially the reasons for the commission in v. 7, with the commission in vv. 9-15, and the reasons for the commission in v. 9. Distinction between a commission to go to the pharaoh, vv. 9-10, and a commission to go first to the elders, vv. 16-17, does not contribute to this division.) Elements from J include 3:1-5 (6a), 6b, 7-8, 16-22; 4:1-16 (17), 18. Elements from E are 3:9-15 and perhaps 3:6a and 4:17. Cf. Noth (*Exodus,* 34, 38), who also suggests 3:1b and 4b for E. On 4:10-16 as part of J, cf. Noth (*Exodus,* 34, 46-47).

Structure in E:

I. Introduction	3:1b, 4b, 6a
II. Vocation dialogue	3:9-15 and perhaps 4:17
A. Commission	9-10
B. Objection	11
C. Reassurance	12
1. Promise for presence	12aα
2. Sign	12aβ-b
D. Objection — leading question	13
E. Reassurance	14-15

The introductory speech in 3:6a may belong to E as a structural doublet of the speech in v. 5 (cf. the renewed introduction to the speech in v. 6a). The content of the speech, however, is not a doublet to v. 5 and could belong equally well to J. Vv. 1b and 4b are not structural doublets to the J material. If the speech in v. 6a should be attributed to E, however, it would imply some kind of narrative introduction. In any case, the principal section of E lies clearly in the DIALOGUE of vv. 9-15. The COMMISSION in vv. 9-10, objection in v. 11, and reassurance in v. 12 follow the pattern described above in a rather simplified fashion. The commission to Moses that this section poses stands out in comparison to the J counterpart: Moses himself, rather than Yahweh, will lead the people out of Egypt. But the difference is not substantial (so Noth, *Exodus,* 34, 38). The unique item of E is the leading question in v. 13 and the response series in vv. 14-15 (see the comments above).

The structure in J:

I. Introduction	3:1-5 (6)
II. Vocation dialogue	3:7-8, 16-22; 4:1-16 (17), 18
A. Commission	7-8, 16-22
1. Promise of exodus	7-8
2. Commission instructions	16-22
B. Objection	4:1
C. Reassurance: signs	2-9
D. Objection	10
E. Reassurance: promise of presence	11-12
F. Objection	13
G. Reassurance	14-17
1. Promise of presence	14-15
2. Definition of relationship	16
3. Sign	17
III. Conclusion	18

J begins with the Theophany Report, then moves abruptly to the series of speeches in the vocation dialogue. The structure of the final stage of the text thus derives from J. The dialogue in J opens in vv. 7-8 with a promise for the exodus, followed immediately by the commission in vv. 16-22. Absence of an introduction to a distinct speech in v. 16 can be explained by understanding vv. 7-8 with their introduction as the proper beginning of the speech. The commission sending Moses first to the elders of Israel and then, with their assistance, to the pharaoh lies at the basis of the J tradition and is primary for the exodus-Moses collection (cf. Seebass, 22). Following the commission is a threefold repetition of the objection-reassurance series.

The final sequence, 4:13-17, and perhaps the preparation for the sequence in 4:10-12, introduce Aaron into the narrative rather abruptly. He is not a principal for action but a subject for discussion. With a somewhat artificial repetition of the promise for presence "with Aaron's mouth and with Moses' mouth" (in v. 15b; cf. also v. 12), this stage should probably be seen as a secondary growth in the tradition (Noth, *Exodus*, 46-47). Significantly, the discussion about Aaron subordinates him to Moses (v. 16). V. 17 may more properly belong to this stage of expansion in J than to the E material.

One must also ask whether the E material should not be considered simply as an expansion of the J saga. No firm antecedent lays a foundation for the exchange in vv. 9-15. The E commission in vv. 9-10 appears immediately after the J promise for the exodus, without distinct introduction to a speech, suggesting that the order, promise-commission, is important. Since E has no promise for the exodus, it would appear to depend on the promise already present in J. Further, like vv. 16-22 in J, the commission speech in vv. 9-10 seems to depend on the speech introduction in v. 7. Moreover, following the wordplay on the name, no further development of E can be seen. Does the wordplay in E have any real independence from the development of the J dialogue? (Contrast Richter, 110, who argues that it does.)

The J saga already reflects a stage in the collection of Israel's sacred traditions when previously distinct traditions have been harmonized (cf. 3:20-22, part of a speech anticipating two distinct conclusions to the sign cycle). It seems probable, therefore, that traditions in 3:1–4:18 existed at an oral level before their formulation in the J source. The clearest evidence lies in element I, the THEOPHANY REPORT, originally a tradition independent of the Moses (→) vocation account (see Gressmann, 23-39). Appearance of a messenger and the accompanying phenomenon belong to this stage. Whether the CALL TO ATTENTION and following instructions in vv. 4-5 and the SELF-INTRODUCTION in v. 6 also belong to an oral theophany tradition cannot be determined with clarity. At least v. 6 seems to be rather late in the history of tradition and anticipates references to the God of the fathers in the vocation dialogue. Evidence does not support reconstructing a narrative about the discovery of a holy place by a Midianite hero (against Noth, *Exodus,* 38-40).

We should also recognize that the Moses vocation tradition had a long oral history distinct from the theophany before it reached written form in J. (Cf. Seebass, 22. See also Gressmann, Schmid.) For example, the mountain of God setting in 3:1-6 would not be the original locale for the vocation tradition. To the contrary, the tradition presupposes more immediate access to the elders of Israel. Indeed, one may ask whether the cycle of plagues in 7:7–10:29 did not grow from the seed of tradition about signs to the elders as preserved in this text (→ The Exodus Saga, Chapter 1A).

Genre

Both the basic J narration of the vocation tradition and the E material that focused on the name are characterized by structural and diction patterns typical for vocation genres. The pattern of structure — commission, objection, reassurance through promise of presence or signs or both — appears in the Gideon vocation narrative, Judg 6:11-24 (so Richter, Kutsch), as well as in various prophetic texts (Isa 6:1-13; Jer 1:4-10; Ezek 1:4–3:15).

In its final stage the unit functions as a part of a larger whole, including Exod 1:8-12; 4:27-31; 5:1–6:1; and 7:7–10:29. Its classification here would be one element of a larger popular SAGA. The J and E versions of the vocation tradition taken by themselves do not develop a complete plot. Though parallel in structural pattern to the Gideon narrative, they provide a significant narration of events. Thus their VOCATION ACCOUNTS may not be identified on the basis of a narrative pattern of events (so Richter, 116, against Habel). Whatever event-related narrative plot may lie behind the texts, it is now structurally subordinated to the focus on the speeches. But despite their truncated form and at the same time because of their expanded and heightened focus on the VOCATION DIALOGUE, these versions belong to the variations within the genre of VOCATION ACCOUNT. For a discussion of genre problems in the larger unit, → The Exodus Saga, Chapter 1A.

As an independent tradition, however, this material probably circulated as an oral vocation account. The span of tension characterizing the plot of the narrative would have been built around the commission-objection-reassurance scheme, with the climax of the plot the final reassurance sending the leader to his task and the execution of the task itself (4:27-31 or 5:1–6:1; cf. Judges 6–7).

Characteristic diction for the vocation structure includes the verbs *hlk*, "to go" (Exod 3:10, 16; 4:12; Judg 6:14; cf. Isa 6:8-9; Jer 1:7), *šlḥ*, "to send" (Exod 3:10, 12, 13, 14, 15; 4:13; Judg 6:14; cf. Isa 6:8, 9; Judg 6:16; and similarly Exod 4:12, 13, contrasted to *'ittĕkā 'ănî* ["I am with you"] in Jer 1:8; cf. also references to the mouth of the man commissioned in Exod 4:10, 11, 12, 15, 16; Jer 1:9; Isa 6:7; Ezek 3:2); the noun *'ôt*, "sign" (Exod 3:12; 4:2-9, 17; Judg 6:12); and the objection introduction "O my Lord!" (*bî 'ădōnāy;* Exod 4:10, 13; Judg 6:15). Cf. Richter.

The narrative tradition behind the introduction reflects characteristics typical for a THEOPHANY REPORT (cf. Jeremias, Schmid). The theophany tradition may have been used as a foundation story for a local sanctuary as in Gen 12:6-7; 28:10-17 (thus Noth, *Exodus,* 38-40; Plastaras; Gressmann). But its character cannot be clearly defined (Richter). An ETYMOLOGICAL ETIOLOGY based on a wordplay between *sĕneh,* "bush," and *sînay,* "Sinai" (thus Gressmann; Noth, *Exodus,* 39-40; Richter) may appear in this tradition. But the narrative was not originally an ETYMOLOGICAL ETIOLOGY.

Verse 1 can be defined as a stylized exposition, a formula employed to open a narrative or a major segment in a narrative (Richter). The CALL TO ATTENTION and RESPONSE (v. 4) appear frequently as the opening element of a DIALOGUE (Richter). V. 5 is paralleled by Josh 5:15, with only minor exceptions in style and orthography. But the Joshua text is not a satisfactory independent witness to the expression as a distinct formula (so Richter). If a formula appears in this text, it cannot now be defined with precision.

Verse 6 contains a SELF-REVELATION FORMULA (Zimmerli). The promise for salvation in vv. 7-10 may reflect influence from the Priestly oracle of salvation in a complaint ritual (so Plastaras). It is not, however, to be categorized as a part of a complaint ritual itself. Moreover, its contact with juridical formulation seems minimal (against Plastaras). V. 11 contains the two chief elements of a SELF-ABASEMENT FORMULA (Coats, "Formulas"). The ASSISTANCE FORMULA in v. 12 is a regular part of vocation genres (Preuss).

In the introduction to messages, to be delivered by Moses to his people, a stereotyped expression marks the message's commission. Closely related to the more widely spread (→) messenger formula, this statement appears in the second person, addressed by the commissioner to his messenger: *kōh-tō'mar 'el-bĕnê yiśrā'ēl,* "Thus shall you say to the sons of Israel" (Exod 3:15, 16, 18; cf. Gen 50:17; Exod 19:3; 1 Sam 18:25; 2 Sam 7:8; 11:25; 1 Kgs 12:10; 2 Kgs 22:18; Jer 23:35, 37; 27:4; 37:7; 45:4; Ezek 33:27; 1 Chr 17:7; 2 Chr 10:10; cf. Richter).

In Exod 3:6, 13, 15, 16, one can see variations of the formula for the patriarchal traditions, "God of your fathers" (cf. Richter). In addition, 3:8, 17 contain variations of the widely spread exodus formulae (Humbert; Wijngaards; Childs, "Deuteronomic Formulae"; Richter). Vv. 8 and 17 also contain two formulae from the conquest theme. The first is a stereotyped hymnic exaltation of the promised land and, through it, an exaltation of the God who gave the land (cf. Exod 13:5; 33:3; Lev 20:24; Num 13:27; 14:8; 16:13-14; and relatively widespread in Dtr). The second reflects memory of the diverse population in Palestine before the conquest (Exod 13:5, 11; cf. Deut 20:17; Josh 3:10; 9:1; cf. Richter).

Setting

The present form of the narrative reflects a redactional setting, concerned to set various exodus traditions together in a meaningful whole. This setting applies to the Aaronic expansion and the E material, as well as to the basic J form of the tradition. The redactional setting may be cultic in character. But some indication of transmission in a popular setting can also be seen (→ The Exodus Saga, Chapter 1A). Moreover, the vocation tradition doubtlessly existed at an earlier level among circles concerned to confirm Moses' position as legitimate, charismatic leader (cf. Exod 3:18). A broader setting for the genre can be seen perhaps in Genesis 24, the commission of a messenger or ambassador, with the principal setting for the genre in the situation requiring the messenger to narrate his commission as a witness to his legitimate office (thus Habel; but contrast Childs, "Deuteronomic Formulae," 36).

Intention

The E expansion reflects a theological concern to explain the name of God by reference to the ASSISTANCE FORMULA (similarly Richter). The Aaronic expansion introduces Aaron into the tradition in order to show his subordination to Moses (in contrast, cf. Exodus 6). The basic account itself initiates the exodus narration and cannot be understood apart from 5:1–6:1 and the plague cycle in 7:7–10:29. Its intention for the complex (also its intention at an earlier, oral level of transmission) is to confirm Moses' position as leader in the exodus by narrating the origin of his commission (Richter, Habel). That position must be understood not so much from the prophetic characteristics in the vocation pattern but from dependency of both the Mosaic traditions and various prophetic narratives on a common heroic conception of the leader.

Bibliography

R. Abba, "The Divine Name Yahweh," *JBL* 80 (1961) 320-28; B. J. Beitzel, "Exodus 3:14 and the Divine Name: A Case of Biblical Paronomasis," *Trinity Journal* 1 (1981) 5-20; B. S. Childs, "Deuteronomic Formulae of the Exodus Traditions," in *Hebräische Wortforschung* (*Fest.* W. Baumgartner; ed. G. W. Anderson, et al.; VTSup 14; Leiden: Brill, 1967) 30-39; G. W. Coats, "Self-Abasement and Insult Formulas," *JBL* 89 (1970) 14-26; H. Gressmann, *Mose und seine Zeit: Ein Kommentar zu den Mose-Sagen* (FRLANT 18; Göttingen: Vandenhoeck & Ruprecht, 1913); N. Habel, "The Form and

Significance of the Call Narratives," *ZAW* 77 (1965) 297-323; P. Humbert, "Dieu fait sortir," *TZ* 18 (1962) 357-61, 433-36; J. Jeremias, *Theophanie: Die Geschichte einer alttestamentlichen Gattung* (WMANT 10; Neukirchen: Neukirchener, 1965); D. J. McCarthy, "Exod 3:14: History, Philology, and Theology," *CBQ* 40 (1978) 311-22; J. Magonet, "The Bush That Never Burnt: Narrative Techniques in Exodus 3 and 6," *HeyJ* 16 (1975) 304-11; L. M. von Pakozdy, "Die Deutung des יהוה-Namens in Exodus 3:14," *Judaica* 11 (1955) 193-208; J. Pedersen, "Passahfest und Passahlegende," *ZAW* 52 (1934) 161-75; H. D. Preuss, ". . . ich will mit dir sein!" *ZAW* 80 (1968) 139-73; W. Richter, *Die sogenannten vorprophetischen Berufungsberichte: Eine literaturwissenschaftliche Studie zu I Sam 9,1–10,16, Ex 3f. und Ri 6,11b-17* (FRLANT 101; Göttingen: Vandenhoeck & Ruprecht, 1970); H. Schmid, *Mose: Überlieferung und Geschichte* (BZAW 110; Berlin: Töpelmann, 1968); W. H. Schmidt, "Der Jahwename und Ex 3,14," in *Textgemässe Aufsätze und Beiträge zur Hermeneutik des Alten Testaments (Fest. E. Würthwein*; ed. A. Gunneweg and O. Kaiser; Göttingen: Vandenhoeck & Ruprecht, 1979) 123-38; H. Seebass, *Mose und Aaron, Sinai und Gottesberg* (AETh 2; Bonn: H. Bouvier, 1962); A. M. Vater, "Narrative Patterns for the Story of Commissioned Communication in the Old Testament," *JBL* 99 (1980) 365-82; J. Wijngaards, "הוציא and העלה: A Twofold Approach to the Exodus," *VT* 15 (1965) 91-102; N. Wyatt, "The Development of the Tradition in Exodus 3," *ZAW* 91 (1979) 437-42; W. Zimmerli, "I Am Yahweh," in *I Am Yahweh* (tr. D. W. Stott; ed. W. Brueggemann; Atlanta: John Knox, 1982) 1-28, 138-43.

ADDENDUM. A. G. van Daalen, "The Place Where YHWH Showed Himself to Moses: A Study of the Composition of Exodus 3," in *Voices from Amsterdam: A Modern Tradition of Reading Biblical Narratives* (SBLSS; ed. and tr. Martin Kessler; Atlanta: Scholars Press, 1994); M. N. Puerto, "La vocación de Moisés: Perspectivas metodológicas," *EstBib* 52 (1994) 133-66; H.-C. Schmitt, "Das sogenannte vorprophetische Berufungs-schema: Zur 'geistigen Heimat' des Berufungsformulars von Ex 3,9-12; Jdc 6,11-24 und 1 Sam 9,1–10,16," *ZAW* 104 (1992) 202-16; N. Wyatt, "Significance of the Burning Bush," *VT* 36 (1986) 361-65.

ANNOTATION. Schmitt's contribution is important form-critically; van Daalen and Weimar employ narratology and the study of literature, with aspects relevant for form criticism; Puerto demonstrates methodological approaches on the unit. A number of other articles discuss special questions, above all of the meaning of the name Yahweh.

TRANSITION, 4:19-23

Structure

This unit is a transition between the vocation tradition set in Midian and execution of the commission in Egypt. It comprises two principal elements of structure: Element I.A, a summary of the preceding material, focuses on the vocation tradition. As a divine speech, I.A recapitulates the commission in general terms: "Go, return to Egypt." A 2nd m. s. imperative from the verb *hālak,* "go," is characteristic diction for vocation tradition. The specific reason for the commission is a death report (cf. Exod 1:6; 2:23), and the death report presupposes the marriage narrative and its setting in Midian as an introductory context for the VOCATION ACCOUNT. Element I.B then narrates the proper execution of the commission: Moses went back to Egypt. Element II, the summary of following traditions, is cast simply as a divine speech. It too recapitulates the commission, but spells out details more extensively than I.A. The instructions for Moses' task begin with an infinitive construct from the verb *hālak,* "go," and an accusative of direction: "When you go, return to Egypt. . . ." The remaining speech focuses on the plague series.

Both elements presuppose a late stage of growth in the history of the exodus traditions. The vocation event occurred clearly in Midian, a contrast to the ambiguous setting of the (→) vocation account itself. The plague traditions end in the Passover event, a contrast to the ambiguous ending of the plague cycle itself (→ 7:7–10:29). Moses takes his wife and sons, not just Gershom (cf. 18:3). Thus a relatively broad scope of tradition organized as a theme is in view.

The unit cannot be satisfactorily divided among sources or pruned of secondary additions. The tension between the execution of commission with its notation that Moses returned to Egypt, I.B, and the commission to go to Egypt in II must be understood as the result of the distinct function each element accomplishes. Otherwise, the unit shows no traces of internal growth or earlier stages of construction. It is a basic unit, perhaps the work of Rje, perhaps the work of J.

Genre

Not an independent genre, this unit is composed typically of two elements of transition, a summary of the preceding materials and one of the following materials; it presupposes a larger collection of material (→ 1:1-14). It may be called a SUMMARY STORY OR REPORT.

Setting

The unit belongs to the redactional process that brought together diverse traditions into a single complex, a setting already in existence as early as J.

Intention

The intention of this transition, along with 2:23-25, is to cement the Moses vocation tradition into an artificial setting involving Moses in Midian. To resolve the contradiction between the Midian setting for the vocation event and the execution of the commission in Egypt, element I marks a conclusion to Moses' experience in Midian (I.B) and element II anticipates the plague events in Egypt (→ The Exodus Saga, Chapter 1A).

CIRCUMCISION ETIOLOGY, 4:24-26

Structure

I. Exposition	24a
II. Narration	24b-26a
A. Crisis	24b
B. Resolution of crisis	25-26a
1. Zipporah's action	25a
a. Circumcision of son	25aα
b. Symbolic circumcision	25aβ
2. Speech	25b
a. Introduction	25bα
b. Performative words	25bβ
3. Results	26a
III. Etiological conclusion	26b

This story has no integral connection with its context (so Childs, *Myth*, 60). It does not build on the oppression motif. It draws nothing from the Moses in Midian tradition, despite the reference to Zipporah (against Gressmann; Kosmala; Schmid, *Mose*). Its setting is not in Midian. It does not presuppose the marriage tradition, even though Zipporah, the bride from that tradition, appears in 2:21, 18:2, here, and in no other text (against Schmid, *Mose,* 32). There is no reference to the father-in-law or marriage responsibility, indeed, no specification of Moses as a principal figure in the narration (cf. MT). The designation of a son for Zipporah moves the tradition rather far from a wedding night scene. (Cf. Noth, *Exodus,* 50, whose suggestion that reference to the son may be a secondary addition to the tradition does not resolve the problem; so Kosmala.) Even the crucial phrase *ḥătan dāmîm,* "bridegroom of blood," does not necessitate contact with the Moses marriage tradition. Yet, despite its traditio-historical isolation, the position of this story in the redaction of the Exodus text is appropriate. The setting is a place for stopping overnight on a journey. Moses' return to Egypt provides an adequate context for that journey. Further, the transition unit observes that Moses takes his family with him. Moreover, this position is at an obvious break in the redactional structure of the Exodus text, a natural opening for including a segment of foreign material.

The structure of the unit comprises three principal elements: I, an introductory exposition of setting; II, a narration of crisis and resolution of crisis; and III, an etiological conclusion, focused on the phrase *ḥătan dāmîm,* "bridegroom of blood." One must ask whether this tradition, more than Exod 2:21 or 18:2, does not provide the original traditio-historical rootage for Zipporah. Since the unit fits into a redactional seam and seems foreign in worldview to tradition normally in J, it has apparently been worked secondarily into the J traditions (see Childs, *Myth,* 60 n. 1).

Several attempts to reconstruct an earlier stage of the narrative have been made (for a review and critical evaluation, see Childs, *Myth,* 58-63). That an earlier form of the tradition existed, unattached to the broader range of exodus traditions, seems certain. But to reconstruct a text considerably more complex than the one now preserved in the MT, based on a conflict between numen and bridegroom over the *ius primae noctis,* is tenuous (cf. Childs, *Myth,* 58-63; idem, *Exodus,* 95-101; Kosmala).

Genre

In its present stage the unit can be classified as an ETIOLOGY (see Childs, *Myth,* 59; for a quite different perspective see Childs, *Exodus,* 95-101). The kernel of the story lies in a narration of crisis and its resolution through a performative ritual. Moreover, since the symbolic words in v. 25 cannot be isolated from the etiological conclusion in v. 26, we should conclude that the narrative grows out of the etiology. The etiological conclusion itself contains a typical introduction in the particle *'āz* (so Childs, *Myth,* 59).

An earlier form of the tradition may have pitted a numen of the night against a human victim, perhaps because the victim had not been circumcised (cf. Childs, *Myth,* 60-61; Kosmala). Such a narrative would be more closely related to myth than to tale. But still its character would be etiological, its focus on the circumcision ritual (cf. Gen 32:22ff.). If an earlier level were mythological, the present level has historicized it by placing it into the context of the Moses traditions. At this point it must be considered part of the Moses

SAGA (so Childs, *Myth,* 62-63). Whether it had already become part of the SAGA before its adaptation for the exodus traditions cannot be determined.

Setting

The performative ritual at a particular locality suggests that the story was preserved at a particular cultic center (Noth, *Exodus,* 49; Schmid, *Mose*). The identity of that center cannot be determined. Whether it might have still been known when the story was incorporated into the exodus scheme is not clear.

Intention

Both a hypothetical earlier level and the etiological narrative as it now stands offer an etiological explanation of the performative words involved in the circumcision, presumably cultic in character (cf. Schmid, *Mose*). Whatever the words meant, they gained their significance from the rite of circumcision. At an earlier period, the story may have functioned as an explanation for the shift of circumcision from adults to infants (so Plastaras; see, however, the cautious remarks by Childs, *Exodus,* 97-98).

Bibliography

B. S. Childs, *Myth and Reality in the Old Testament* (SBT 1/27; London: SCM, 1962); H. Gressmann, *Mose und seine Zeit: Ein Kommentar zu den Mose-Sagen* (FRLANT 18; Göttingen: Vandenhoeck & Ruprecht, 1913); H. Kosmala, "The 'Bloody Husband,' " *VT* 12 (1962) 14-28; E. Kutsch, "Der sogenannte Blutbräutigam: Erwägungen zu Ex 4.24-26," *ZDMG Supplement* 4 (1980) 122-23; H. Schmid, "Mose, der Blutbräutigam: Erwägungen zu E 4.24-26," *Judaica* 22 (1966) 113-18; idem, *Mose: Überlieferung und Geschichte* (BZAW 110; Berlin: Töpelmann, 1968); G. Schneemann, "Deutung und Bedeutung der Beschneidung nach Ex 4,24-26," *TLZ* 105 (1980) 794.

ADDENDUM. H.-C. Gossman, "Metamorphosen eines Dämons: Ein Beitrag zur Rezeptionsgeschichte von Ex 4,24-26," in *Begegnungen zwischen Christentum in Antike und Mittelalter* (Fest. H. Schreckenburg; ed. Dietrich-Alex Kock and Hermann Lichtenberger; Göttingen: Vandenhoeck & Ruprecht, 1993); C. Houtman, "Exodus 4:24-26 and Its Interpretation," *JNSL* 11 (1983) 81-105; W. H. Propp, "The Bloody Bridegroom (Exodus 4:24-26)," *VT* 43 (1993) 495-518; B. P. Robinson, "Zipporah to the Rescue: A Contextual Study of Exodus iv 24-6," *VT* (1986) 447-61.

ANNOTATION. Besides a number of unlisted, mostly short, contributions to this unit, the articles by Gossman, Houtman, Propp, and Robinson are important generally and also for aspects in form criticism.

ACCOUNT OF COMMISSION EXECUTION: REPORT TO ELDERS, 4:27-31

Structure

I.	Introduction of Aaron	27-28
	A. Speech: instructions for action	27a
	B. Execution of instructions	27b
	C. Summary report to Aaron	28
	1. Words	28a
	2. Signs	28b
II.	Execution of commission	29-31
	A. Statement of change in setting	29
	B. Report to the elders in narration	30
	1. Words	30a
	2. Signs	30b
	C. Narration of response	31

Two distinct elements, distinguished by a change in scene in v. 29, compose this unit. The first element introduces Aaron into the vocation tradition as a principal by means of a speech from God, directing his meeting with Moses (I.A; see 4:14), along with a narration of the execution of those instructions (I.B). Element I.C incorporates Aaron into the action of the vocation commission by narrating a summary of the commission itself. Aaron has now been brought up-to-date. The second element moves Moses and Aaron to the elders of Israel in Egypt (II.A). The narration of the commission before the elders (II.B) follows a line of development around words God spoke to Moses and signs he gave him, just like the report to Aaron in I.C. The unit concludes by noting that the elders responded to the commission favorably (II.C).

Three notations about place confuse the character of the unit. The Lord's instructions (v. 27a) suggest that the meeting between Moses and Aaron should occur in the wilderness. Thus the unit appears in a break between the VOCATION ACCOUNT with a Midianite setting and an ACCOUNT of the commission's execution in Egypt (cf. 4:19-23) and functions as part of Moses' journey back to Egypt (cf. 4:24-26). Yet the ACCOUNT of instructions executed (v. 27b) sets the meeting on the mountain of God; it is thus tied closely with a VOCATION ACCOUNT already associated with the tradition behind 3:1-6. The third place, pinpointed by the change of setting in v. 29, is Egypt. Since the unit focuses on execution of the commission, carried out in vv. 30-31, Egypt must be seen as the primary locale for the unit. The full range of ambiguity about setting for the vocation tradition thus also appears here. Moreover, element I, focused on Aaron, and all allusions to Aaron in element II appear to be secondary additions to the ACCOUNT, related to the Aaronic expansion in 4:13-17 (so Noth, *Exodus,* 51; Schmid; Plastaras). An earlier level of the unit would have contained only a note about change in setting, Moses' (rather than Aaron's) report to the elders of Israel, and a record of positive response. At this level only the change in locale reflects the ambiguity of location in the vocation tradition.

Literary analysis reflects the traditio-historical analysis: Vv. 27-28, along with all references to Aaron in vv. 29-31, are secondary additions to J, with the basic report a part of the primary traditions of J (so Noth, *Exodus,* 51).

Genre

The unit has its roots clearly in the vocation tradition and does not constitute an independent pericope. It must be understood simply as an ACCOUNT of execution for the commission established in 3:1–4:18. Thus no distinct genre observations are possible. It may be called a SUMMARY STORY OR REPORT.

Setting

The redactional process that placed the Moses vocation tradition in Midian, yet closely related to events executed in Egypt, must be responsible for this material as a distinct unit. It would have no setting independent of the vocation account, no life independent of the vocation tradition.

Intention

The unit narrates proper execution of instructions from the commission Moses carries to the elders, 3:1–4:18. If the Aaronic material is indeed secondary in the unit, its intention would be to introduce Aaron as a principal for action into a tradition originally involving only Moses. Significantly, Aaron plays no active role in the vocation account. The position of the unit at this point in the larger complex of traditions derives from the necessity to change the setting of action from Midian to Egypt. Cf. Exod 7:6-7, where an ACCOUNT of execution for the vocation commission occurs within the formal structure of the VOCATION ACCOUNT.

Bibliography

H. Schmid, *Mose: Überlieferung und Geschichte* (BZAW 110; Berlin: Töpelmann, 1968); J. M. Schmidt, "Aaron und Mose: Ein Beitrag zur Überlieferungsgeschichte des Pentateuchs" (Diss., Hamburg, 1963).

ACCOUNT OF COMMISSION EXECUTION: NEGOTIATIONS WITH THE PHARAOH, 5:1–6:1

Structure

I. Negotiation dialogue	5:1-5
A. Speech: Moses and Aaron to Pharaoh	1

For this ACCOUNT, note the regularly occurring NARRATIVE introduction, I.A.1–v. 1a, in this and many other texts also about speeches. These introductions represent the NARRATIVE FRAME of the texts. They reveal the hands of their narrators/writers without which we would not possess what is narrated. The speeches themselves consist of four distinct series: I, developing negotiations between Israel's representative and the pharaoh; II, presenting the pharaoh's response to the negotiations as a change in policy; III, showing the Israelite elders' appeal about the change in policy; and IV, a final collection of speeches with Israel's reaction, Moses' response to God, and God's promise for the exodus. The only parts of the entire unit not constructed as a speech or a narrated introduction to a speech are II.C, a narration of instructions executed, and III.C, a narration of the conclusion to the negotiations. Even the last narration incorporates a citation of an earlier speech (cf. vv. 6-9). Moreover, the change in policy described in the scene contrasts with the final scene of negotiation between Pharaoh and Moses (→ 12:33-36) and constitutes a structural inclusion (so Weimar and Zenger, 46-47). The point of the inclusion emphasizes the shift of Israel from service to the Egyptians to service for Yahweh.

The text cannot easily be divided among the sources. Since v. 4 appears to duplicate v. 5 in the structure of the series, it might be bracketed as a secondary addition, perhaps part of E (so Noth, *Exodus,* 53). The series must be assigned, with perhaps the exception of v. 4, entirely to J (so Noth).

The last stage in the history of tradition for the unit was an introduction of Aaron as one of the negotiators (so Noth). Presentation of the preceding stage, with Moses as the only negotiator, would have involved the same three series of speeches. The third series, with a summons to trial (vv. 20-21), a complaint as the response to the trial summons (vv. 22-23), and a promise for salvation — the exodus (6:1) — focuses on Moses' leadership and belongs originally to this stage. The summons in v. 21 presupposes Moses' active role not just in sending the elders to the pharaoh but in making contact with the pharaoh himself (cf. 3:19-15 and v. 4 in this unit).

Even Moses' role as negotiator appears artificial and secondary, however. Not only do the foremen approach the pharaoh directly for appeal and further negotiation (vv. 15-16), but Moses (along with Aaron) is then introduced abruptly, waiting outside the place of negotiation for the results of the foremen's work. Moreover, vv. 1-5 place Moses and Aaron superficially as principals for the negotiations, with the Israelites as a whole or their representatives originally intended as a point of reference for the plural verb in v. 3 (so Noth, *Exodus*, 54). The earliest stage of tradition may have narrated only that the Israelite foremen or elders conducted negotiations. Structure at this stage would have included only elements I and II (so Noth; cf. Smend for a different evaluation of the question).

If this tradition history is correct, we could conclude that the kernel of tradition in this series served as the seed for traditions that are obviously related: 1:8-12; 3:1–4:18; and 7:7–10:29. We could hypothesize the following history. First, a narrative presented the elders negotiating with the pharaoh for release of the Israelites. The oppression motif, 1:8-12, is already crucial at this stage (cf. Noth, *A History,* 71). Then Moses was introduced, commissioned to bring Yahweh's words and signs to the elders before negotiations started. With Moses come various heroic motifs, such as the signs intended at the earliest level only to convince the elders to respond in faith to the Lord's commission represented to them by Moses (cf. the commission in 3:16–4:9). Finally, Moses appears alone as negotiator and sign worker before the pharaoh (cf. the commission in 3:9-15). The signs are designed to convince the pharaoh to release the Israelites. The sign cycle would thus be an extension not of the Passover plague (so McCarthy, against Noth, *Exodus*, 68-69) but of the signs originally intended to convince the elders that Yahweh commissioned their release (cf. 4:1-9).

In this outline of tradition, the Aaronic expansion corresponds with the similar Aaronic expansion in the VOCATION ACCOUNT, 4:14-17, as well as in 4:27-31 and the sign cycle, 7:7–10:29. The account that brings Moses and Aaron directly before the pharaoh points to the account of Moses' commission in 3:9-15. The presence of the elders in the negotiations recalls the commission that sends Moses first to the elders and only with their assistance to the pharaoh. Even the tradition at its earliest hypothesized stage, reconstructed to present the elders or foremen as chief negotiators, shows crucial contact with the VOCATION ACCOUNT. For example, 5:3, with an allusion that suggests a primitive tradition about God appearing to all the Israelites (so Noth, *Exodus,* 52, 55), is duplicated almost exactly in 3:18. The motif that pitches Israel's appeal to the pharaoh for permission to sacrifice in the wilderness, present in both texts, becomes substantial for the sign cycle. This motif should not be taken as an allusion to Sinai or to any other particular festival or sacrifice identifiable in subsequent traditions (against Schmid; cf. Plastaras). Rather, it describes a plan of deception for effecting Israel's release (cf. 5:9 and a consistent refrain in the sign cycle suggesting that the plans for a festival are contrived). Finally, the negotiations represented in both this text and the sign cycle suggest that the efforts to gain the pharaoh's permission to leave end in failure. (On the climax of the sign narrative as a secret escape in keeping with the motif of deception, see the discussion below.)

Genre

This unit, at least in its present stage, is not independent. To be sure, a crisis develops around the challenge to Moses' leadership in 5:20-21, and 5:22–6:1 presents a resolution of the challenge. But the arc of tension here is peripheral to the basic thrust of the unit, negotiation for Israel's release from oppression. Indeed, the resolution in 6:1 points forward to that release. In its present stage, then, this unit must be classified as an ACCOUNT dependent on the VOCATION ACCOUNT in 3:1–4:18. Its apparent relationship with 1:8-12; 3:1–4:18; and 7:7–10:29 suggests that it serves as one element of a more extended popular history (see Eissfeldt, *Intro.*, 50-52). Popular history is, however, an inadequate term to define genre. It points rather to the role of this unit in SAGA. (Popular history has more in common with saga than with historically reliable records, according to Eissfeldt.) The SAGA would have narrated an account of Moses' negotiations with the pharaoh as the genesis of national consciousness (cf. The Exodus Saga, Chapter 1A). As Moses tradition, the saga can thus be classified as HEROIC.

If this designation of the earliest level as SAGA is correct, one further problem would need consideration. Negotiations between the Israelites and the pharaoh end in failure, even at an early level in the tradition history. Resolution of the crisis posed by oppression and resolved by an exodus from Egyptian bondage would not have been the result of negotiations. (See the discussion of the climax to the plague cycle below.)

The series of speeches in vv. 1-5 is related to (→) disputation. But the function of the series is not to present sides in an argument. It seems more appropriate, therefore, to classify the series as NEGOTIATION, a combination of speeches describing an effort to win concession from an antagonist who stands in higher authority than the protagonists (cf. esp. v. 3). V. 21 is construed as a formal SUMMONS TO TRIAL (Boecker). Vv. 22-23 are constructed in the present sequence of the text as a RESPONSE to the summons. But they also reflect the pattern of COMPLAINT followed by divine response. Two questions introduced by the interrogative particle *lāmmâ*, "why," and a description of the plight calling forth the complaint characterize the first element, while the second, a response from the deity in first-person address, should be seen as an ORACLE OF SALVATION (Begrich).

Other formulas include the MESSENGER FORMULA (5:1, 10; note that the message in vv. 10-11 derives not from Yahweh but from the pharaoh, thus preserving the original character of the formula as an element of speech in a secular setting). A stereotyped INSULT FORMULA appears in 5:2 (Coats, *Moses,* 82; idem,

Moses Tradition, 117-18). Questions in 5:4, 14 are closely related to a formal (→) accusation, although the foremen could hardly be seen as accusing the pharaoh. Perhaps a closer point of contact lies in the (→) complaint questions (cf. 5:22) or a simple (→) appeal (cf. 5:15). The pharaoh's judgment, 5:7-9 and 17-18, follows a recognizable pattern of indictment-judgment, although in both texts the *'al-kēn* does not introduce the judgment but stands as part of the INDICTMENT.

Setting

The latest stage of tradition reflects the same redactional process that brought various elements of exodus traditions together as an extended popular history (cf. The Exodus Saga, Chapter 1A). That it may have been preserved in a cultic setting as a celebration of the exodus seems possible. But another alternative lies in the popular preservation of national lore reflected, for example, in 10:2. The setting for the hypothesized HEROIC SAGA would more likely be the family circle reflected in 10:2.

Intention

In its present stage, the text accounts for an execution of the commission to Moses and Aaron leading to an increase in oppression (cf. 1:8-12) and finally the exodus. At earlier levels, the tradition may have focused more directly on Moses' negotiations, their failure, and perhaps the following consequences that effected Israel's exodus such as a secret escape (cf. 11:1–12:36).

Bibliography

J. Begrich, "Das priesterliche Heilsorakel," in *Gesammelte Studien zum Alten Testament* (TBü 21; Munich: Kaiser, 1964) 217-31 (repr. from *ZAW* 52 [1934] 81-92); G. W. Coats, *Moses: Heroic Man, Man of God* (JSOTSup 57; Sheffield: Sheffield Academic Press, 1988); idem, *The Moses Tradition* (JSOTSup 161; Sheffield: Sheffield Academic Press, 1993); O. Eissfeldt, *The Old Testament: An Introduction* (tr. P. R. Ackroyd; New York: Harper & Row, 1965); R. Smend, *Yahweh War and Tribal Confederation: Reflections upon Israel's Earliest History* (tr. M. Rogers; Nashville: Abingdon, 1970); P. Weimar and E. Zenger, *Exodus: Geschichten und Geschichte der Befreiung Israels* (SBS 75; Stuttgart: KBW, 1975).

ADDENDUM. G. W. Coats, "Self-Abasement and Insult Formulas," *JBL* 89 (1970) 14-26; T. B. Dozeman, *God at War: A Study of Power in the Exodus Tradition* (New York: Oxford Univ. Press, 1996); M. C. Lind, *The Theology of Warfare in Ancient Israel* (Scottdale, Pa.: Herald, 1980); F. Stolz, *Jahwes und Israels Kriege* (ATANT 60; Zürich: Theologischer Verlag, 1972).

MOSES-AARON VOCATION ACCOUNT, 6:2–7:6

Structure

The relationship between this unit and 5:1–6:1 is brittle. A first-person speech of God, 6:2ff. can be understood as a response to the challenge to Moses' leadership in 5:21 and to Moses' COMPLAINT in 5:22-23 (so Greenberg, "Thematic Unity," 152). Yet 6:1 already fills that position. Moreover, the unit in 6:2–7:6 constitutes a doublet to 3:1–4:18. The break between 5:1–6:1 and 6:2–7:6 is thus a major point in the organization of the Pentateuch (→ The Exodus Saga, Chapter 1A). The relationship between 6:2–7:6 and 7:7–10:29 (cf. also chs. 11 and 12) is much closer and indeed parallels the relationship between 3:1–4:18 and 4:27-31; 5:1–6:1. Both have similar relationships to the introductory leitmotif in 1:1-14.

Structure in 6:2–7:6 is more complex than its parallel in 3:1–4:18. It combines a wider variety of speeches or series of speeches connected into a dialogue with recapitulation of earlier speeches, distinct types of narration, and a genealogy. Nevertheless, the basic vocation pattern, commission-objection-reassurance, can still be seen. The introductory element (I) is simply speech, with a commission for delivering a message to the Israelites. This speech parallels the speech in 3:7-17, as well as some motifs from the THEOPHANY REPORT in 3:1-6. Most significant are the SELF-REVELATION FORMULAS (cf. 3:6), reference to the patriarchal tradition (cf. 3:6) and the conquest tradition (cf. 3:8), emphasis on the name Yahweh (cf. 3:14-15), and Moses' commission to go to the elders (cf. 3:16-17) with a promise for the exodus (cf. 3:8, 17). For this unit, the emphasis on the name Yahweh constitutes not a new revelation to Moses and Aaron but an explanation of revelation given to the patriarchs under the name 'El Shaddai (cf. Lohfink). In contrast to the parallel, this unit does not have a (→) theophany report as introduction. It also places heavy emphasis on the covenant as a reason for God's concern.

Element II narrates the execution of the commission, with a negative response of the people (cf. the positive response of the people in 4:31, outside the formal structure of the VOCATION ACCOUNT). Element III moves to the VOCATION DIALOGUE (//3:7–4:17). The COMMISSION in 6:10-11 corresponds to the commission to send Moses directly to the pharaoh in 3:10, the objection in 6:12 to the objection in 4:10, 13. Moses cannot go to the pharaoh because of his slow speech, his "uncircumcised lips."

The parallel with 3:1–4:18 breaks sharply with element IV. Instead of re-assurance for the objection in the context of a dialogue, a narration element re-capitulates the commission. The break is significant since it introduces Aaron as a full partner in the commission and lays the foundation for a list of Aaronic genealogy, element V.

The list itself presupposes a traditional order of Israelite tribes (cf. the first three elements in the list, Reuben, Simeon, Levi, in vv. 14-16). The list of sons' names and deference to a Canaanite woman in the Simeon element (v. 14a, "These are the heads of their fathers' house" [*'ēlleh ro'šê bêt-'ăbōtām*]) parallels the formula in v. 25, the conclusion for a Levite list (cf. Neh 12:7, 12, 22, 23; 1 Chr 5:24; 7:7, 9). The character of the list as GENEALOGY appears in the structure for each entry in the list: an introduction, e.g., "the sons of Reuben," precedes a list of the entry's sons, with a conclusion, e.g., "these are the families of Reuben," to close the segment.

The principal variation appears with Levi. Between the list of Levi's sons and the conclusion for the list appear a notation about Levi's age (v. 16b) and an expansion of the list to include a second generation of Levites (vv. 17-19a). With one exception, the same pattern (introduction — list of the sons — conclusion) appears for the second generation. The exception is a notation of age instead of a conclusion for the middle figure, Kohat (v. 18; cf. v. 16b). Following the conclu-sion to the Levite list in v. 19b a series of expansions pushes the genealogy to the fifth generation. The third generation develops only one son from the second generation. Significantly, that son is Kohat, the one entry in the second genera-tion whose age was noted instead of a regular conclusion. Three of Kohat's sons appear in the third generation, with the regular conclusion dropped. The entries in vv. 21 and 22 have only an introduction and a list of sons. Amram, the first en-try (v. 20), has a MARRIAGE REPORT for an introduction and concludes with a notation of age (cf. vv. 16b, 18). → Age Formula. Significantly, the fourth gen-eration concerns Aaron, one of Amram's sons. The structure of this entry again substitutes a MARRIAGE REPORT for an introduction. The Korahite GENEALOGY in v. 24, also part of the fourth generation, follows none of the patterns clearly developing from the beginning of the genealogy. Although it does appear in the regular introduction — list — conclusion fashion, it would appear to be an addi-tion to the list, arising perhaps from the Korah tradition in Num 16:1. Finally, the fifth generation contains only Aaron's son. In progressively narrowing stages, each marked by an age notation or a (→) marriage report, or both, the GENEALOGY focuses on Aaron and his son.

The GENEALOGY is not part of vocation patterns and cannot be attributed to an original form of this particular vocation tradition. The secondary charac-ter of the list and Aaron's role generally for the vocation tradition can be de-tected in this text not only by the break in the vocation pattern with the incor-poration of the GENEALOGY. Also vv. 2-12 concern only Moses, with Aaron abruptly introduced in v. 13 without previous preparation (cf. 4:14-17). The disunity reflects a problem in the history of the Moses vocation tradition: Under what circumstances did Aaron enter the tradition? (Contrast the emphasis placed on the names Moses and Aaron in the recapitulation of the commission, v. 13, with the emphasis on Moses in vv. 28-29.) The emphasis reflects the impact of the GENEALOGY on the structure of the unit.

Element VI recapitulates element III (cf. v. 26 with v. 6, vv. 28-29 with v. 11, and v. 30 with v. 12). The nominal sentence structure of v. 26 emphasizes its character as recapitulation: "These are Aaron and Moses, to whom the Lord said. . . ." The explicit intention for the recapitulation is to incorporate Aaron into the commission. Thus the combination of names in v. 26 places Aaron before Moses (cf. 4:27-31). Aaron is considered from this point forward a principal in the action. Only after the recapitulation can the vocation dialogue be resumed with God's speech of reassurance. The speech parallels the reassurance speech in 4:14-17. Aaron is the instrument for Moses' speech. But rather than the subordination in 4:14-17, describing Moses as God to Aaron and Aaron as Moses' mouth, this text makes Moses God to Pharaoh and Aaron serves as Moses' prophet. The unit closes with a narration in 7:6 reporting that the commission was properly executed.

The late stage of tradition in 6:2–7:6, including the Aaron element, confirms a consensus among critics that this text belongs to P. It embraces a wide scope of tradition history. Combining stages of tradition about Moses' commission that originated on two different levels, it considers only one of the stages as the kernel of the unit, the focus of the account (against Habel). In contrast to 3:1–4:18, it places the call of Moses not in Midian but in Egypt. Finally, the signs given Moses in 4:2-9 do not function in this unit as a demonstration for appeal to the elders of Israel, but rather are fully the weapons for inducing Pharaoh to release Israel (cf. 7:8-13). Indeed, the signs belong to God, not to Moses (cf. 6:6; 7:3). (Against Habel, who sees 7:8-9 as part of the P vocation account fulfilling the structural pattern calling for signs.) For earlier stages in the vocation tradition, cf. 3:1–4:18.

Genre

As a whole, this text belongs to the genre of ACCOUNT because it focuses on the legitimacy of Moses' leadership and also on the legitimacy of Aaron (cf. Intention). In it, however, the more basic VOCATION ACCOUNT genre is significantly modified. Most of all, part V, the GENEALOGY, does not belong to the form of the genre at all. Moreover, the text does not develop a span of tension between crisis and resolution. It does not work out a plot, although commission, objection to the commission, and final execution of the commission all appear here. Indeed, the principal item of narration from the parallel in 3:1–4:18, the THEOPHANY REPORT, has been suppressed here for a SPEECH from God. As with 3:1–4:18, this text is an element in a larger popular history (→ 3:1–4:18). But the character of heroic narration apparent in the parallel has been suppressed.

The speech in 6:2-8 reflects influence from a complaint liturgy (cf. v. 5) and suggests that the promise in vv. 6-8 should be seen as a Priestly (→) oracle of salvation (thus Plastaras). If this observation is accurate, one should never-theless avoid pressing the similarity too far (cf. 3:7-10).

The GENEALOGY has important parallels in Gen 46:8ff. and Num 3:17 for the order of names in the second generation (on genealogies generally, cf. Johnson, Wilson). The SELF-REVELATION FORMULAS (vv. 2bβ, 6aα, 8bβ, 29β) point to some influence from the THEOPHANY REPORT of the parallel in 3:1-6. A God unknown previously by a particular name reveals the name for his dev-otees (Zimmerli, "I Am Yahweh"). The formulas appear at the beginning and the end of the message to be delivered to the elders (vv. 6aα, 8bβ), recalling a similar position at the beginning and end of law groupings in the Holiness Code. The promise for deliverance by reference to the covenant God has with the patriarchs and the corresponding promise of land recall Lev 26:40-45. The COVENANTAL FORMULA in v. 7, defining relationships between people and God, has a parallel in Lev 26:45. Cf. Smend. A KNOWLEDGE FORMULA, also characteristic for P, closes the final speech of the unit in 7:5 (cf. Zimmerli, "Word").

Setting

For discussion of setting and intention in the vocation tradition, → 3:1–4:18. The unit now shows the particular setting of the Priestly source, a theological reflection about the vocation tradition particularly from the perspective of the Aaronic circles. The reflection is not limited to the vocation tradition, how-ever, but sets this tradition in relationship to a larger whole. The genealogy de-rives from the same circle.

Intention

This unit, like 3:1–4:18, intends to show the legitimate role of leadership that Moses carries into the exodus. But in distinction from 3:1–4:18, the focus of this unit also embraces Aaron. Aaron's position in the exodus shares the legiti-macy attributed by tradition to Moses. Indeed, this unit has an intention that is distinct from the expansion of the JE material that includes Aaron in its pur-view: the definition of relationship between Moses and Aaron that subordi-nates Aaron to Moses (4:16) has been altered to remove the obvious subordi-nation. Moses receives the word and delivers it to Aaron his prophet. But Moses is not God to Aaron.

As a distinct generic element in the pericope, the GENEALOGY empha-sizes the function this text has for legitimizing Aaron.

Bibliography

P. Auffret, "The Literary Structure of Exodus 6:2-8," *JSOT* 27 (1983) 46-54; M. Greenberg, "The Thematic Unity of Exodus iii–xi," in *Fourth World Congress of Jew-*

ish Studies (vol. 1; Jerusalem: World Union of Jewish Studies, 1967) 151-54; N. Habel, "The Form and Significance of the Call Narratives," *ZAW* 77 (1965) 297-323; M. Johnson, *The Purpose of the Biblical Genealogies with Special Reference to the Setting of the Genealogies of Jesus* (SNTSMS 8; London: Cambridge Univ. Press, 1969); N. Lohfink, "Die priesterschriftliche Abwertung der Tradition von der Offenbarung des Jahwenamens an Mose," *Bib* 49 (1968) 1-8; J. Magonet, "The Rhetoric of God: Exodus 6:2-8," *JSOT* 27 (1983) 56-67; H. Seebass, *Mose und Aaron, Sinai und Gottesberg* (AETh 2; Bonn: H. Bouvier, 1962); R. R. Wilson, "The Old Testament Genealogies in Recent Research," *JBL* 84 (1975) 169-89; idem, *Genealogy and History in the Biblical World* (YNER 7; New Haven: Yale Univ. Press, 1977); J. Wimmer, "Tradition Reinterpreted in Exodus 6.2-7.7," *Augustinianum* 7 (1967) 405-18; W. Zimmerli, "I Am Yahweh," in *I Am Yahweh* (tr. D. W. Stott; ed. W. Brueggemann; Atlanta: John Knox, 1982) 1-28, 138-43; idem, "The Word of Divine Self-Manifestation (Proof Saying): A Prophetic Genre," in ibid., 99-110, 154-56.

ADDENDUM. P. Auffret, "Remarks on J. Magonet's Interpretation of Exodus 6.2-8," *JSOT* 27 (1983) 69-71; J. Magonet, "A Response to P. Auffret's 'Literary Structure of Exodus 6.2-8,'" *JSOT* 27 (1983) 73-74; A. Marx, "La généalogie d' Exode vi 14-25: sa forme, sa fonction," *VT* 45 (1995) 318-36; J.-L. Ska, "La place d'Ex 6:2-8 dans la narration de l'exode," *ZAW* 94 (1982) 530-48; S. Steingrimsson, *Vom Zeichen zur Geschichte: Eine literar- und form-kritische Untersuchung von Ex 6,28–11,10* (ConBOT 14; Lund: Gleerup, 1979).

ANNOTATION. From more publications than listed, the following are particularly important for this commentary. The studies by Marx, Ska, and Steingrimsson discuss matters of form/structure, genre, function, and tradition history. The discussion between Auffret and Magonet focuses on literary/rhetorical structure.

THE LEGEND OF MOSES' — AND AARON'S — EMPOWERMENT: THE SIGN CYCLE, 7:7–10:29

Structure

The cycle of scenes recounting Moses' dealings with the pharaoh can readily be distinguished from its context. The limits are marked by the exposition for the cycle in 7:7, announcing who the principals of the cycle are and what they did, and the conclusion in 10:28-29 (and 11:9-10), noting the consequences of the relationship between the principals. Yet the cycle cannot be separated from its context as an independent tradition. The cycle of scenes in this unit depends on the traditions about Moses' and Aaron's vocation (3:1–4:18 and 6:2–7:6). Indeed, the major range of motifs in the cycle — signs, negotiations, appeal to a festival in the wilderness with implications of deception, and finally failure of the negotiation — is developed in the vocation texts or the execution of the vocation commission in 5:1–6:1 (→ The Exodus Saga, Chapter 1A).

Moreover, the following unit, 11:1–12:36, presupposes the cycle of signs. Its structure is a conscious imitation of a sign scene, and it functions, at least in the final stage of the Pentateuch, as a structural conclusion of the cycle. Indeed, the summary conclusion to all the signs in 11:9-10 binds the beginning of the eleventh sign into the cycle. (For a discussion of structure in 11:1–12:36, see the analysis below.) The tension between the sign cycle and the Passover sign constitutes a major problem in interpreting the exodus traditions.

The simplest structure for a single scene can be seen in 7:8-13. (For reasons to include this sign as part of the cycle, see McCarthy, 338-47; similarly, Noth, *Exodus,* 71-72; against Fohrer, 59-60.) A speech from God to Moses (and Aaron) gives instructions regarding the procedure for effecting a sign. A brief narration notes the execution of the instructions, and finally the response of the pharaoh and his people to the sign is set out. This structure can be expanded with a speech from God to Moses that sends Moses (and Aaron) to the pharaoh before the sign occurs. Moses (and Aaron) can carry an oracle of indictment and judgment (the judgment will be the sign) for the pharaoh's previous failure to respond (cf. 7:14-24), or a demand for release of the people and a warning of the consequences (the consequences will be the sign) if the demand is not met (cf. 7:25–8:11). The response of the pharaoh can be a simple rejection of the demand (cf. 7:11-13) or a series of negotiation speeches with Moses (and Aaron) before the demand is rejected (cf. 8:4-7). The rejection is characterized by a hard-heart motif, either *kbd* or *ḥzq*, and functions in the structure of each scene as a transition to the following scene (see Eising, 86). Finally, an intercession motif raises the tension of each scene since it demonstrates pharaoh's increasing dependency on Yahweh and his representatives (see Eising, 86). The intercession also facilitates the transition from one plague to the next. Although a few scattered elements in addition round out the largest structure in several scenes (cf. 9:31-32; 10:6, 7, 11b), these elements appear at transitional joints and are incidental for the structure.

Structure in the cycle as a whole follows a symmetrical and well-defined scheme (so Noth, *Exodus*, 67-68; McCarthy; Greenberg). The symmetry can be defined as a structuring of elements within a particular scene, and indeed, the length of the scene itself to correspond with a parallel scene paired in a concentric pattern. Thus scenes I and X, II and IX, III and VIII, IV and VII, and V and VI have parallel elements structured in the same pattern, but no two pairs have identical patterns (so McCarthy, 341). For a different description of the symmetry, cf. Greenberg, "Thematic Unity," 153; idem, "Redaction," 243-52; Weimar and Zenger, 36-47.

The concentric pairs do not always correspond exactly. The breaks, however, are generally incidental, as for example the presentation of a coming sign as an alternative consequence for the pharaoh's disobedience or as a judgment following indictment based on past disobedience (cf. III and VIII). The break in parallel for II and IX is more problematic. The order varies more sharply, and the length of the one scene does not correspond to the length of the other. Scene IX, however, presupposes at least a message commission formula and a speech from Moses to the pharaoh as part of the instructions for Moses' action (cf. v. 1a, normally part of a message commission formula). The scene is thus elliptical. This observation does not allow reconstructing the scene on the basis of the parallel in II. But it does emphasize the necessity for recognizing the concentric structure of the cycle. The remaining pairs correspond in placement of elements and generally in length. The position of references to Pharaoh's hard heart, and indeed, the selection of the word for describing the hard heart, illustrate the point.

The principal conclusion from this observation is that even for the final stage of the text, the structure for the sign cycle excludes the Passover scene (so McCarthy). To be sure, the Passover scene, at least in 11:1-8, is bound to the sign cycle by the conclusion in 11:9-10. But a marked tension between the Passover and the sign cycle can still be detected. Insofar as the cycle of sign scenes is concerned, the climax for negotiations described there does not come in the Passover event.

Specification of the proper conclusion for the cycle of signs is problematic. It does not come with the peak of symmetry in scenes V and VI. The parallels are not maintained woodenly but permit distinctive developments that point toward a climax at the end of the cycle. Thus the Egyptian magicians first duplicate Moses' signs. Then they fail and confess that the finger of God is at work. Finally, covered with boils, they cannot stand before Moses (not before the pharaoh) and leave the scene entirely (cf. 9:11). The pharaoh begins the cycle with a categorical denial of Moses' demands. Then he moves through a sequence of concessions, each allowing more freedom for Israel and confessing more guilt for Egypt. At the beginning of the cycle, Moses and Aaron function together, with Aaron responsible for the sign. In the later scenes Moses works alone, suggesting that the cycle increases its emphasis on the unique status of Moses. Finally, the signs move from petty annoyances related to popular magic to signs effecting physical discomfort, loss of property, death to Egyptians who do not take Moses seriously, and defeat of the Egyptians' gods (darkness as defeat of the sun god). The cycle thus builds around a dual scheme: a concentric arrangement of elements in the sequence of scenes, and a heightening conflict between Moses (Aaron) and the pharaoh, anticipating some kind of resolution.

The conclusion for the cycle of signs appears in 10:28-29. The negotiations are broken off; Moses cannot again appear before the pharaoh to warn or demand. The complexity of the conclusion for the plague cycle appears clearly at this point. For despite the ban on Moses' reappearance before the pharaoh, the speech in 11:4-8a places Moses again in the pharaoh's presence (cf. v. 8b) and a new sign is announced. Moreover, the summary conclusion in 11:9-10 again flags the end of the signs (cf. v. 10a: "Moses and Aaron did all these wonders before the pharaoh"). The position of this conclusion after the first part of the firstborn sign binds scene XI to the cycle and suggests that negotiations involving all signs are broken off.

The purpose of the signs in part is God's self-revelation to Israel and Egypt (cf. 7:17; 8:6, 18; 9:14, 29; 10:2). An expressed purpose in addition is ridicule for Egypt through coming generations. Indeed, the signs imply an intention to achieve recognition of Israel's God by all hearers, Israelites and Egyptians alike. But for the structure of the scenes, for the negotiations between Moses and Pharaoh, the signs function as weapons to convince the pharaoh that he should release Israel. They thus undergird the demand for release of the slaves with a demonstration of authority. The authority belongs to both Yahweh and Moses. The signs qualify the power of both Yahweh and Moses before the pharaoh. It is significant that in some cases (cf. 7:17-18; 9:1-7) the subject of the action is not altogether clear; it may be either Yahweh or Moses (see Noth, *Exodus,* 73, 79). Moreover, the demand for release is in itself contrasted with the service the pharaoh demands from the slaves. By divine decree, Israel shall no longer serve the pharaoh. Israel shall serve Yahweh in the wilderness (see Weimar and Zenger, 37-41). The pharaoh responds to the demand for release in order to serve Yahweh as a subtle plot to deceive, and the narrative shows the pharaoh's perception to be accurate (see Plastaras, 140-41). That purpose fails, however, just as in 5:1–6:1. After the sign cycle (10:28-29) and the additional sign announcement for the firstborn (11:9-10), Israel remains in oppression. The pharaoh's heart remains hard. Thus the tension built by the successive scenes of signs breaks. But it does not break in Israel's favor.

Structural doublets in the sign cycle support source analysis. P appears in 7:7, 8-13, 19-20a, 21b-22; 8:1-3, 11aβ-b, 12-15; 9:8-12, 22-23a, 35; 10:12-13a, 20, 21-23, 27. P's conclusion to the cycle is in 11:9-10 (cf. Fohrer, 68).

The structure of P is as follows:

I. Exposition		7:7
II. Sign cycle	(P references from 7:8–10:27)	
A. Rod to snake		7:8-13
1. Speech		8-9
a. God to Moses and Aaron		8
b. Speech		9
1) Message commission formula		9aα
2) Instructions for action		9aβ-b
2. Execution of instructions		10
3. Narration of response		11-13
a. Egyptian magicians' trick		11-12
b. Pharaoh's hard heart — *ḥzq*		13
B. Water to blood		7:19-20a, 21b-22
1. Speech		19
a. God to Moses		19aα
b. Speech		19aβ-b
1) Message commission formula		19aβ1
2) Instructions for action		19aβ2-b
2. Execution of instructions		20a, 21b
3. Narration of response		22
a. Egyptian magicians' trick		22a
b. Pharaoh's hard heart — *ḥzq*		22b
C. Frogs	8:1-3, 11aβ-b (*NRSV* 8:5-7, 15aβ-b)	
1. Speech		1
a. God to Moses		1aα
b. Speech		1aβ-b
1) Message commission formula		1aβ1
2) Instructions for action		1aβ2-b
2. Execution of instructions		2
3. Narration of response		3, 11aβ-b
a. Egyptian magicians' trick		3
b. Pharaoh		11aβ-b
D. Gnats	8:12-15 (*NRSV* 8:16-19)	
1. Speech		12
a. God to Moses		12aα
b. Speech		12aβ-b
1) Message commission formula		12aβ1
2) Instructions for action		12aβ2-b
2. Execution of instructions		13
3. Narration of response: Egyptian magicians' trick fails		14
4. Speech		15a
a. Magicians to Pharaoh		15aα
b. Confession		15aβ
5. Narration of response: hard heart — *ḥzq*		15b
E. Boils		9:8-12

69

      P's version of the sign cycle opens with the exposition in 7:7. The cycle itself develops in a compact, uniform pattern. A speech from God to Moses introduces each scene. The first four cast the speech as a message to be delivered to Aaron, with instructions for Aaron's role in the coming sign. In the first scene, the speech is addressed to both Moses and Aaron, although the MESSAGE COMMISSION FORMULA immediately following the introduction presupposes the pattern of the next three scenes. The fifth scene begins with a speech addressed to both Moses and Aaron, instructing both to effect the sign. (The continuation of the instructions places primary emphasis on Moses.) The final three scenes drop Aaron, casting Moses alone as the instrument of the plague. Thus, despite P's emphasis on Aaron at other parts of the exodus traditions, it preserves a focal role for Moses in the sign cycle.

The opening speech is followed by an account of the execution of the instructions, then a narration of response to the sign. The first three report that the Egyptian magicians duplicate Moses' work. The fourth notes the failure of the magicians' efforts. The fifth describes the plight of the magicians before Moses and their exit from the cycle. In addition, each scene regularly reports the pharaoh's response in stereotyped terms. All but the third note that his heart is hard (ḥzq). In addition, the first five scenes note that the pharaoh would not listen, just as God said. In the third scene, 8:11, P's conclusion is preserved only in the note that the pharaoh did not listen, just as God said. In the last three scenes and the conclusion, reference to the pharaoh's not listening is replaced by a note that he did not send the Israelites away. In the last two scenes and the conclusion, the note that God said the pharaoh would not listen is dropped.

A progression of drama appears in P despite the uniform pattern of structure. The magicians begin as successful counterparts to Moses, then drop from view in failure before the conclusion of the cycle (cf. the discussion above). Of more importance, the signs increase in severity as the cycle progresses. The progression presupposes an eventual break in tension. But as in 10:28-29 (J), so for P the cycle ends without permission for Israel to leave (cf. 11:9-10). P cannot say that negotiations between Moses and the pharaoh fail. Moses does not negotiate. He effects a sign without demand, and the pharaoh responds. For P the cycle of signs appears to be nothing more than a multiplication of plagues against Egypt. Nevertheless, the conclusion in 11:9-10 recalls the tradition that negotiations failed. Israel is still under oppression. The tension between movement toward release of Israel and multiplication of signs without effect on the pharaoh is not resolved within the structure of the cycle. Moreover, for P, contrary to the final stage of the text, the cycle excludes the Passover sign as its proper resolution (so 11:9-10).

J appears in 7:14-18, 20b-21a, 23-29; 8:4-11a, 16-28; 9:1-7, 13-21, 23b-34; 10:1-11, 13aβ-19, 23-26, 28-29.

The structure of J is as follows:

I. Exposition	(5:1–6:1? or 7:7 P)
II. Sign cycle	(J references from 7:14–10:26)
A. First scene: rod to snake?	(missing in the preserved text)
B. Second scene: water to blood	7:14-18, 20b-21a, 23-24
1. Speech	14-18
a. God to Moses	14aα
b. Speech	14aβ-18
1) Report of Pharaoh's past response — kbd	14aβ-b
2) Instructions for speech	15-18
a) Message commission formula	15-16aα1
b) Message	16aα2-18
(1) Indictment	16aα2-b
(a) Citation of earlier speech	16aα2-aβ

E cannot be adequately separated from J (see Noth, *Exodus,* 69-71, though contested by Fohrer, followed by Childs, *Exodus,* 131). Moreover, J's version of the sign cycle is not complete. That 5:1–6:1 may represent J's exposition of the cycle (so Schmid, 47) seems unlikely since more than exposition appears there; in addition to an introduction of the principals in the sign cycle, 5:1–6:1 develops negotiations between the Israelites and the pharaoh, ending in failure. If an exposition can be assumed, however, J would preserve the same basic exposition — cycle — conclusion scheme also present in P. Moreover, the water-to-blood scene presupposes that negotiations between Moses

74

and the pharaoh had already begun. The point of reference for the presupposition is not the negotiation scene in 5:1–6:1 but an account of Moses' rod turning into a snake (against Noth, *Exodus,* 73; cf. the allusion to the rod in the expansion of the MESSAGE COMMISSION FORMULA in v. 16 and the indictment with its citation in v. 17). J must have had some kind of scene parallel to 7:8-13. If the assumption is justified, and if the signs involving flies and the death of cattle can be taken as doublets to the signs of gnats and boils in P (cf. Plastaras), J's version of the sign cycle would also parallel P with eight basically identical signs. The water-to-blood sign shows internal evidence for problems in tradition history: (1) Is the water fouled by turning it to blood or by dead fish? (vv. 17-18) (cf. Noth, *Exodus,* 72-74). (2) Does the oracle of God, commissioned for delivery to the pharaoh by Moses in vv. 17-18, depict God striking the water with his rod? Or has the oracle shifted from God's address to the pharaoh through Moses to an address directly from Moses to the pharaoh? (cf. Noth, *Exodus,* 73). Can this point be resolved by alluding to the prophetic tendency to use a divine first person for prophetic speech and action? The fragmentation of J also involves loss of notice about an execution of commission in the frog scene. The locust scene has no concluding narration of the pharaoh's response, and the darkness scene has neither an opening speech nor a concluding narration of response.

Despite the fragmentation, a structural pattern quite different from P develops in the J cycle. It too has uniformity. Each scene (except the darkness scene) begins with a speech. God sends Moses to the pharaoh with a demand that Israel be released for a festival in the wilderness and a threat that a sign-plague will occur should the pharaoh not comply, or an oracle of judgment for not complying. (Aaron plays an inconsistent role in the series and should be evaluated as a secondary part of the tradition.) Each scene (except the frogs scene) notes that the sign occurs. In five of the eight scenes, the pharaoh responds to the sign by summoning Moses for negotiations or a confession of guilt and pleas for intercession. In four the scene ends with a notation that the pharaoh's heart was hardened *(kbd),* and he refused to send the people away. Motifs like the demand for release so that the people can sacrifice in the wilderness and the growing assertions by the pharaoh that Moses must be trying to deceive him (cf. 10:10) derive from the execution of the vocation commission in 5:1–6:1. Thus, in a fashion similar to P, the J sign cycle progresses in intensity toward its conclusion. (On the influence of prophetic legend in the structure of J's plague scenes, see Childs, *Exodus,* 146-49.)

In contrast to P, however, the J cycle constructs elements of each scene on the basis of a concentric pattern. The evidence for a concentric pattern is not as extensive in J as it is in the final stage of the text. Part of the reason is that the uniform elements from P have been regularly combined with a relatively uniform pattern in J. Thus the redactor responsible for combining the two would have been aware of the concentric design (so McCarthy). But the basic concentric pattern for the cycle seems to have been present, at least in part, in J.

The conclusion from this observation, as in the final stage of the text, is that the sign cycle in J does not include the Passover. Indeed, the conclusion in

10:28-29 excludes the Passover scene in 11:1-8 as a part of the sign cycle, contrary to the final redaction. The climax for the sign cycle in J does not lie in the Passover scene. Again, the tension between the signs and the negotiations with Pharaoh is not resolved by the sign cycle. At the end of the series Israel remains under Egyptian oppression.

The consistent tension between the sign cycle and the Passover denies arguments that the sign cycle grew out of the Passover tradition (so McCarthy, against Noth, *Exodus,* 68-69). The kernel for the cycle must be sought instead in the vocation tradition, 3:1–4:18, and in its execution, 5:1–6:1. Moreover, the cycle may have been developed out of the vocation tradition in a basic concentric structure before it gained final shape in J. J's familiarity with the Passover scene in 11:1-8 points to a tension between the two traditions, not a preference of the one to the exclusion of the other.

Genre

For determining the genre of the whole unit 7:7–10:29, one must distinguish between its function in the total context of the vocation-execution tradition and its generic nature as a narrative of its own in that context. Whereas the unit functions in context as the intensifying unfolding of the execution of the vocation in the Moses SAGA, its own genre is not determined as a further version of that SAGA but by the focus on the typical mode in which it is cast.

Virtually all commentators emphasize that the entire unit and its individual parts have in common the focus on the signs and wonders, especially on the wondrous and miraculous power of Moses — and in part Aaron — as the executor(s) of Yahweh's confrontation with Pharaoh. "The reality and power of Yahweh's presence is demonstrated to Pharaoh and to the Egyptians by the miraculous" (Durham, *Exodus,* 91) — to which must be added the role of Moses and Aaron, without whom the unit would not exist in the first place, as the executors of this power.

Constitutive in the miracles of the signs is, then, that increasingly Moses himself is empowered by Yahweh to perform and cause miracles beyond contestation for the execution of his vocation. Notwithstanding the variations in plot, the entire unit and its individual episodes depend in all their literary layers on this focus.

The emphasis on the miraculous dimension in reality, certainly in human affairs, characterizes the plague narratives as LEGEND in general, and as belonging to the known genre of LEGENDS of the prophets, or prophetic legends, specifically.

Childs has given a succinct discussion of the generic provenance of the plague narrative (*Exodus,* 142-51). After discounting proposals for genre such as the linking of events in real history (history writing), novelistic love of embellishment (tale or fiction), the mythical or apocalyptic or battle motif, wisdom, cultic, or legal setting or the tradition of prophet versus king, Childs, starting from studies by Koch and Rofé, sees "a connection between the plague stories and the prophetic legend" (*Exodus,* 144). Yet distinctive for the prophetic legend of the plague stories is that "the plague is produced by the direct action of Moses and Aaron, not by the prophetic word which is subsequently fulfilled. The power is not a prophetic word which ultimately brings an event to pass, but in the prophet himself who possesses the charisma to unleash at will. . . . We have, therefore, in the plague stories a totally different picture of Moses' role from that of the legend in which the prophet is basically a messenger of the word" (145-46). After further analysis, Childs postulates that J adapted an already existing tradition of this type of prophetic legend, a tradition, however, that "cannot be accounted for by supposing the influence of some special sociological setting . . . but leads . . . to a primary, non-derivable stage" (149).

The MESSAGE COMMISSION FORMULA appears widely in the cycle (cf. 7:9, 15-16, 19, 26; 8:1, 12, 16; 9:1, 13). In 7:9, 15-16; 8:16; 9:1, 13, the formula is associated with brief instructions for a particular action: "Go to the pharaoh . . . and say to him. . . ." Such instructions for action should not be seen as a distinct element but only as an introduction to the message commission formula. In 10:1 the instructions for action anticipate a message commission formula, and the message delivered in vv. 3-6a presupposes a similar element.

The MESSENGER FORMULA appears regularly in J (cf. 7:17, 26; 8:16; 9:1, 13; 10:3). The structure of a PROPHETIC ORACLE OF JUDGMENT, with its two parts (indictment — judgment) appears in close conjunction with the MESSENGER FORMULA (7:16-18; 9:17-19). The KNOWLEDGE FORMULA occurs in 7:17; 8:6, 18; 9:14, 29; 10:2. In 7:17; 8:6, 18, the formula is followed by an explicit definition of the event that will establish the knowledge (cf. Zimmerli, "Knowledge"). Several series of speeches in dialogue are similar in function to the negotiation speeches in 5:1–6:1 (cf. 8:4-7, 21-25; 9:27-30; 10:8-11a, 16-17).

ANNOTATION. The discussion of genre, offered before the discussion of the formulae of the unit, replaces the discussion by Coats in his typescript. Based on the larger context of the unit and on the variations and inconsistencies of the pattern in the individual units, Coats had said that "no single scene in this cycle of signs can be categorized as a genre in itself," and "even in its unity, the series resists genre definition. It is dependent on a larger context." It should be evident, however, that one cannot say that this large narrative does not belong to a narrative genre, quite apart from the fact that its genre has been well determined.

Setting

Discussion of setting for this cycle of signs is bound to the discussion of setting for the larger unit of exodus traditions (cf. The Exodus Saga, Chapter 1A). It is important to note here, however, that traditions can have more than one setting. The question here is not about setting for the exodus traditions, but about setting for this text and the larger unit it is part of. The larger unit may have had a role to play in the cult (thus Pedersen). This may have been the case especially for the P document. But a more probable setting for the J material as well as any earlier stages would be the family. The sign cycle, and the larger history it is part of, were popular national lore, transmitted in the family from father to son (cf. 10:2).

Intention

For J and any earlier stages of the sign cycle, the intention is to heighten the tension already described in 5:1–6:1, the initial contact between Moses and the pharaoh. The heightening tension leads toward a break. The goal of the commission from the vocation tradition is to effect Israel's release from oppression. The sign cycle should contribute to that goal. Yet the signs end in failure, and Israel remains under oppression. The tradition has not moved beyond the point reflected in 5:1–6:1. The climax of the exodus traditions does not appear here.

Perhaps in an effort to soften the failure of the negotiation cycle, the text points beyond the exodus to a different intention. The signs will be passed down from father to son in order to ridicule the Egyptians. God plagued Egypt not once but eight or nine or ten times. Moreover, repetition of the cycle tradition will serve to elicit knowledge of God, commitment to Israel's God as Lord. The cycle has thus a decidedly theological function.

Bibliography

H. Cazelles, "Rédactions et Traditions dans l'Exode," in *Studien zum Pentateuch* (ed. G. Braulik, et al.; Vienna: Herder, 1977) 37-58; F. E. Eakin, "The Plagues and the Crossing of the Sea," *RevExp* 74 (1977) 473-82; H. Eising, "Die ägyptischen Plagen," in *Lex Tua Veritas* (*Fest.* H. Junker; ed. H. Gross and F. Mussner; Trier: Paulinus, 1961) 75-87; G. Fohrer, *Überlieferung und Geschichte des Exodus* (BZAW 91; Berlin: Töpelmann, 1964); M. Greenberg, "The Redaction of the Plague Narrative in Exodus," in *Near Eastern Studies in Honor of William Foxwell Albright* (ed. H. Goedicke; Baltimore: Johns Hopkins Univ. Press, 1971) 243-52; idem, "The Thematic Unity of Exodus iii–xi," in *Fourth World Congress of Jewish Studies* (vol. 1; Jerusalem: World Union of Jewish Studies, 1967) 151-54; D. M. Gunn, "The Hardening of Pharaoh's Heart: Plot, Character, and Theology in Exodus 1–14," in *Art and Meaning: Rhetoric in Biblical Literature* (ed. D. J. A. Clines, D. M. Gunn, and A. J. Hauser; JSOTSup 19; Sheffield: JSOT Press, 1982) 72-96; M. S. Luker, "The Figure of Moses in the Plague Traditions" (Diss., Drew, 1968); D. J. McCarthy, "Moses' Dealings with Pharaoh," *CBQ* 27 (1965) 335-47; E. Otto, "Erwägungen zum überlieferungsgeschichtlichen Ursprung und 'Sitz im Leben' des jahwistischen Plagenzyklus," *VT* 26 (1976) 3-27; J. Pedersen, "Passahfest und Passahlegende," *ZAW* 52 (1934) 161-75; H. Schmid, *Mose: Überlieferung und Geschichte* (BZAW 110; Berlin: Töpelmann, 1968); J. M. Schmidt, "Erwägungen zum Verhältnis von Auszugs- und Sinaitradition," *ZAW* 82 (1970) 1-31; A. M. Vater, "A Plague on Both our Houses: Form and Rhetorical Observations on Exodus 7–11," in *Art and Meaning*, 62-71; P. Weimar and E. Zenger, *Exodus: Geschichten und Geschichte der Befreiung Israels* (SBS 75; Stuttgart: KBW, 1975); R. R. Wilson, "The Hardening of Pharaoh's Heart," *CBQ* 41 (1979) 18-36; Z. Zevit, "The Priestly Redaction and Interpretation of the Plague Narrative in Exodus," *JQR* 66 (1975/76) 193-211; W. Zimmerli, "Knowledge of God According to the Book of Ezekiel," in *I Am Yahweh* (tr. D. W. Stott; ed. W. Brueggemann; Atlanta: John Knox, 1982) 29-98, 143-54, esp. 46ff.

ADDENDUM. A. M. Cartun, " 'Who Knows Ten?' The Structural and Symbolic Use of Numbers in the Ten Plagues: Exodus 7:14–13:6," *USQR* 45 (1991) 65-119; L. Schmidt, *Beobachtungen zu der Plagenerzählung in Exodus 7:14–11:10* (StudBib 4; Leiden: Brill, 1990); J. Van Seters, "The Plagues of Egypt: Ancient Tradition or Literary Invention?" *ZAW* 98 (1986).

ANNOTATION. Next to the recent commentaries and monographs, the following studies must be especially noted: Otto's and Van Seters's for form criticism, Schmidt's for source criticism, and Cartun's for the rhetorical function of the numbering of the plagues.

LEGEND OF THE DEATH OF THE FIRSTBORN: PASSOVER SIGN, 11:1–12:36

Structure

I. Opening scene	11:1-10
A. Speech	1-2
1. Introduction: God to Moses	1aα
2. Speech	
a. Announcement of sign	1aβ-b
b. Message commission formula: Moses to the people, with introduction of spoil motif	2
B. Description of relationships between Israelites and Egyptians and the great importance of Moses in the sight of the Egyptians	3
C. Speech	4-8a
1. Introduction: Moses	4aα
2. Speech	4aβ-8a
a. Messenger formula	4aβ
b. Oracle	4b-8a
1) Announcement of sign	4b-7a
a) Against Egypt	4b-6
b) Exception: Israel	7a
2) Knowledge formula	7b
3) Results of the sign	8a
a) Introduction: Egyptians to Moses	8aα1
b) Citation	8aα2

a. Instructions for Passover	21aβ-22
1) For procuring and sacrificing a lamb	21aβ-b
2) For protection ritual	22
b. Reason for the Passover	23
c. Ordinance for Passover	24-25
d. Provision for explanation of the festival with Passover name etiology	26-27a
C. Execution of the commission to the people	27b-28 (//12:50-51)
III. Conclusion	12:29-36
A. Narration of the Passover sign	29-30
B. Speech	31-32
1. Introduction: Pharaoh to Moses and Aaron	31aα1
2. Concession for exodus without conditions	31aα2-32
C. Narration of sign's consequences	33-36
1. Unleavened bread etiology	33-34
a. Egyptians' pressing Israel to leave in haste	33a
b. Reason: a citation	33b
c. Preparation for departure with unleavened bread	34
2. The exodus with spoil	35-36

In the final stage of the text, the firstborn scene is not an independent unit of tradition but the conclusion to the sign cycle in 7:7–10:29. Thus element I begins abruptly, with no introductory exposition. It moves instead immediately to a speech from God to Moses, vv. 1-2. The speech presupposes the sign cycle by using the particle 'ôd: "Yet one plague *more*. . . ." Moreover, the structure of element I suggests an imitation of a sign scene typical for the cycle in 7:7–10:29 (cf. Otto, 17-18; Schmid, *Mose,* 43). The opening SPEECH commissions Moses to announce a sign, and the speech in vv. 4-8 develops motifs characteristic for the speeches announcing signs in the sign cycle: a messenger formula introduces the announcement. The body of the speech details a sign against the Egyptians and notes the immunity of the Israelites. A KNOWLEDGE FORMULA, along with the consequences of the sign, concludes the message. Cf. 8:16-19 (*NRSV* 20-23). The closing speech in 12:31-32 (III.B) also picks up the sign cycle by playing on the negotiation-concession chain (cf. 8:4, 24 [*NRSV* 8, 38]; 9:27-28; 10:8, 24). Indeed, the chain of concessions reaches its climax here since for the first time the pharaoh does not combine his concession to Moses with explicit or implicit exceptions.

Despite the contact this scene obviously has with the sign cycle, the unity between the two is superficial. The scene opens with a speech commissioning Moses to address an announcement of a new plague, not to the pharaoh, as in previous scenes, but to the people. This break in the parallel might be attributed to the concluding speeches in 10:28-29, prohibiting further audiences Moses might have with the pharaoh. But the speech is nonetheless vague. A new sign is announced, but the details of the sign do not appear. Rather, the speech sets out instructions for the people to despoil the Egyptians. The second speech, 11:4-8a, has an ambiguous introduction: no addressee is named. Its position following the commission for Moses to speak to the people implies that the addressee should be the people. The speech would thus be an execution of the commission in vv. 1-2. But the speech has nothing to do with the instructions for despoiling the Egyptians. It details the firstborn sign against the Egyptians and thus follows the pattern from other sign scenes for a speech to be delivered to the pharaoh. The speech, however, is not part of a commission to Moses for subsequent delivery to the pharaoh, as in the sign cycle. The closing lines of the speech, vv. 7b-8a, and the narration in v. 8b clarify the ambiguity by showing that Moses addresses the speech to the pharaoh, despite the prohibition for further contact in 10:28-29 (Noth, *Exodus*, 92-93; Plastaras; and Otto make vv. 7b-8a secondary).

The announcement of a sign in element I presupposes some account of the sign's execution. Element I, however, gives a general summary of the sign cycle as a whole, with a notation that *all* signs were executed and *none* broke the hard heart of the pharaoh. With no explicit reference to the sign against the firstborn, in contrast to the material in 12:1-36, these verses appear to be intrusive in the unit. Their position here points to the tension between the sign cycle and the firstborn scene noted in the discussion of 7:7–10:29. For the final stage of redaction, element II binds the announcement of the firstborn sign to the sign cycle and suggests that this sign, like all the others, failed to produce the desired results. The description of the sign execution and its consequences, in 12:1-36, would stand outside the summary statement and thus not be subject to the implications of failure it carries.

Element II continues the firstborn scene with two speeches, both with ritual instructions. The final element, 12:29-36, concludes not only the firstborn scene but the entire chain of exodus narration.

Source analysis clarifies the complex structure of the unit. P appears in 11:9-10 and 12:1-20. In addition, the speech in 12:21-27a should probably be attributed to P because of its structural unity with 12:1-20 (so May; cf. the discussion below). Finally, the conclusion in 12:27b-28 marks the end of the exodus narration for P.

Structure in this P material is as follows:

I.	Opening speech	12:1-20
	A. Introduction: God to Moses and Aaron	1
	B. Speech	2-20
	1. Definition of festival month	2
	2. Message commission formula:	
	Moses and Aaron to all the Israelites	3aα
	3. Message: Passover ordinance	3aβb-11
	4. Announcement of sign	12-13
	5. Ordinance for Unleavened Bread	14-20
II.	Speech: execution of the commission	12:21-27a
	A. Introduction: Moses to all the elders	21aα
	B. Speech	21aβ-27a
	1. Instructions for Passover (ordinance)	21aβ-22
	2. Reason	23
	3. Ordinance for the Passover	24-25

One should see 11:9-10 not as part of the Passover tradition for P but as the conclusion for the sign cycle in 7:7–10:29*. It functions in a parallel position to 10:28-29 (J) and shows that for both J and P the Passover stands after the sign cycle as a distinct structural and tradition element (see Otto, 12). The general summary of *all* signs in 11:10 would thus not include the firstborn sign for the Priestly source.

The Passover, and indeed, the exodus event itself P describes entirely in terms of the ritual patterns in the speeches of 12:1-27a and the concluding statement of execution in vv. 27b-28. The first speech from God to Moses and Aaron commissions a speech to the people with instructions for preparing and executing the Passover (vv. 3-11; cf. 12:43-49; 13:3-10), an announcement of the sign (vv. 12-13), and parallel provisions for the Unleavened Bread Festival (vv. 14//17, 15//19, and 16//18, at least in specifications for the first and last days of the festival). The introduction for both the Passover INSTRUCTIONS (v. 2) and the Unleavened Bread INSTRUCTIONS (v. 14) and the conclusions for the Passover (v. 11bβ) and the Unleavened Bread (v. 20) mark the basic outline of the speech. The second speech, vv. 21-27a, parallels the Passover section of the first (v. 21aβ-b//3b-6; 22//7; 23//12-13. Cf. also vv. 24//14). The introduction to the speech suggests, however, that its position in the unit is not as a doublet to the first speech but as an execution of the commission given to Moses and Aaron in the first speech (against Noth, *Exodus,* 97-98). Under such a structural pattern, one would expect some duplication of tradition and even of direct wording. The successful execution of the commission given to the people in this speech is narrated in vv. 27b-28. This statement constitutes P's conclusion to the exodus narration. A longer form of the same conclusion appears in 12:50-51 and shows that execution of the Passover instructions constitutes P's presentation of the exodus event itself, the climax of the crisis posed by Egyptian oppression in 1:1-7, 13-14.

The structure of J in 11:1-8 and 12:29-36 is as follows:

I. Speech	11:1-2
A. Introduction: God to Moses	1aα1
B. Speech	1aα2-2
1. Announcement of sign	1aα2-b
2. Message commission formula: Moses to the people	2a
3. Purpose of the message (despoiling)	2b
II. Description of relationships between Israelites	
and Egyptians and of Moses' greatness	3
III. Speech	4-8a
A. Introduction: Moses	4aα
B. Speech proper	4aβ-8a
1. Messenger formula	4aβ
2. Oracle	4b-8a
a. Announcement of sign	4b-7a

The firstborn scene in J is an imitation of a scene from the sign cycle in 7:7–10:29* (see Childs, *Exodus,* 191). The initial commission to Moses announces a sign, with Moses subsequently appearing before the pharaoh to deliver the commission. As in J's sign scenes, so here the sign will draw an explicit distinction between the Egyptians and the Israelites. The pattern of the sign scene develops its natural completion in 12:29-30, a report that the sign occurred as announced, and in vv. 31-32, the final speech in negotiations between Moses and the pharaoh that now ends in success (cf. the discussion of J in the sign cycle). The contrast between Moses' presentation before the pharaoh here and the close of negotiations in 10:28-29 (J) shows that for J the sign cycle and the firstborn tradition stand in tension (contrast Otto, 18). The close of the pharaoh's speech in 12:32, an appeal for blessing, has a parallel in the concession speeches of the sign cycle, since there the pharaoh appeals for intercession and forgiveness (cf. 9:27-28; 10:16-17). The appeal specifically for blessing here is characteristic for J's theology (cf. Wolff). Vv. 33-34 set the stage for the exodus with a motif of haste for the Israelites under pressure from the Egyptians, while vv. 35-36 describe the exodus event itself in terms of the despoiling motif. Israel escapes the burden of Egyptian oppression and takes the spoil of their oppressors with them.

The initial speeches are problematic. In J's sign cycle the opening speech detailed the coming sign as part of the message Moses was to deliver to the pharaoh. Here the opening speech has no details of the sign. The plague sign will be effected against the pharaoh (v. 1), but the message Moses is commissioned to deliver should go to the people, not the pharaoh. The instructions to the people anticipate the despoiling, with the narration in v. 3 structured on the basis of the heroic stature of Moses not only for Israel but also for Egypt. It is then clear that the text does not cast the despoiled objects as gifts freely given, but as objects *requested* by the people. The details of the sign come in the second speech. The speech has an incomplete introduction, but its closing lines and the narration in 11:8b show that the speech was delivered not to the people but to the pharaoh. The difficulty can be explained, at least in part, as the result of a complex history of tradition behind the J text. Two distinct traditions about the exodus event have come together. The dominant one concerns the sign against the firstborn Egyptians. For this tradition, the exodus occurred when the pharaoh, along with his people, sent the Israelites away in response to the death of the firstborn. This tradition stands in tension with the sign cycle at every major point.

Moreover, the firstborn tradition may not have been attached from the beginning to the Passover. Indeed, some tension between firstborn and Passover can still be seen (see Childs, *Exodus,* 189-95; Otto, 19). The conclusions to the sign cycle in 10:28-29 and 11:9-10 highlight that tension and lead to the observation that the Passover was probably a tradition originally independent of the sign cycle (cf. Noth, *A History,* 65-71; McCarthy). Moreover, an ancient tradition about the Passover ritual, perhaps older than the exodus event itself and unrelated to a celebration of the exodus, probably lies behind this stage of the text. According to this tradition, the protective ritual, practiced by a family or a larger group of families, would have been used to protect the flocks at the time of pasture change. That ritual would have been appropriated at a later time by Israel for the celebration of the exodus since the exodus involved a major change of location for the Israelites (cf. Rost).

In addition to the Passover tradition about the exodus, traces of a distinct, originally independent tradition about the exodus can be seen. When negotiations for release failed, Moses instructed the Israelites to despoil the Egyptians. No new negotiations would be necessary, for the despoiling motif presupposes that the Israelites escaped from Egypt in secret with spoil taken by deception from Egyptian citizens (cf. McCarthy; Coats, "Despoiling"). Evidence for this tradition is preserved in the instructions and the description of relationships, 11:1-3, and in the conclusion to the scene, 12:35-36 (cf. 3:21-22 and 14:5).

An Unleavened Bread Festival, originally distinct from the Passover, can be identified in the ritual ordinances of this text (cf. Otto, 19). Like the Passover, the Unleavened Bread Festival may have been older than the exodus, an agricultural rite used for celebrating the spring growth (cf. Noth, *Exodus,* 89). Like the Passover, this rite would have been adopted by the Israelites for celebrating the exodus event. It is possible that the motif of despoiling may have been closely connected to the Unleavened Bread Festival before Unleavened Bread and Passover, celebrated at roughly the same time in the course of the year, came together.

If a tradition about the exodus as a secret escape from Egypt with spoil taken by deception could be identified, it would not have the same point of tension with the sign cycle that the Passover tradition obviously has. Moreover, it would correspond with the virtually unanimous tradition that Israel did not escape Egyptian oppression as a result of negotiations with the pharaoh. Both the sign cycle in 7:7–10:29 and the initial series of negotiations in 5:1–6:1 end in failure. The deception involved in the despoiling would correspond to the deception motif also present in the negotiation tradition, centered in the appeal to go on pilgrimage to sacrifice in the wilderness. If a saga lies behind 5:1–6:1, the conclusion for it, the climax of the oppression crisis in the exodus traditions, would be the secret escape with spoil. Despite failure in the negotiations, Israel could escape Egyptian oppression without the pharaoh's permission,

85

without his knowledge. The spoil, made possible only by God's intervention, would dramatize the escape for the delight of future generations (cf. Coats, "Despoiling").

Genre

Genre definition for the firstborn scene is as complex as the structure analysis. The final stage of the text does not constitute an independent unit of tradition, open to genre definition in itself. Rather, it stands as the conclusion to the chain of texts beginning in 1:1-14, including the vocation unit and the sign cycle. It would be the final execution of the commission given to Moses in the vocation tradition. The complex structure suggests, moreover, that the unit is a hybrid text, unlike either P or J, constructed as a unique piece by combining two quite distinct formulations of tradition about the firstborn sign. Efforts to define the genre of this stage accomplish little more than demonstrations of the complex combination of J and P.

The Priestly version of the firstborn tradition is a completely different genre from J. The conclusion in 11:9-10 constitutes a principal break between the sign cycle and the firstborn scene; for P, contrary to the final stage of the text, the Passover is not simply an extension of the sign cycle. The first speech begins without exposition and constitutes a cultic ritual text. 12:2-11 and 14-20 are constructed in parallel, with formulations suggesting a festival ORDINANCE, a law constructed as a speech to institute a festival (cf. Plastaras). The introductions in vv. 2 and 14 are similar: "This month shall be for you . . ." *(haḥōdeš hazzeh lākem);* "This day shall be for you . . ." *(wĕhāyâ hayyôm hazzeh lākem).* (Cf. Exod 32:5; Lev 23:5, 8, 23, 27, 32, 34, 35; Num 28:16, 17ff.). In v. 14 reference to the Unleavened Bread Festival as a festival to God *(ḥag la'dōnāy)* (cf. Exod 10:9; 13:6; 32:5; Lev 23:6, 34, 39, 41; Num 29:12; Deut 16:10ff.) and the designation of the ordinance as an ordinance forever *(ḥuqqat 'ôlām)* in both vv. 14 and 17 (cf. Exod 27:21; 28:43; Lev 3:17; 7:36; 10:9; 16:31; 17:7; 23:14, 21, 31; 24:3ff.) again point to the speech as a ritual text, a specification of cultic procedure. The conclusion to the Passover section of the speech, in v. 11b, is a typical designation for festival law: "It is the Passover for God" *(pesaḥ hû' la'dōnāy).* (Cf. Exod 29:14, 18, 22, 25, 28; Lev 4:21, 24; 5:9, 19; 8:21, 28.) Finally the cultic ORDINANCE builds around the verb *ḥāgag,* "to observe a feast." In 12:14 it is a 2nd m. pl. Qal perfect (cf. Lev 23:41; Num 29:12) or imperfect with a suffix. Cf. also Exod 23:14; Lev 23:39, 41; Deut 16:15. The closest parallel in content for this speech would be the cultic calendars, Exod 34:18-20; Lev 23:4-8; Deut 16:1-8.

The two ordinances have been joined by the announcement of the sign in vv. 12-13. The SELF-REVELATION FORMULA in the middle of the announcement (v. 12b) belongs directly with the ordinance institution (cf. Lev 23:22, 43). The second speech parallels the first, at least through v. 24. Vv. 26-27a attach an ETIOLOGY for the name of the Passover Festival, based on a wordplay with the verb *pāsaḥ,* "to pass over" (cf. Long, Soggin).

There is no clear evidence of the ritual institution speech in J (unless the speech in vv. 21-27a should be appropriated for J). To the contrary, the J text presents the firstborn scene as an imitation of a sign scene, thus presupposing the material to be dependent in some manner on the sign cycle. No independent genre characteristics appear in the J material. It seems to be virtually an appendix to the sign cycle, an explanation that a tradition about Israelite efforts to escape oppression, which had focused on the apparent failure of these efforts, in fact ended pointing out their success. The firstborn scene for J would at best be a continuation of the execution for Moses' vocation commission, already discussed for 5:1–6:1 and 7:7–10:29 (→ The Exodus Saga, Chapter 1A). The tradition about a secret escape with spoil taken from the Egyptians would also represent not an independent genre but the original conclusion for the negotiation tradition and the popular history it is now part of. The etiological element for unleavened bread in the festival celebration of the exodus would not qualify the unit as an etiological narrative. Behind the popular history, perhaps ending in the despoiling escape from oppression, may lie a national saga, recounting efforts to negotiate Israel's release with its implications of deception (Israel would certainly not have come back from such a pilgrimage) and an eventual escape without the pharaoh's knowledge.

The formulae in the unit, employed to imitate a sign scene, have been fully discussed in the section on 7:7–10:29.

ANNOTATION. As with many studies by other authors, Coats's, in part unique, distinction of the differences between the final text and its P and J predecessors as well as his discussion of the genre characteristics of the P version deserve particular attention. But his denial of the genre of the final and the J versions appears unwarranted.

Explicitly linking the firstborn scene with the sign cycle of 7:7–10:29 and what is typical for that cycle, the narrative of this scene would also belong to the genre of LEGEND, should the assertion of this genre for that cycle be valid. Cf. already the typically legendary characterization of the admiration of the Egyptians for the Israelites — and for the "great importance" of Moses "in the land of Egypt, in the sight of Pharaoh's officials and the sight of the people" in II (J), the opening scene in 11:3, in addition to all other indicators for the miraculous dimension of the J narrative.

The versions of J and P have in common that the traditions of the Unleavened Bread, the Passover, and the death of the firstborn/the houses of the Egyptians, however independent originally, are solidly embedded in the narrative of the preparation for and the event of the exodus, regardless of possibly preliterary stages of their combination with the exodus tradition. The same fact is also evident in the final text, notwithstanding the clear shifts in its composition and focus due to its combination of J and P in it.

The genre of the narrative in the tradition history of its literary layers is therefore determined by their focus on the legendary, i.e., the wondrous, even miraculous nature of the events and of Moses' role in them, including those parts of the narrative in which the origin of and instructions for unleavened bread and the Passover Festival are historicized through their connection with the final plague and the exodus in legendary dimensions.

Setting

The setting for the final stage of the text reflects the redactional process that brought J and P together into a single line of narrative. The unique interests of the redactor can be seen in this instance by the position of P's conclusion to the sign cycle. The Priestly version of the firstborn tradition reflects the cultic setting of festival law. The specific circumstances of the setting can be defined as a proclamation by a cultic leader before the congregation (cf. 32:5). Thus the material in P appears entirely as a speech without narration or exposition. For P the conclusion of the exodus traditions is a cultic event. At this stage in the history of the exodus traditions, then, a cultic setting seems certain (cf. Pedersen). Indeed, since in P no trace of the despoiling motif can be seen, and the Unleavened Bread Festival has been suppressed in favor of the Passover, P must preserve the exodus tradition from a cultic setting in the Passover celebration. Even the reference to transmission by family questions (v. 26) has been overlaid by the cultic setting dominant in the entire scope of P (Soggin). The children now ask: "What do you mean by this service?"

Setting for the J material cannot be separated from the exodus traditions at large and should probably be placed in the family process of transmission. The firstborn tradition cannot be completely separated from the cultic celebration of Unleavened Bread (Otto, 26) and suggests that both settings were involved in preserving the tradition employed by J. Perhaps the despoiling tradition was at one time celebrated in a cultic festival as well.

Intention

In the final stage of the material this unit binds the firstborn sign to the sign cycle as one of the failures in negotiating Israel's release. Its intention would be to depict Israel's release despite the failure. Yet the scene is split by the conclusion in 11:9-10 and leaves the impression of tension between the signs and the eventual success of Israel's pressure on the pharaoh. That tension is not resolved. The intention of the P text is to attach the exodus event to a ritual institution for the Passover (and Unleavened Bread) despite the failure of the negotiations. The ritual ordinances in 12:1-20 function as the basis for instituting the festival itself (cf. Plastaras), for observing it perpetually, and certainly also for their ongoing instruction. The brief etiology in 12:26-27a for the name of the festival does not point to the basic intention of the unit, nor does it show the motivating force for the origin of the material (cf. Long). The J text is much more clearly concerned to spell out the consequences of failure in the negotiations. The firstborn scene reopens the negotiations despite the prohibition in 10:28-29. At this point, however, the negotiations succeed. The despoiling tradition behind the firstborn scene accounts for Israel's exodus without reopening the negotiation process and thus resolves the tension between the sign cycle and its apparent conclusion. Its intention is to say that Israel escaped despite Pharaoh's refusal to accede to Israel's request for permission to leave. The escape without the pharaoh's knowledge might have been an anticlimax to the negotiation scenes, an undramatic departure. The spoil, however, makes the final scene dramatic for future tradition. Israel escapes as victor over Egypt, capable of obtaining spoil, if not by military might at least by deception.

Bibliography

G. W. Coats, "Despoiling the Egyptians," *VT* 18 (1968) 450-57; J. Halbe, "Erwägungen zu Ursprung und Wesen des Massotfestes," *ZAW* 87 (1975) 324-46; O. Keel, "Erwägungen zum Sitz im Leben des vormosaischen Pascha und zur Etymologie von פֶּסַח," *ZAW* 84 (1972) 414-34; E. Kutsch, "Erwägungen zur Geschichte der Passafeier und das Massotfestes," *ZTK* 55 (1958) 1-35; D. J. McCarthy, "Moses' Dealings with Pharaoh," *CBQ* 27 (1965) 336-47; B. O. Long, *The Problem of Etiological Narrative in the Old Testament* (BZAW 108; Berlin: Töpelmann, 1968); H. G. May, "The Relation of the Passover to the Festival of Unleavened Cakes," *JBL* 55 (1936) 65-82; E. Otto, "Erwägungen zum überlieferungsgeschichtlichen Ursprung und 'Sitz im Leben' des Jahwistischen Plagenzyklos," *VT* 26 (1976) 3-27; J. Pedersen, "Passahfest und Passahlegende," *ZAW* 52 (1934) 161-75; L. Rost, "Weidewechsel und altisraelitischer Festkalender," *ZDPV* 66 (1943) 205-16; J. Schreiner, "Exodus 12, 21-23 und das israelitische Pascha," in *Studien zum Pentateuch* (*Fest.* W. Kornfeld; ed. G. Braulik; Vienna: Herder, 1977) 69-90; J. Van Seters, "The Place of the Yahwist in the History of Passover and Massot," *ZAW* 95 (1983) 167-81; J. A. Soggin, "Kultätiologische Sagen und Katechese im Hexateuch," *VT* 10 (1960) 341-47; H. W. Wolff, "The Kerygma of the Yahwist" (tr. W. A. Benware), *Int* 20 (1966) 131-58; repr. in W. Brueggeman and H. W. Wolff, *The Vitality of Old Testament Traditions* (2nd ed.; Atlanta: John Knox, 1982) 41-66, 148-54.

ADDENDUM. S. Bar-On, "Zur literarkritischen Analyse von Ex 12,21-27," *ZAW* 107 (1995) 18-31; J. Van Seters, "The Plagues of Egypt: Ancient Tradition or Literary Invention?" *ZAW* 98 (1986) 31-39; P. Weimar, "Zum Problem der Entstehungsgeschichte von Ex 12,1-14," *ZAW* 107 (1995) 1-17.

ANNOTATION. The study by Van Seters is important form-critically, the one by Bar-On literary-critically, and the one by Weimar for its discussion of structure within 12:1-14, its tripartite development, and especially of P.

SUMMARY OF THE EXODUS TRADITIONS, 12:37-42

Structure

I. Itinerary formula	37a
II. Participants in the exodus	37b-38
III. Etiology for unleavened bread	39
IV. Date for the exodus	40-41

The structure of this material demonstrates no intricate development of narrative motifs from one element to the next, no movement of plot or arc of tension from crisis to resolution. The exodus narration does not continue into these verses. Rather, the unit comprises a loose collection of summary statements about the exodus traditions. The first, v. 37a, is an itinerary formula, similar to other formulas found not in the exodus traditions but throughout the wilderness traditions (cf. 13:20; 15:22a, 27; 16:1; 17:1abα; 19:2; Num 11:35; 12:16; 20:1, 22; 21:4a, 10, 11, 12, 13, 16, 18b, 19, 20; 22:1; cf. also Gen 46:1a). It comprises two parts, a notice of departure from one site and a notice of arrival at another (cf. Coats, "Wilderness Itinerary"). It marks the initial movement of the Israelites from Egypt into the wilderness and thus stands for the exodus itself. But its relationship with other formulas throughout the wilderness theme shows the contact this collection of statements has with both the exodus and the wilderness themes.

The second element contains a summary review of the participants in the exodus, both people and cattle. It thus picks up the motif of concession from the sign cycle: Moses pressed the pharaoh for permission to take all the Israelite community on the pilgrimage, men, women, children, and animals. The nominal syntax of the sentence highlights its summary character; it does not narrate a new set of events but reviews material. The verb "to go up" (*'ālâ*), in the second syntactical position of the sentence, is characteristic of the exodus formulas (cf. Wijngaards).

The third element explains the necessity for using unleavened bread during the exodus-wilderness journey: The Israelites were unable to bring leaven with them because they were expelled from Egypt in haste before they had time to make proper provisions. This note thus picks up 12:33-34 and presupposes the firstborn scene. Although it makes no reference to cultic celebration of the exodus, it cannot be separated from the Unleavened Bread Festival.

The fourth element dates the exodus event by first noting the total number of years spent in Egypt and then specifying the exodus as the end of the period. Citation of the total number of years is in itself a summary of the exodus traditions (cf. Deut 2:7; 8:2, 4; Josh 5:6; Amos 2:10; 5:25; Neh 9:21).

The last element in the unit contains two basically parallel statements of festival ordinance. The first ties the ordinance with a reason for the festival's observance: "to bring them out from the land of Egypt." The second requires celebration of the festival "by all the people of Israel throughout their generations." Otherwise the statements are identical: "It is a night of watching for God." The watch-night festival cannot be separated from the Passover celebration. Thus both the Unleavened Bread and the Passover celebrations of the exodus are picked up in the summary.

Loose collections of material such as this one defy careful source analysis since no large narrative context provides thorough control for distinctions. This material should most probably be assigned to P or perhaps to a post-P redaction of exodus tradition. It is possible that J material appears in part (cf. v. 39), although the summary character of the material could account for both J and P style. The summary statements pick up older traditions, such as the ones discussed above in 7:7–10:29 and 11:1–12:36, but no evidence of an older summary can be seen.

Genre

This COLLECTION does not represent an independent genre. It is a summary of distinct statements held together narratologically. The statements as distinct elements can be identified as formulas and stereotyped expressions, at least in part. V. 37a is an ITINERARY FORMULA (cf. Gen 46:1a) similar to the type of statement that defines the structure of Assyrian annals (cf. the annals of Shalmaneser III) and even Gen 14:1-16. V. 39 is an ETIOLOGY, although it uses none of the etiological formulas. Its loose connection with the context emphasizes its character here simply as etiology. V. 42 is a festival ORDINANCE, like the statements in 12:2 and 14. Its function is to institute the festival watch night. This kind of summary may be called SUMMARY STORY OR REPORT.

Setting

The unit derives from the redactional work that brought the exodus traditions together under one theme and set them into relationship with the wilderness theme of traditions. Material from other settings could readily be adopted for this kind of unit: a cultic ordinance for the watch-night festival or an etiology for the unleavened bread.

Intention

The unit summarizes the exodus traditions and anticipates stages in the wilderness traditions. It intends, therefore, to set the transition between the exodus and wilderness themes (cf. 1:1-14). The wilderness itinerary points especially to the role this unit plays as a bond between the two major themes.

Bibliography

G. W. Coats, "A Structural Transition in Exodus," *VT* 22 (1972) 129-42; idem, "An Exposition for the Wilderness Traditions," *VT* 22 (1972) 288-95; idem, "The Wilderness Itinerary," *CBQ* 34 (1972) 135-52; J. Wijngaards, "הוציא and העלה: A Twofold Approach to the Exodus," *VT* 15 (1965) 91-107.

ADDENDUM. R. Schmitt, *Exodus und Passa: Ihr Zusammenhang im Alten Testament* (OBO 7; Göttingen: Vandenhoeck & Ruprecht, 1982). This work deals with the tradition history of the Passover and its relationship to P.

STORY OF PASSOVER ORDINANCE, 12:43-51

Structure

I. Speech	43-49
A. Introduction: God to Moses and Aaron	43aα
B. Speech	43aβ-49
1. Introduction to the ordinance	43aβ
2. Ordinance	43b-48
a. Prohibition of foreigner	43b
b. Circumcision of slave	44
c. Prohibition of sojourner or hired servant	45
d. Order for eating the Passover (expressed both positively and negatively)	46-47
e. Circumcision of stranger	48a
f. Prohibition of uncircumcised	48b
3. Conclusion to the ordinance	49
II. Execution of instruction	50-51

This unit of Passover ORDINANCE is isolated from the principal Passover ritual in 12:1-11 and from the closely related speech in 12:21-27a by the conclusion to the exodus traditions in 12:29-36 and by the collection of summary statements in 12:37-42. Both its isolation and its position in an organizational seam suggest that its distinctive contribution to the Passover ordinance derives from its character as a secondary growth in Passover tradition (cf. 4:24-26, also in a redactional seam).

The ORDINANCE, element I, appears as a speech from God to Moses and Aaron, just like the ordinance in 12:1-11. The speech itself begins with a nominal clause, v. 43a, defining the subject of the speech as an ordinance for the Passover. The conclusion in v. 49 specifies the validity of the ordinance for both native and stranger and suggests that the principal focus of the ordinance falls on the role of nonnatives in the Passover celebration (cf. Num 9:11-14; 15:16, 29). The ordinance itself vacillates between PROHIBITION against participation in the Passover by certain figures in Israel's community — the foreigner *(ben-nēkār),* the sojourner or hired servant *(tôšāb wĕśākîr),* the uncircumcised *('ārēl)* — and definition of circumcision as a necessary part of preparation. Circumcision can establish eligibility, especially for the slave purchased with silver *(miqnat-kāsep)* and a stranger *(gēr).* Cf. the reference to the stranger *(gēr)* in v. 49. The ORDER for eating the Passover, set in the middle of the unit (vv. 46-47), introduces incidental requirements, not noted in 12:1-11, and then emphasizes the importance of keeping the festival. The unique item in this ordinance, then, is the emphasis on circumcision as a preparation for the Passover by slaves and strangers. Indeed, the PROHIBITION against participation by the uncircumcised in v. 48b and the concluding formula in v. 49 emphasize the importance of circumcision for all who participate, both stranger and native.

The ordinance belongs entirely to P or perhaps a secondary element in P (so Noth, *Exodus*, 92, 99). Its position in an organizational seam and the absence of any reference to circumcision as a prerequisite for the Passover elsewhere in the OT, except perhaps Josh 5:2-11, suggest that the Passover ritual was not originally concerned to stipulate circumcision for all participants.

The conclusion in element II, 12:50-51, appears to be an indication that the Passover ordinance was properly carried out. But its reference to the exodus (v. 51) stands in contrast to the ordinance specification of participants in the Passover as natives of the land (cf. esp. v. 48aβ, *kě'ezraḥ hā'āreṣ*). The conclusion should be seen, then, as a longer form of P's statement about the exodus event itself in 12:27b-28 (so Coats, "Exposition").

Genre

The speech is a CULTIC ORDINANCE for a particular rite. The conclusion in vv. 50-51 incorporates the ordinance into the narrative about the exodus (cf. Kuhl).

Setting

The ordinance with its emphasis on circumcision derives from the cultic institution responsible for the Passover and reflects the interests of a community concerned to define itself over against nonnative, uncircumcised population elements (cf. Childs, *Exodus*, 202).

Intention

Since this speech focuses not so much on the rite itself but on circumcision as a preparation for the rite, and appears to be a secondary growth in the Passover tradition, one could conclude that the ordinance has been appropriated as the basis for circulating the circumcision stipulation. The ordinance requires circumcision for participation in the Passover Festival.

Bibliography

G. W. Coats, "An Exposition for the Wilderness Traditions," *VT* 22 (1972) 288-95; C. Kuhl, "Die 'Wiederaufnahme' — ein literarkritisches Prinzip?" *ZAW* 64 (1952) 1-11.

ADDENDUM. W. Johnstone, "The Two Theological Versions of the Passover Pericope in Exodus," in *Text and Pretext: Essays in Honour of Robert Davidson* (JSOTSup 138; ed.

Robert P. Carroll; Sheffield: JSOT Press, 1992), 160-78. This discussion relates to the issues of sources (D and P) and their structure in Exodus.

STORY OF CULTIC ORDINANCES, 13:1-16

Structure

I. Speech		1-2
A. Introduction: God to Moses		1
B. Ordinance: consecration of firstborn		2
1. Basic command		2aα1
2. Reason		2aα2-b
II. Speech		3-16
A. Introduction: Moses to the people		3aα1
B. Ordinances		3aα2-16
1. First ordinance: Unleavened Bread		3aα2-10
a. Exhortation to keep the festival		3aα2-aβ
1) Imperative to remember		3aα2
2) Definition of the memorial day		3aα3
3) Reason		3aβ
b. Prohibition of leaven		3b
c. Definition of the memorial day		4
d. Command to keep the festival		5
1) Beginning point (presupposition)		5a
2) Basic command		5b
e. Length of festival		6-7a
f. Prohibition of leaven		7b
g. Provision for explanation of festival		8
h. Provision for sign		9
i. Concluding command		10
2. Second ordinance: consecration of firstborn		11-16
a. Command to keep the rite		11-12
1) Beginning point (presupposition)		11
2) Basic command: definition of firstborn		12
b. Provision for redeeming firstborn		13
1) Ass		13a
2) Man		13b
c. Provision for explanation of the rite		14-15
d. Provision for sign		16

Three distinct but related cultic ordinances in this collection appear to be isolated from the larger context of tradition themes by a summary of the exodus in 12:37-42 and by the introduction to the wilderness theme in 13:17-22. The Passover ordinance in 12:43-51 shares some structural similarities and an isolated position in an organizational seam with this unit.

Element I of the collection highlights the isolation. Without exposition, without reference to the exodus theme or the wilderness theme, the speech introduces a command for consecrating all firstborn. The COMMAND comprises two sentences. The first is an unconditional positive demand, expressed by a 2nd m. s. imperative: "Consecrate all firstborn to me." The second, a nominal sentence following the imperative, can be understood as the reason for the demand: "*Because* the opener of every womb among the Israelites, whether man or beast, is mine." Cf. the definition of the firstborn in 13:12 and the definition of the festival day in 32:5.

The first ordinance, vv. 1-2, is introduced as a speech from God to Moses. The remaining two ordinances appear together as a speech from Moses to the people (element II), thus apparently as transmission of the message from the first speech (see Childs, *Exodus,* 203). The first ordinance in element II, vv. 3-10, makes no reference to the firstborn rite. It is rather an ordinance for the Unleavened Bread Festival (cf. Exod 12:14-20; Deut 16:3-8). The basic structure of the ORDINANCE involves an EXHORTATION (2nd m. s. imperative) to remember the festival (v. 3a) and a PROHIBITION of leaven (v. 3b). The pattern is repeated in vv. 4-7 with a specification of date for the festival (v. 4), a COMMAND to keep the festival (a 2nd m. s. perfect follows a note that celebration should begin with entry into the land), a definition of length for the festival, and a prohibition of leaven. Vv. 8-9 attach a provision for explaining the festival to children as a celebration of the exodus (cf. v. 4) and a sign for memorializing the exodus. The speech closes the first ordinance with a new COMMAND to keep this ordinance (v. 10).

The second ordinance returns to the firstborn consecration. It begins with a command parallel to the one in v. 5: a 2nd m. s. perfect follows a note that celebration of the rite should begin with entry into the land. The ordinance continues with a provision for redeeming the firstborn of ass and man (v. 13) and ends with a provision for explaining the rite to children as a celebration of the firstborn scene in the exodus traditions and a sign for memorializing the exodus (//vv. 8-9).

These verses constitute an addition to the exodus traditions, perhaps Deuteronomistic in origin (cf. Noth, *Exodus,* 93, 101-2; for a slightly different position see Caloz). That vv. 11-16 attach an explanation for the firstborn rite from the exodus traditions while vv. 1-2 make no reference to the exodus suggests that the firstborn rite may have originally been a pastoral ceremony, unrelated to the exodus (cf. Exod 22:23 [*NRSV* 24]; 34:18-20; Lev 27:20; Num 3:40-51; 18:15-17; Deut 15:19; in contrast, cf. Num 3:12-13; 8:16-18).

Unity among the three ordinances is superficial. Ordinances one and three concern the firstborn rite. Ordinance three links the rite to the death of the firstborn in the exodus and thus brings the firstborn rite into contact with the ordinance for the Unleavened Bread Festival, also a celebration of the exodus.

Genre

The unit comprises three distinct CULTIC ORDINANCES, each designed to establish observance of a particular rite or festival. In addition, ordinances two and three have an etiological motif. But the ordinances are not primarily etiological.

Setting

All three ordinances belong to the cult, specifically to celebrations of the exodus (Unleavened Bread Festival). The family would offer a complementary setting (contrast Soggin). The first ordinance, however, may have been originally celebrated as a pastoral rite, quite apart from its exodus contacts.

Intention

The ordinances function primarily to institute the rite or festival they present. It is important to note also that the etiological elements suggest a catechetical function (cf. Soggin, Long).

Bibliography

M. Caloz, "Exode, XIII, 3-16 et son rapport au Deutéronome," *RB* 75 (1968) 5-62; B. O. Long, *The Problem of Etiological Narrative in the Old Testament* (BZAW 108; Berlin: Töpelmann, 1968); J. A. Soggin, "Kultätiologische Sagen und Katechese im Hexateuch," *VT* 10 (1960) 341-47.

ADDENDUM. W. Gross, "Die Wolkensäule und die Feuersäule in Ex 13 + 14: Literarkritische, redaktionsgeschichtliche und quellenkritische Erwägungen," in *Biblische Theologie und gesellschaftlicher Wandel* (*Fest.* Norbert Lohfink; ed. George Braulik, et al.; Freiburg: Herder, 1993) 142-65. This is a discussion of literary-critical, source-critical, and redactional-historical issues.

WILDERNESS TRADITIONS

Chapter 3

THE FRAMEWORK,
EXOD 13:17–DEUT 34:12

BIBLIOGRAPHY

R. Bach, "Die Erwählung Israels in der Wüste" (Diss., Bonn, 1952); C. Barth, "Zur Bedeutung der Wüstentradition," in *Volume du Congrès, Genève 1965* (VTSup 15; Leiden: Brill, 1966) 14-23; K. Budde, "Das nomadische Ideal im Alten Testament," *Preussische Jahrbücher* 85 (1896) 57-79; R. P. Carroll, "Rebellion and Dissent in Ancient Israelite Society," *ZAW* 89 (1977) 176-204; B. S. Childs, *The Book of Exodus* (OTL; Philadelphia: Westminster, 1974); G. W. Coats, "Conquest Traditions in the Wilderness Theme," *JBL* 95 (1976) 177-90; idem, "An Exposition for the Wilderness Traditions," *VT* 22 (1972) 288-95; idem, *Rebellion in the Wilderness: The Murmuring Motif in the Wilderness Traditions of the Old Testament* (Nashville: Abingdon, 1968); idem, "The Traditio-Historical Character of the Reed Sea Motif," *VT* 17 (1967) 253-65; idem, "The Wilderness Itinerary," *CBQ* 34 (1972) 135-52; G. I. Davies, "The Wilderness Itineraries: A Comparative Study," *TynBul* 25 (1974) 46-81; idem, "The Wilderness Itineraries and the Composition of the Pentateuch," *VT* 33 (1983) 1-13; I. Engnell, "The Wilderness Wandering," in *A Rigid Scrutiny: Critical Essays on the Old Testament* (ed. and tr. J. T. Willis; Nashville: Vanderbilt Univ. Press, 1969) 207-14; J. W. Flight, "The Nomadic Idea and Ideal in the OT," *JBL* 42 (1923) 158-226; G. Fohrer, *Überlieferung und Geschichte des Exodus* (BZAW 91; Berlin: de Gruyter, 1964); M. V. Fox, "Jeremiah 2:2 and the 'Desert Ideal,'" *CBQ* 35 (1973) 441-50; V. Fritz, *Israel in der Wüste: Traditionsgeschichtliche Untersuchung der Wüstenüberlieferung des Jahwisten* (Marburg: N. G. Elwert, 1970); J. Gray, "The Desert Sojourn of the Hebrews in the Sinai-Horeb Tradition," *VT* 4 (1954) 148-54; H. Gressmann, *Die Anfänge Israels* (2nd ed.; Die Schriften des Alten Testaments in Auswahl I/a; Göttingen: Vandenhoeck & Ruprecht, 1922); idem, *Mose und seine Zeit: Ein Kommentar zu den Mose-Sagen* (FRLANT 18; Göttingen: Vandenhoeck & Ruprecht, 1913); A. Haldar, *The Notion of the Desert in Sumero-Accadian and West-Semitic Religions* (UUÅ 3; Uppsala: Lundequistska, 1950); W. Harrelson, "Guidance in the Wilderness," *Int* 13 (1959) 24-36; H.-H. Mallau, "Die theologische Bedeutung der Wüste im AT" (Diss., Kiel, 1965);

U. W. Mauser, *Christ in the Wilderness* (SBT 39; London: SCM, 1963); W. L. Moran, "The End of the Unholy War and the Anti-Exodus," *Bib* (1963) 333-42; M. L. Newman, *The People of the Covenant: A Study of Israel from Moses to the Monarchy* (New York: Abingdon, 1962); M. Noth, *Exodus: A Commentary* (tr. J. S. Bowden; OTL; Philadelphia: Westminster, 1962); idem, *A History of Pentateuchal Traditions* (tr. B. W. Anderson; Englewood Cliffs, N.J.: Prentice-Hall, 1972); idem, "Der Wallfahrtsweg zum Sinai," *PJ* 36 (1940) 5-28; J. C. M. Plastaras, *The God of Exodus* (Milwaukee: Bruce, 1966); J. R. Porter, "The Role of Kadesh-Barnea in the Narrative of the Exodus," *JTS* 44 (1943) 139-43; G. von Rad, "The Form-Critical Problem of the Hexateuch," in *The Problem of the Hexateuch and Other Essays* (German 1938; tr. E. W. T. Dicken; New York: McGraw-Hill, 1966) 1-78; P. Riemann, "Desert and Return to Desert in Pre-Exilic Prophets" (Diss., Harvard, 1964); M. de Roche, "Jeremiah 2:2-3 and Israel's Love for God during the Wilderness Wanderings," *CBQ* 45 (1983) 364-76; F. Schnutenhaus, "Die Entstehung der Mosetraditionen" (Diss., Heidelberg, 1958); H. Seebass, *Mose und Aaron; Sinai und Gottesberg* (AETh 2; Bonn: H. Bouvier, 1962); S. Talmon, "The 'Desert Motif' in the Bible and in Qumran Literature," in *Biblical Motifs: Origins and Transformations* (ed. A. Altmann; Cambridge: Harvard Univ. Press, 1966) 31-63; A. C. Tunyogi, *The Rebellions of Israel* (Richmond: John Knox, 1970); idem, "The Rebellions of Israel," *JBL* 81 (1962) 385-90; R. de Vaux, "L'itinéraire des Israéliens de Cadès aux plaines de Moab," in *Hommages à André Dupont-Sommer* (ed. A. Caquot and M. Philonenko; Paris: Adrien-Maisonneuve, 1971) 331-42; S. J. De Vries, "The Origin of the Murmuring Tradition," *JBL* 87 (1968) 51-58; J. T. Walsh, "From Egypt to Moab: A Source Critical Analysis of the Wilderness Itinerary," *CBQ* (1977) 20-33; J. A. Wilcoxen, "Some Anthropocentric Aspects of Israel's Sacred History," *JR* 48 (1968) 333-50.

THE WILDERNESS SAGA

Structure

I. Transition	Exod 13:17-22
II. Enemy, spring, food	Exod 14:1–18:27
A. Enemy	14:1–15:21
1. Legend	14:1-31
2. Songs	15:1-21
a. Song of the Sea	15:1-19
b. Song of Miriam	15:20-21
B. Spring	15:22-27
C. Food	16:1-36
D. Spring	17:1-7
E. Enemy	17:8-16
III. Praise of Yahweh and judicial organization	Exod 18:1-27
IV. Sinai	Exod 19:1–Num 10:35
V. Food, enemy, spring	Num 11:1–25:17
A. Food	11:1-35

The wilderness theme of traditions reveals a more loosely structured narration than the exodus theme (see Childs, 254). Indeed, the loose structure may point to a significant function of the theme as transition between exodus and conquest (see Noth, *Traditions,* 58-59). If, however, the wilderness theme does function as transition and stands structurally in a secondary position (so, Noth, *Traditions,* 58), it is not thereby an unimportant section of narrative (against Noth, *Traditions,* 58). To the contrary it develops an explicit theological affirmation of central importance to the entire Pentateuch/Hexateuch: God leads his people. In this theme, his guidance overcomes the privations caused by enemies and the lack of food and water. It is the guidance leitmotif that provides structural cohesion for the individual units in the theme (→ Exod 13:17-22).

In addition to the motif of guidance, the wilderness theme draws on an itinerary chain for its structure (see Coats, "Itinerary"; Davies). The chain itself does not, however, provide substance for the patterns of structure in the theme. To the contrary, itinerary formulas appear as secondary items in individual tales, virtually disconnected pieces used simply as framework for the content of the theme. Moreover, the first links in the chain appear in the exodus summary (cf. 12:37), and the last in the transition to the conquest (→ Josh 3:14ff.). The chain is nevertheless an indication of breadth for the theme. Its individual links bind diverse traditions, such as narrative and law, Moses and Joshua, even Sinai and conquest, into the body of the wilderness theme.

An initial problem posed by the wilderness traditions is a definition of the beginning and ending of the theme. The itinerary chain provides some clue for coming to terms with the question. Both the beginning of the chain and the redactional devices such as summary or exposition suggest that the wilderness theme begins immediately after the account of Israel's departure from Egypt. The sea legend in Exodus 14 would thus be properly part of the wilderness theme, not part of the exodus (see Coats, "Reed Sea Motif"). Moreover, the transition pieces suggest that the theme does not end until Israel moves across the Jordan. There are conquest stories in Numbers, but they do not constitute a new structural unit (see Coats, "Conquest Traditions"). It seems clear, then, that the wilderness theme runs through Numbers, with its conclusion extended to include Deuteronomy (→ The Moses Saga, Chapter 1B).

The major substance of the theme comprises narratives concerned with Israel's privations during the wilderness trek. Yahweh leads, protecting his people from enemies, hunger, and thirst (cf. also Deut 29:4). Indeed, the dominant theme is the crisis posed by enemies (see the structural balance suggested by the outline). These narratives appear under the stamp of two patterns (see Coats, *Rebellion;* Childs, 258). The first presents events in the wilderness in a positive light. Confronted by some type of crisis, Israel raises a complaint before Yahweh, and Moses represents their cause. Yahweh responds to the complaint by instructing Moses, and the crisis is resolved. In the second pattern, the people's complaint follows much the same line, but it now slides over into rebellion. The murmuring motif, so characteristic for the wilderness theme generally, provides structure for most of the units in this pattern (for details see Coats, *Rebellion;* Childs, 254-64). It is not adequate to draw an easy structural analysis for the wilderness theme generally around the center represented by Sinai or the golden calf incident. To say that all of the narratives before Sinai appear in pattern I (so Childs, 260) overlooks the possibility that some elements of the murmuring may not be complete (→ Exodus 14). The distinctions in individual units may thus not derive from a significant theological role for the apostasy with the calf but from various redactions of the units. The important position of Sinai in the structure of the wilderness theme would seem more likely the result of stylistic structuring around a central body of material (see the outline).

The wilderness traditions develop as much focus on threats posed by various enemies as they do on narratives of hunger or thirst. In addition, the theme also embodies the Sinai traditions simply as one among several items in the wilderness itinerary. This fact does not deny the problems with the Sinai traditions developed by various scholars in the past decades (see Childs, 337-39). It does suggest, however, that the final form of the Pentateuch/Hexateuch does not consider Sinai as a distinct theme vis-à-vis the wilderness or the exodus (→ The Sinai Traditions, FOTL IIB). To the contrary, Sinai, along with the traditions clustered around it, is but a stage in the wilderness migration. Moreover, it suggests that even in the face of the tradition history that brought Sinai into contact with the wilderness, the Sinai tradition cannot be easily shunted aside as if the law of Sinai were separate from the accounts of God's action in the exodus, the wilderness, and the conquest (→ The Pentateuch/Hexateuch, FOTL I; contrast von Rad).

The Priestly account of the wilderness is distinct from J. Its structure follows this pattern:

I. Transition	Exod 13:17-19
II. Enemy, hunger	Exodus 14*, 16*
III. Sinai	Exod 24:15–31:17, 34:29–Num 10:28
IV. Enemy, thirst	Numbers 13–14 (also J),
	15, (also in ch. 16), 17–19, 20 (also J)
V. Conquest traditions	Num 25:6–27:11; 28–31; 33–36
VI. Legend about Moses' successor	Num 27:12-23

In the Priestly narratives, the dominating leitmotif is God's leadership through the wilderness coupled with his assistance in meeting the problems posed by the wilderness (cf. Exod 13:17-20). Moreover, the itinerary chain provides cohesion for the stories and can be considered a device employed by P for limiting the extent of the theme (thus part of P_s; see Noth, *Traditions*, 223-27). It is just at this point, however, that two crucial problems for interpreting the Priestly wilderness materials appear. (1) Some of the itinerary tradition may not belong originally to this secondary Priestly chain. To the contrary, some formulas seem to be more intrinsically part of narrative material, even part of J or pre-J oral tradition (see Fritz, 38ff.). Yet whatever earlier itinerary tradition may be present has been incorporated into a single, rather tightly unified framework (so Coats, "Itinerary"). Even should some of the itinerary tradition not stand originally as P or P_s, it has now been incorporated into the Priestly structure. (2) Where, then, does the wilderness theme begin and end for P? Does it exclude the sea narrative of Exodus 14 (so Childs, 223)? This hypothesis, though significant for both its exegetical and its theological consequences, does not meet the crucial issues of the text (for details see Coats, "Itinerary"). The evidence in the text shows that for P (as well as JE) the sea cannot be separated from the exodus theme. But the impact of this point is not that it thereby is structured into the exodus theme and receives its formative imagery and theological tendency from exodus tradition. The impact, to the contrary, is that the wilderness is not a separate and independent theme vis-à-vis the exodus. The ending for P's account of the wilderness theme is fortunately not so difficult to determine. Num 27:12-23 reports the conclusion of Moses' career, a parallel to the death report in Deuteronomy 34. With Moses' demise comes a transition of power to Joshua.

The stories within P again appear in both patterns noted above, the one essentially positive, the other essentially negative. On the one hand, the negative stories show the formative influence of the murmuring motif. But here the murmuring stories are not as focused as in J. Rather, they depict generalizing tendencies, an Israel guilty of sin without the precision in defining the sin so characteristic of J. The new attachment of the murmuring pattern to the role of Moses (see Childs, 262) would be part of that generalizing trend. On the other hand, P retains at least some signs of the positive tradition. Exodus 16, the Priestly presentation of the manna, holds the manna at a distance from the murmuring rebellion. Indeed, the preservation of manna as a reminder for future generations suggests that the positive quality of the tradition held an important function for the cult (→ Exodus 16). In addition to the stories about the wilderness period, P places significant focus on Sinai as the structural center of the theme. This point can be demonstrated by the role of Exodus 25–29, if not also the P and P_s materials in Exodus 35–40, Leviticus, and Numbers 1–10 (→ The Sinai Traditions, FOTL IIB).

In JE the structure is as follows:

I. Transition	Exod 13:20-22
II. Enemy, thirst, hunger, thirst, enemy	Exodus 15*, 16*, 17*
III. Military, judicial organization	Exodus 18
IV. Sinai	Exod 19:1–24:14; 32:1–34:28

V. Hunger, enemy	Numbers 11*, 12*, 13–14, 16*, 20–21*, 22–24, 25*
VI. Conquest	Numbers 32
VII. Death of Moses	Deuteronomy 34

The Yahwistic account of the wilderness theme begins in Exod 13:21-22 and runs through the Moses death report in Deuteronomy 34. The limitations of the theme in J and P are thus parallel, showing that the final redactor had no problem in choosing an ending, no theological revision to reflect in his choice. There is no clear evidence that J employed an itinerary framework as a means for connecting his stories, although the attachment of individual stories to a place (cf. Exodus 17) may suggest that an itinerary tradition lies behind the structure. Moreover, the stories encompassed by the Yahwist reflect the two patterns already noted as typical for the wilderness theme. While the competition between the two patterns doubtlessly derives from growth of the wilderness traditions at an oral level (cf. Childs, 258), it constitutes a primary characteristic of J. J's Dathan-Abiram story may reveal the original element of rebellion against Moses, and thus against Yahweh, from which the patterns spread to other units (for details, particularly concerning the reasons, see Coats, *Rebellion*). In addition to the two patterns, J's wilderness theme incorporates a large body of distinct tradition: the military, judicial review of Exodus 18, the Balaam story of Numbers 22–24, even the report of encounter in Numbers 20–21. Again, at the center of the theme, the Sinai narrative and the traditions associated with it form a structural fulcrum (see the comments above).

There must have been earlier layers of traditions about Israel's life in the wilderness from which the Yahwist drew his material. Indeed, something of this earlier history may be seen in the relationship between the murmuring tradition and the Dathan-Abiram story in Numbers 16 (so Coats, *Rebellion;* but see the important critique by Childs, 262). Yet recovery of the earlier stages remains hypothetical. Moreover, the structure that gives cohesion to individual stories in the wilderness theme may have been part of the pre-Yahwistic tradition (so Fritz, 107-13). That this pre-Yahwistic narrative was written does not seem likely. It is also possible that the early tradition was characterized by an election theme, an account of Yahweh *finding* Israel in the wilderness (so Bach). But again, evidence to support the possibility is thin (see Childs, 263).

Genre

Observation about the genre of the entire wilderness theme, or the theme in P or J, may not be particularly appropriate. The wilderness theme is part of a larger whole and thus functions as an element within the whole (→ The Pentateuch/Hexateuch, FOTL I; and above, The Moses Saga, Chapter 1B). Yet some suggestion may be helpful. The final form of the wilderness theme, dominated by the itinerary tradition, can be related to the ANNALS of kings (see Coats, "Itinerary"). Thus in the same manner that a king recounts his exploits in a connected review of events at key places, so the narrator recounts God's exploits or Moses' unique leadership.

ANNOTATION. The discussion about genre of this narrative comes into sharper focus when one considers whence and whither God leads his people, precisely in the context of the entire Pentateuch/Hexateuch. The theme of God's leadership is inseparably controlled by the concept that Israel was under way, literally territorially. It means especially that Israel was not aimlessly wandering around in the wilderness but despite all wandering aiming at the promised land. The Israelites were no eternal homeless vagrants. The time and particularly the locales are transitional, subject to Israel's movement. The itinerary stands in the service of this kind of movement. The theme of God's leadership, also in the itinerary movement through the wilderness, stands equally clearly in the service of Israel's movement toward their, and God's, goal.

A narrative about the intentional movement of a population, not forced as in deportation or expulsion, from its departure from one long inhabited territory toward its arrival for settling in another territory is a SAGA of — a one time — transmigration.

This characteristic is generic, and distinctly different from the military campaign reports in royal annals that have nothing in common with transmigration. Nevertheless, the royal annals are relevant with regard to the aspect of military campaigns, their encounters with obstacles along their itineraries, and the role of deities in such campaigns. These aspects are also relevant for the SAGA of Israel's transmigration from Egypt to Moab and the promised land. For more detailed discussion, cf. FOTL IV, on Numbers).

Setting

The process of organizing traditions into a relatively unified theme, joined to other significant themes, derives from the redactional, theological work responsible for the larger whole (→ The Pentateuch/Hexateuch, FOTL I; and above, The Moses Saga, Chapter 1B). There can be no doubt that the influence of the cult can be seen at work in the organization. This point arises not only in the murmuring tradition as a revision of the earlier forms of wilderness stories (see Coats, *Rebellion*), but also in the itinerary chain (Noth, "Der Wallfahrtsweg"), and certainly in the Sinai traditions (→ Exodus 32–34).

Intention

The wilderness traditions clearly do provide a bridge between exodus and conquest. This goal must have been built into the theme from the beginning. But the fact of its bridging function does not deny its importance (→ The Jacob Saga, Genesis 37–50). To the contrary, it provides the literary affirmation for Israel's conviction that Yahweh led his people through a hostile wilderness, protected them from varied enemies, provided for their needs in the face of privations, and finally set them before the entrance to the promised land.

ADDENDUM. G. W. Coats, *Moses: Heroic Man, Man of God* (JSOTSup 57; Sheffield: Sheffield Academic Press, 1988).

Chapter 4

THE INDIVIDUAL UNITS

TRANSITION TO THE WILDERNESS TRADITIONS, 13:17-22

Structure

I.	Explanation of route through the wilderness	17-18a
	A. Negative statement	17a
	B. Reason: a citation	17b
	C. Positive statement	18a
II.	Manner of departure from Egypt	18b
III.	Joseph's bones	19
	A. Narration of event	19a
	B. Reason: a citation	19b
IV.	Itinerary formula	20
V.	Pillar of fire and cloud	21-22

This unit has some contact with the preceding exodus traditions (vv. 17aα, 18b). But its principal orientation anticipates the following traditions about God's leading his people through the wilderness (cf. 1:7-14). Like 12:37-42, it comprises a series of loosely connected statements. The first, vv. 17-18a, is an explanation for the extended route through the wilderness reflected by the wilderness itinerary formulas (cf. 12:37a). The second element ties the wilderness route to the exodus theme by noting the manner of Israel's departure from Egypt.

The third element picks up a redactional motif from Gen 50:25 (cf. also Josh 24:32) and emphasizes this unit as a redactional element, a link between narrative units rather than a narrative itself. The citation in v. 19b is drawn from Gen 50:25. The fourth element moves the itinerary tradition, introduced in Exod 12:37a, to its second stage and anticipates 14:1-2. Finally, vv. 21-22 introduce the leitmotif for the coming wilderness tradition, describing the symbols of cloud and fire pillars for God's leading his people (cf. Exod 14:19-20, 24; 33:9-10; Num 12:5; 14:14; Deut 31:15; Ps 99:7; Neh 9:12).

Source-critical distinctions in this material are difficult to establish (cf. Exod 12:37-42). Vv. 20-21 seem clearly to be J (so Noth, *Exodus*, 105, 109-19). The other verses, isolated from major narrative units, and indeed not closely unified among themselves, remain uncertain. Because of contact with the itinerary route, they may be P or the work of a post-P redaction (so Coats). These verses would be similar to 1:1-7, 13-14 in that a brief review of preceding tradition is coupled with a basic leitmotif for the following tradition. In contrast, the J material in vv. 20-21, like 1:8-12, simply sets the leitmotif for the following traditions without allusion to the exodus.

These verses draw on old tradition. But an older statement of wilderness leitmotif as an organizational introduction cannot be identified.

Genre

The loose and short COLLECTION of statements in this section develops the leitmotif for the wilderness theme of tradition simply by reporting events that prove general but characteristic for the entire theme, or by using one of the ITINERARY FORMULAS characteristic for structuring the entire theme (cf. 1:1-14). It is at best a synthetic or mixed genre; it may be called a SUMMARY STORY OR REPORT.

Setting

The collection derives from the redactional setting responsible for organizing originally independent wilderness traditions into a unified theme and setting them into relationship with the exodus traditions.

Intention

This collection of statements sets the major leitmotif for the coming theme of wilderness traditions. Its contact with both the exodus theme and the wilderness theme shows its function as a transition between the two major themes of tradition (cf. also 12:37-42).

Bibliography

G. W. Coats, "A Structural Transition in Exodus," *VT* 22 (1972) 129-42; idem, "An Exposition for the Wilderness Traditions," *VT* 22 (1972) 288-95.

THE LEGEND OF THE CRISIS AT THE SEA, 14:1-31

Structure

The sea narrative is the structural and traditio-historical sequel to the exodus narrative in 7:7–10:29 and 11:1–12:36 (cf. McCarthy). The impact of this observation is not that the sea narrative is the climax of the exodus theme (against McCarthy; cf. Coats, "Reed Sea Motif"). The exodus narrative reaches its own climax in 12:33-36 and is separated structurally from the sea account by the transitions in 12:37-42 and 13:17-22 (cf. Coats, "Exposition"). Rather, the impact of the observation is that the exodus theme and the wilderness theme, though developing distinct affirmations about Israel's history, cannot be deemed originally independent themes of tradition.

Moreover, the sea narrative is the initial unit of tradition introduced by the transition in 13:17-22. The opening speech ties to the itinerary chain in 12:37a and 13:20 (cf. Coats, "Wilderness Itinerary"), and the narrative as a unit employs the general theme of God's leadership and the specific motif symbolizing that leadership as a pillar of cloud.

The structure of the unit comprises four principal elements: I, an exposition introduces the narrative with a notice about principals and the focal crisis of the plot; II, the complication of plot develops the crisis to a peak of tension; III, the denouement breaks the crisis and lowers the tension to a point of resolution for the entire narrative; IV, the conclusion notes the major consequences of events presented by the narrative.

This structure is obscured, however, because of several structural doublets. The unit opens with an exposition in a speech, vv. 1-4a, and follows immediately with an exposition in narration, v. 5. The duplication suggests source complications, not easily resolved by structural analysis or style patterns (cf. Coats, *Rebellion;* von Rabenau). P appears in vv. 1-4, 8, 9aβ-b, 15-18, 21aα ("Then Moses stretched out his hand over the sea"), 21b-23, 26-27a ("So Moses stretched forth his hand over the sea"), 28-29.

The structure in P is:

I. Exposition	14:1-4
A. Speech	1-4a
1. Introduction: God to Moses	1
2. Speech	2-4a
a. Itinerary instructions	2
b. Reason for the instructions	3-4a
1) Citation	3
2) Hard-heart motif — *ḥzq*	4aα
3) Knowledge formula	4aβ
B. Execution of instructions	4b
II. Complication of the plot	8, 9aβ-b, 10-12 (also J)
A. Egyptian action	8, 9aβ-b
1. Hard-heart motif — *ḥzq*	8aα
2. Pursuit	8aβ
3. Manner of Israel's departure	8b
4. Confrontation	9aβ-b
B. Israel's reaction	10-12 (see J)
III. Denouement of the plot	15-18, 21a, 21b-23, 26-27a, 28-29
A. Speech	15-18
1. Introduction: God to Moses	15aα
2. Speech	15aβ-18
a. Question: favorable response to petition	15aβ
b. Instructions for action	15b-16
1) Message commission formula: Moses to the people	15bα

The P material may not be preserved in a complete edition. Element III presupposes not only a statement of Egyptian action in element II, but also a statement of Israelite reaction (cf. Coats, *Rebellion*). Otherwise, P reveals a structure basically identical to the one that characterizes the final stage of the text.

The exposition in P is surprisingly cast as a speech, not as narration. It nevertheless functions as exposition since it defines the principals for the coming narrative (God and Moses, the people of Israel, and the pharaoh with his people) and sets out the governing crisis that provides plot for the story. Significantly, the crisis is not oppression in Egypt. For P the Israelites are now out of Egypt, out from under the oppression that constitutes the leitmotif for the exodus traditions (contrast Childs, "Traditio-Historical Study"). The crisis here is confrontation between Israel and Egypt in the wilderness. The threat is not that Israel would be returned to servitude. The threat is a military battle with odds greater than Israel can handle. Moreover, the military character of the tradition is characteristic for the wilderness theme (v. 8b; cf. 13:18), as highlighted by other accounts of threat from a battle with an enemy (cf. 17:8-16). The military crisis is foreshadowed in God's speech to Moses through the citation from the pharaoh: "The pharaoh will say of the people of Israel: 'They are entangled in the land; the wilderness has shut them in.'." It is carried out throughout the narrative by the motif of pursuit: the pharaoh follows Israel into the wilderness like a victorious army (cf. 15:9). But the outcome is also foreshadowed by the hard-heart motif, reminiscent of the exodus traditions, and a KNOWLEDGE FORMULA (cf. vv. 4a, 17-18).

The opening speech (I.A) contains instructions to be delivered to the people. Although no reference to departure from Etham appears here (cf. 13:20), the instructions nevertheless hide a stage of the wilderness itinerary chain since they cite a new site for encampment, and the ITINERARY in 15:22 continues from that point (cf. Coats, "Wilderness Itinerary"). The exposition closes with a brief notation that the instructions are carried out (I.B).

The crisis is heightened in II by a narration of the pharaoh's pursuit, in accord with the speech in vv. 3-4a. The hard-heart motif appears again in v. 8aα (cf. v. 4aα) and recalls the refrain from P's version of the sign cycle. The sea tradition in P is thus not independent of the exodus theme (so Childs, *Exodus,* 222-23). Yet the connection between the hard-heart motif and the pharaoh's pursuit into the wilderness demonstrates that the issue is no longer failure in efforts to persuade the pharaoh to release Israel. The hard-heart motif is used in a new context, with a new structural function, as an explanation for the pharaoh's fatal wilderness confrontation.

Element III begins with an allusion to a cry, not readily identified with the cry in v. 10 (cf. Coats, *Rebellion).* The allusion may presuppose that the people cry to Moses, and Moses mediates the cry to God. In any case, the allusion itself, constructed as a question, prefaces a favorable response to Israel's plight that should be considered a typical response to a request for aid (cf. 17:2). God then provides the needed aid for resolving the crisis by giving instructions to Moses. The hard-heart motif and a new knowledge formula recall patterns from the sign cycle. As in the sign cycle, so here God instructs Moses to use the rod to effect Israel's benefit (cf. also Exod 17:5, 9; Num 20:9, 11). As in the sign cycle, so here the rod belongs to Moses (contrast Exod 17:9). Yet, whether these points mean that the pericope is cast by P as an exodus story or whether there is no essential discontinuity between wilderness and exodus for P is not clear. There is an organizational distinction, but not one that is so sharply drawn (cf. v. 4a).

Narration of instructions executed sets the stage for the climax. The sea parts, Israel crosses on dry land between walls of water, and the Egyptians pursue. The final speech closes the span of tension by providing instructions for closing the walls of water on the hapless Egyptians. The instructions are executed, the Egyptians defeated, and the Israelites saved from the first crisis in the wilderness.

In vv. 5-7, 9aα, 10-14, 19b-20, 21aβ ("And God drove the sea back by a strong east wind all night"), 24-25, 27aβ-b ("And the sea returned to its wonted flow . . ."), 30-31, J has a similar structure:

I. Exposition of principal characters and their action	14:5
A. Report of Israel's flight	5a
B. Changed-heart motif	5b
1. "The heart of the pharaoh and his servants	
was changed . . ."	5bα
2. Speech	5bβ
a. Introduction: Pharaoh and his servants	5bβ1
b. Question: self-accusation	5bβ2
II. Complication of the plot in a crisis	6-7, 9aα, 10-12
A. Egyptian action	6-7, 9aα
1. Preparation for pursuit	6-7
2. Pursuit	9aα
B. Israel's reaction	10-12 (also P)
1. Discovery of crisis	10a-bα

J has essentially the same structure as P: The first element, an exposition, sets out the principal characters and marks the crisis of the narrative. The second heightens the crisis to its peak. The third resolves the crisis. The final element concludes the narration by noting the consequences of the events described there.

As with P, so with J the crisis providing plot for the narrative is not oppression in Egypt. The exodus theme of traditions does not include the sea narrative (cf. The Exodus Saga, Chapter 1A). The crisis for this narrative is a confrontation between the Egyptians and Israel in the wilderness (cf. I.B). The complication of the crisis, element II, is more complex than in P. It begins in the same way: the Egyptians pursue the Israelites into the wilderness. Then the scene changes to the Israelites, who cry out to God (for help). V. 10bβ might have been taken as part of the introduction to the speech in vv. 11-12 (cf. the expanded introduction in the sign cycle, e.g., 9:5). At most the introduction anticipates a complaint. But the introduction and speech in vv. 11-12 change directions: rather than expressing an appeal to God for help, the speech is addressed to Moses. The four parts of the speech, especially the ironic question and the question of accusation, belong to the patterns of the wilderness murmuring motif (cf. Coats, *Rebellion*). The ironic question ties the murmuring motif to the basic crisis of the unit: Israel faces the threat of death from the

Egyptians in the wilderness. But this crisis is overshadowed by a new crisis: The Israelites challenge Moses' position of leadership, indeed, the exodus event itself: "Is not this what we said to you in Egypt, 'Let us alone and let us serve the Egyptians'? It would have been better for us to serve the Egyptians than to die in the wilderness." The accusation presupposes that Moses will defend himself against the charge, but no defense appears. Element III moves back to the basic crisis of the narrative with a response to the expected appeal for help. The opening refrain of Moses' speech, "Fear not," picks up the motif of fear from v. 10 (see the comments on holy war motifs below).

The narration of God's response to the crisis is also complex. The angel may be a later symbol for the leadership of God, intended to supplant the pillar of cloud (cf. Dus). At least the combination of the two appears to be a traditio-historical problem rather than a literary-critical one. The narration continues with a description of an east wind blowing against the sea. But no reference is made in J to a path in the sea. Rather, the results of the wind blowing the sea back are clogged chariot wheels. The Egyptians are disarmed (cf. Hay). When the sea returns to its normal position it does not cover the Egyptians. Rather, the Egyptians flee into it. The images are basically those of holy war in character, although v. 27 moves toward a mythopoeic image similar to the one in the Song of Miriam (15:21b).

Despite the complexities, however, the narrative clearly reports that God resolved the crisis by defeating the enemy, the Egyptians, in the sea. The conclusion, element IV, presents Israel's response to the resolution as a response of fidelity and commitment, strikingly in contrast to the murmuring speech in 14:11-12.

Behind this narrative lies a long history of oral tradition. Two points in that history must be emphasized: (1) The basic plot of the story emphasizes God's victory over the enemy and Israel's response of fidelity. The murmuring-rebellion motif represents a reinterpretation of the tradition at a relatively late pre-J period (cf. Coats, *Rebellion*). (2) The basic plot of the story in J, and probably in the pre-J oral tradition, made no reference to a path of dry land in the sea for Israel to cross (cf. 15:21). Combination of the victory over Israel's enemy at the sea and the path in the sea for Israel to cross reflects influence on the sea tradition from the story about crossing the Jordan (Joshua 3-4; so Coats, "Song of the Sea"). The earliest stage of this tradition, although cast in a completely different genre, can be seen in Exod 15:21.

Genre

The final stage of this unit is essentially a combination of two distinct narrative units. Both P and J reveal a relatively tight development of plot, especially in light of the long history of the tradition that lies behind the narratives. There are few characters. The span of tension develops from exposition through heightened crisis to resolution without playing on subplots. In contrast to the extensive narration in the Moses vocation tradition, but analogous to the exodus from Egyptian oppression, this unit maintains its original character as a LEGEND for which the miraculous nature of the event is constitutive.

115

The KNOWLEDGE FORMULA (vv. 4aβ, 18) is closely tied to the hard-heart motif and recalls the same refrains in the sign cycle, 7:7–10:29. The rod of Moses plays a stereotyped role as an instrument for Moses' action in execution of God's instructions, not only in the sign cycle, but in other wilderness traditions as well (cf. Num 20:1-13). The accusation question in the murmuring motif derives from preofficial legal speech and presupposes a defense in response (cf. Boecker; Coats, *Rebellion*). Holy war formulas, similar to the stipulation in Deut 20:1-4, can be seen in v. 13: "Fear not, stand firm, see the salvation . . ." (cf. Smend; Plastaras, 75; von Rabenau; von Rad). V. 25 also calls on the language of holy war: "Let us flee from before Israel, for God fights for them against the Egyptians" (cf. Josh 10:10; 24:7; Judg 4:15; 7:22; 1 Sam 7:10; 14:20).

Setting

The sea tradition has an obvious cultic setting (cf. Exod 15:21). But traditions can live in more than one setting (cf. Schmidt). This legend might also have had its place in the family as entertainment through collective remembering. The final stage of this text reflects the redactional process that brought J and P together into one text unit. The LEGEND in P, perhaps the one in J as well, may have had a function in the cult, as did the HYMN in 15:21. But it seems more likely that a national orientation like this one would have lived in a popular setting, transmitted in the context of family life (and worship) over several generations.

Intention

The function of this LEGEND is to celebrate the victory of God over the Egyptians at the sea. The celebration reflects not only the concerns of the cult but also the needs of the family (10:2). Moreover, 14:31 shows the relationship between remembering and faith.

Bibliography

H. J. Boecker, *Redeformen des Rechtslebens im Alten Testament* (WMANT 14; Neukirchen-Vluyn: Neukirchener, 1964), tr. T. Moiser, *Law and the Administration of Justice in the Old Testament and Ancient East* (Minneapolis: Augsburg, 1980); B. S. Childs, "A Traditio-Historical Study of the Reed Sea Tradition," *VT* 20 (1970) 406-18; G. W. Coats, "An Exposition for the Wilderness Theme," *VT* 22 (1972) 288-95; idem, *Rebellion in the Wilderness: The Murmuring Motif in the Wilderness Traditions of the Old Testament* (Nashville: Abingdon, 1968); idem, "The Song of the Sea," *CBQ* 31 (1969) 1-17; idem, "The Traditio-Historical Character of the Reed Sea Motif," *VT* 17 (1967) 253-65; idem, "The Wilderness Itinerary," *CBQ* 34 (1972) 135-52; P. Dale, "Traditio-history of the Reed Sea Account," *VT* 26 (1976) 248-49; J. Dus, "Herabfahrung Jahwes auf die Lade und Entziehung der Feuerwolke," *VT* 9 (1969) 290-311; F. Eakin, "The Plagues and the Crossing of the Sea," *RevExp* 74 (1977) 473-

82; idem, "The Reed Sea and Baalism," *JBL* 86 (1967) 378-84; L. S. Hay, "What Really Happened at the Sea of Reeds?" *JBL* 83 (1964) 397-403; A. Lauha, "Das Schilfmeermotiv im Alten Testament," in *Congress Volume, Bonn 1962* (VTSup 9; Leiden: Brill, 1963) 32-46; T. W. Mann, "The Pillar of Cloud in the Reed Sea Narrative," *JBL* 90 (1971) 15-30; D. J. McCarthy, "Plagues and Sea of Reeds: Exodus 5–14," *JBL* 85 (1966) 137-58; J. Pedersen, "The Crossing of the Reed Sea and the Paschal Legend," in *Israel: Its Life and Culture* (tr. A. Moller and A. I. Fausbell; 4 vols. in 2; London: Oxford Univ. Press, 1926-40) III-IV.728-37; J. Plastaras, *The God of Exodus* (Milwaukee: Bruce, 1966); K. von Rabenau, "Die beiden Erzählungen vom Schilfmeerwunder in Ex 13,17–14,31," in *Theologische Versuche* (ed. P. Wätzel and G. Schille; Berlin: Evangelische Verlagsanstalt, 1966) 7-29; G. von Rad, "Beobachtungen an der Moseerzählung, Exodus 1–14," *EvT* 31 (1971) 579-88; J. Scharbert, "Das 'Schilfmeerwunder' in den Texten des Alten Testaments," in *Mélanges bibliques et orientaux en l'honneur de M. Henri Cazelles* (ed. A. Caquot and M. Delcor; Neukirchen-Vluyn: Neukirchener, 1981) 395-417; R. Smend, *Jahwekrieg und Stämmebund: Erwägungen zur ältesten Geschichte Israels* (FRLANT 84; Göttingen: Vandenhoeck & Ruprecht, 1963), tr. M. Rogers, *Yahweh War and Tribal Confederation: Reflections upon Israel's Earliest History* (Nashville: Abingdon, 1970); J. M. Schmidt, "Erwägungen zum Verhältnis von Auszugs- und Sinaitraditionen," *ZAW* 82 (1970) 1-31; H-C. Schmitt, "'Priesterliches' und 'prophetisches' Geschichtsverständnis in der Meerwundererzählung Ex 13,17–14,31: Beobachtungen zur Endredaktion des Pentateuch," in *Textgemäss: Aufsätze und Beiträge zur Hermeneutik des Alten Testaments* (Fest. E. Würthwein; ed. A. Gunneweg and O. Kaiser; Göttingen: Vandenhoeck & Ruprecht, 1979) 139-55; R. Tomes, "Exodus 14: The Mighty Acts of God: An Essay in Theological Criticism," *SJT* 22 (1969) 455-78.

ADDENDUM. P. Auffret, "Essai sur la structure littéraire d'Ex 14," *EstBib* 41 (1983) 53-82; M. Vervenne, "The Protest Motif in the Sea Narrative (Ex 14:11-12): Form and Structure of a Pentateuchal Pattern," *ETL* 63 (1987) 257-71.

ANNOTATION. Vervenne discusses genre, structure, function, motif, and its traditio-historical aspect, whereas Auffret treats the literary/rhetorical structure.

STORY OF THE SONG OF THE SEA, 15:1-19

Structure

I. Introduction: Moses and the people of Israel to God	1a
II. Song	1b-18
A. Introit	1b
1. Opening statement of intent to praise	1bα1
2. Reasons	1bα2-b
a. General statement: "He has triumphed gloriously"	1bα2
b. Specific statement: "Horse and chariotry he has thrown into the sea"	1b

The Song of the Sea, element II, is framed by an introduction, element I, and a gloss, element III. Both the introduction and the gloss are narration, in contrast to the poetic style of the song. The introduction is structured like an introduction to a speech, with the explicit specification that the address it introduces is a song *(haššîrâ)* to be sung *(yāšîr)*. (Cf. Num 21:17; Josh 10:12; 22:1-2; similarly, Judg 5:1.) The gloss explains a point only implied by the song — the people of Israel crossed on dry land in the midst of the sea. The song itself has an opening couplet with a statement of intent to praise (II.A), and two extensive elements of epic narration (II.C, II.E) interspersed with brief hymnic elements (II.B, II.D). The final element (II.F) is somewhat isolated from the body of the poem, but it should nevertheless be seen as the coda.

The statement of intent to praise, II.A, introduces the poem with a first-person cohortative verb, followed by a *kî*-clause explaining general reasons for the praise. The reasons lie in God's action, his victory: "For he has triumphed gloriously. Horse and chariotry he has thrown into the sea."

Element II.B is problematic. In contrast to the first-person declaration about God's victory at the sea in v. 1b, v. 2 contains a first-person ascription of praise to God in general terms, and v. 3 presents a third-person statement about the divine name. Contextual relationship can be established between vv. 1b and 2: With a first-person subject, v. 1b announces intention for praise, with the praise itself introduced in the clause noting reasons for the act. V. 2 expands that praise, again with a first-person subject. V. 3 shows no evidence of the first-person construction and may be isolated from the context as a foreign element. But its description of God as a man of war suggests at least a common motif with the confession of God's victory in v. 1b, and both refer to God in the third person. Vv. 2-3 can then be taken as an elaboration of v. 1b (so Muilenburg).

Element II.C constitutes the first principal unit of the poem. A shift from epic narration describing God's victory over the Egyptians in the third person, vv. 4-5, to an ascription of praise to God in the second person in v. 6 suggests a break in formal structure. Address to God in the second person continues through v. 10. V. 11 concludes the first unit of praise with a second-person ascription to God in the shape of rhetorical questions. It functions perhaps as a coda for the first unit of praise, at least as a transition to the next unit, and should not be considered part of the epic narration in II.E (so Coats, "Song"; contrast Cross, Freedman).

Element II.E constitutes the second major unit of the poem. V. 14 shifts the address to God in the second person to a third-person reference to the peoples of Canaan. Third-person reference to the Canaanites continues into vv. 15-16aα, although the second-person address to God resumes in v. 16aβ. The distinction between vv. 12-13 and 14-16aα seems to be confirmed by metrical analysis (cf. Muilenburg) as well as by the content of the two sections. Still another distinct element of the unit may be reflected in the liturgical movement described in v. 16b. Yet v. 17 continues the second-person address to God by narrating his deeds in the conquest. The entire unit, vv. 12-17, thus functions as a whole, a second-person address to God in praise of his deeds.

Verse 18 is the final coda, a third-person ascription of praise to Yahweh as a king. It does not belong simply to the confession of God's deeds in the conquest, element II.E, but brings the entire poem to its proper conclusion (cf. Psalm 146).

The two elements of epic narration in this poem, joined by hymnic descriptive praise, belong together in the tight structure. The principle for uniting the two elements, focused on the event at the sea and the events of the conquest, is to be found in the traditional unity of the two themes, sea and river (cf. Ps 114:3). Significantly, the point of unity is not exodus and conquest (so Coats, "Song"). In this poem, the two distinct images associated with the sea tradition are preserved side by side: God makes a path in the sea, God destroys the enemy in the sea. The early stages of union between the sea and river traditions thus lie exposed here. In addition, mythical motifs like the struggle between God and the sea, personified as opposing gods, may have exerted their influence. There can be little doubt that mythological images can be seen in allusions to the sea event in Pss 78:12-14 and 114:3 (cf. Lauha, McCarthy). But whether those images play a role here seems doubtful (so Cross, Freedman).

For earlier stages in the history of the sea tradition, → Exod 14:1-31.

Genre

Although the genre of the Song of the Sea may be broadly defined as a HYMN OF PRAISE, it is essentially mixed (cf. Noth, *Exodus,* 123; Muilenburg). V. 1a defines the genre explicitly as a SONG, but more precisely formulated distinctions are necessary to highlight the complexities of the poem. Like v. 21b, the introductory couplet may be considered a song of victory in itself (cf. Mowinckel, 2.26-27). At least it would fall into the general category of declarative praise (so Westermann, 141). Focusing on one particular event, the worshiper declares the intention to offer praise for God's deliverance at the sea. The cohortative introduction (cf. Pss 13:6b [NRSV 6]; 57:8 [NRSV 7]; 89:2 [NRSV 1]; 101:1; 104:33; 108:2 [NRSV 1]; 144:9; as well as Judg 5:3) leads to the principal body of praise in the kî-clause (cf. Psalms 117; 148). In comparison particularly to the Song of Deborah, Judges 5, where no kî-clause marks a principal body of praise in the introductory unit (cf. esp. Judg 5:2-3), v. 1b in the Song of the Sea looks like an independent poem, adapted from its original context and setting for use as the introductory element in this longer frame (cf. Exod 15:21b). The construction of the opening couplet with a cohortative emphasizes the role of the individual and suggests that the lines derive from the individual thanksgiving (so Noth, *Exodus,* 123).

Verse 2 contains characteristics of a THANKSGIVING PSALM (so Noth, *Exodus,* 123). It may be appropriate to describe it as an element of descriptive praise over against the DECLARATIVE PRAISE of vv. 1b and 4-10. V. 3 is again problematic, perhaps an isolated element in the poem drawn from holy war contexts (cf. Josh 17:1; Judg 20:17; 1 Sam 16:18, 17:33; 2 Sam 8:10; 17:8; Isa 3:2). Like vv. 4-10, vv. 12-17 function as (→) declarative praise, although the concentration on events in a series rather than one central event raises the possibility that these verses should be considered descriptive praise. The hymnic transition in v. 11 and perhaps the declaration of victory in v. 6 should also be classified as descriptive praise. V. 18 is drawn from the so-called enthronement psalms. We may conclude that the genre of the Song of the Sea is specifically the type of DECLARATIVE PRAISE in the Hymns of Praise, with elements of descriptive praise in vv. 2, 11, and perhaps v. 6, and an ENTHRONEMENT FORMULA in v. 18.

Setting

The setting for the Song of the Sea is the cult. Its introduction suggests the worship of an individual. Its tie with the Passover celebration seems minimal (cf. Coats, "Song"; Childs, "Study"; against Cross). The position it played in a particular festival should be sought instead within the liturgical structure of the autumnal festival (cf. Muilenburg).

Intention

The poem functions as an individual's expression of praise in a cultic celebration of God's deeds.

Bibliography

T. C. Butler, "The Song of the Sea. Exodus 15:1-8: A Study in the Exegesis of Hebrew Poetry" (Diss., Vanderbilt, 1971); B. S. Childs, "A Traditio-Historical Study of the Reed Sea Tradition," *VT* 20 (1970) 406-18; G. W. Coats, "The Song of the Sea," *CBQ* 31 (1969) 1-17; F. M. Cross, "The Song of the Sea and Canaanite Myth," *JTC* 5 (1968) 1-25; rev. in *Canaanite Myth and Hebrew Epic: Essays in the History of the Religion of Israel* (Cambridge: Harvard Univ. Press, 1973) 112-44; D. N. Freedman, "Early Israelite History in the Light of Early Israelite Poetry," in *Unity and Diversity: Essays in the History, Literature, and Religion of the Ancient Near East* (ed. H. Goedicke and J. J. M. Roberts; Baltimore: Johns Hopkins Univ. Press, 1975) 3-35; idem, "Strophe and Meter in Exodus 15," in *A Light Unto My Path* (*Fest.* J. M. Myers; ed. H. N. Bream, et al.; Philadelphia: Temple Univ. Press, 1974) 163-203; A. Lauha, "Das Schilfmeermotiv im Alten Testament," in *Congress Volume, Bonn 1962* (VTSup 9; Leiden: Brill, 1963) 32-46; N. Lohfink, "Das Siegeslied am Schilfmeer," in *Das Siegeslied am Schilfmeer* (Frankfurt: J. Knecht, 1965) 102-28; D. J. McCarthy, "'Creation' Motifs in Ancient Hebrew Poetry," *CBQ* 29 (1967) 393-406; S. Mowinckel, *The Psalms in Israel's Worship* (tr. D. R. Ap-Thomas; 2 vols. bound as 1; New York: Abingdon, 1962); J. Muilenburg, "A Liturgy of the Triumphs of Yahweh," in *Studia Biblica et Semitica* (*Fest.* T. C. Vriezen; Wageningen: H. Veenman en Zonen N.V., 1966) 238-50; J. D. W. Watts, "The Song of the Sea — Ex XV," *VT* 7 (1957) 371-80; C. Westermann, *Praise and Lament in the Psalms* (tr. K. R. Crim and R. N. Soulen; Atlanta: John Knox, 1981).

ADDENDUM. M. L. Brenner, *The Song of the Sea: Ex 15:1-21* (BZAW 195; Berlin: de Gruyter, 1991); M. Howell, "Exodus 15:1b-18: A Poetic Analysis," *ETL* 65 (1989) 5-42.

ANNOTATION. Brenner's study is form-critically directly important for its focus on structure, genre, intention, and setting, whereas Howell focuses on stylistic poetic devices.

STORY OF THE SONG OF MIRIAM, 15:20-21

Structure

I. Exposition for the poem, in narration	20
II. Song	21
A. Introduction, in narration: Miriam to all the women	21a
B. Song	21b
1. Opening invitation to praise	21bα1
2. Reason	21bα2-bβ
a. General statement: "For he has triumphed gloriously"	21bα2
b. Specific statement: "Horse and chariotry he has thrown into the sea"	21bβ

An ancient poem in v. 21b has been set into a narrative context by the exposition of the principal character, the singer of the poetry, in v. 20, and the speech introduction in v. 21a. The structure of the poem itself is simple. A 2nd m. pl. Qal imperative introduces the poem with a call to the audience for praise (cf. Pss 113:1; 117:1; 135:1ff.). The substance of the praise follows, introduced by a *kî*-clause: *For* he has triumphed gloriously. The second line of the couplet makes the character of the event quite explicit.

This poem is the oldest reference to the event at the sea in the OT, perhaps the oldest piece of literature of any kind in the OT. Its image of the event is not historical but mythopoeic. The enemy is defeated not by loss of chariots in mire (cf. Exod 14:1-31) but by direct intervention of God. The intervention is described in mythopoeic language: "Horse and chariotry he has *thrown* into the sea" (cf. Coats, "Song"). Thus the oldest witness to the event at the sea concentrates on the defeat of the enemy by God's act without reference to a path in the sea for crossing on dry land (cf. the discussion of the history of the tradition in the sections on 14:1-31 and 15:1-19 in this volume).

Genre

The poem is a HYMN OF PRAISE (so Noth, *Exodus,* 121-23), perhaps more specifically defined as a hymn of declarative praise (so Westermann, 85, 89, 231). Since the hymn of praise concentrates on a military victory, it may be qualified as a SONG of victory (so Mowinckel, 2.26-27).

Setting

The poem belongs to the life of the cult. The imperative in the opening couplet presupposes an address to the assembled congregation, in contrast to the 1st s. cohortative introduction to essentially the same couplet in v. 1b where the setting would be individual thanksgiving (so Noth, *Exodus,* 123). A specific cultic festival for the hymn would be difficult to identify, although it, like the Song of the Sea, may have had a role to play in the autumnal festival (cf. the discussion of setting on 15:1-19).

Intention

The hymn offers praise to God by declaration of a particular event from the past known to worshipers as an act of God's intervention on their behalf.

Bibliography

G. W. Coats, "The Song of the Sea," *CBQ* 31 (1969) 1-17; S. Mowinckel, *The Psalms in Israel's Worship* (tr. D. R. Ap-Thomas; 2 vols. bound in 1; New York: Abingdon,

1962); C. Westermann, *Praise and Lament in the Psalms* (tr. K. R. Crim and R. N. Soulen; Atlanta: John Knox, 1981).

ADDENDUM. M. L. Brenner, *The Song of the Sea: Ex 15:1-21* (BZAW 195; Berlin: de Gruyter, 1991). See the ANNOTATION to 15:1-19.

THE MARAH LEGEND OF THE SPRING, 15:22-27

Structure

I. Itinerary	22a-bα
II. Narrative	22bβ-26
A. Exposition	22bβ
B. Complication of plot	23-24
1. Etiology	23
2. Israel's reaction to the crisis, a speech	24
a. Introduction: people murmur against Moses	24a
b. Question: request for aid	24b
3. Moses' reaction to the crisis	25aα
C. Resolution of the crisis	25aβ-26
1. Narration of God's aid	25aβ-b
a. Means for sweetening water	25aβ
b. Statute and ordinance given	25b
2. Speech	26
a. Introduction: God to the people	26aα1
b. Speech	26aα2-b
1) Condition	26aα2-aβ
2) Promise	26bα
3) Reason	26bβ
III. Itinerary: to Elim's springs and palms	27

The Marah spring narrative is framed by two itinerary formulas, essentially unrelated to the narrative itself (→ The Framework, Chapter 3). The narrative comprises three structural elements: II.A, an exposition of the major crisis in the narrative's plot; II.B, a complication of the plot by heightening the crisis; and II.C, a resolution of the crisis.

The exposition describes the crisis by noting that the people journey three days into the wilderness without finding water. The crisis intensifies when, on arrival at Marah, the people discover the water available there to be unpalatable (v. 23a). With its reference to "bitter" water *(mārîm)*, v. 23a constitutes a foundational narration for inferring an etiology for the place-name, Marah, in v. 23b. Moreover, movement to Marah, v. 23a, breaks into the itinerary chain (v. 22). As a result, the itinerary in v. 27 does not note a point of departure (but cf. Num 33:8-9). The isolation of the narrative within the framework of the itinerary is thus heightened.

Israel's reaction to the crisis comes in a speech in v. 24. The introduction to the speech defines the question as murmuring against Moses. But the murmuring introduction should not prejudice interpretation of the question (cf. The Framework, Chapter 3). The people pose a question of complaint (cf. Gen 41:55), in effect, a petition for aid: "What shall we drink?" Moses then relays the request to God (v. 25aα).

The resolution of the crisis is a narration of God's response: He shows Moses a means for sweetening the water (v. 25aβ). Reference to a statute and an ordinance, along with a note about testing, in v. 25b has no apparent relationship with the narrative about crisis over water at Marah. The speech in v. 26 seems to be based on the refrain in v. 25b (so Noth, *Exodus,* 129). It is possible that vv. 25b and 26 allude to a different local tradition. The verb "to test," *nissāhû,* may reflect a wordplay (→) etiology on the place-name Massah.

Verses 25b-26 derive from Dtr (so Noth, *Exodus,* 127). The remaining verses of the narrative, vv. 22b -25a, are J. The itinerary framework belongs to P or a post-P redactor. The history of tradition behind vv. 25b-26 is obscure. All clear references to Massah belong to Dtr or Deuteronomy (cf. Exod 17:2, 7; Ps 95:8; Deut 6:16; 9:22; 33:8). But not one gives a firm control for the expression in v. 25b, and the speech in v. 26 depends on that expression.

A complex history of tradition can, however, still be seen behind the J text. The latest stage stamps the narrative with the murmuring motif, limited to the speech introduction. Behind the murmuring lies a tradition, positive in its description of Israel's relationship with God. Its structure is characterized by crisis in the wilderness, request for God's aid, mediation of the request by Moses, resolution of the crisis through God's aid (on the two patterns see Childs, *Exodus,* 258). The crisis for the aid stage develops around the etiology in v. 23. But the etiology does not depend on the resolution of the crisis. Thus behind the narrative about God's aid lies an older local tradition, an etiology for the place-name. This tradition would not have been tied to Israel or their God (cf. Coats, *Rebellion,* against Fritz).

Genre

The latest stage of this narrative is simply a reinterpretation of the second stage, characterized only by a single word in the introduction of the speech. It thus draws its genre from the second stage. The second stage is not an → ETIOLOGICAL NARRATIVE. Its pattern, but especially its emphasis on the miraculous solution, suggest a national LEGEND of God's aid like the one in Exod 14:1-31. The local tradition behind the aid episode is not a (→) narrative. As it now stands, it is only an ETIOLOGY. The introduction to the formula in v. 23b with the expression 'al-kēn is typical for ETIOLOGICAL FORMULAS (cf. Long).

The statement in v. 25b has the appearance of a stereotyped expression, but no parallels are available. It may do nothing more than establish a foundation for the speech in v. 26 (so Noth, *Exodus,* 129). The SPEECH in v. 26 is a warning (so Noth), but the warning should be more carefully defined. The initial conditions preface a promise (cf. Deut 11:13), and the conclusion of the speech adapts the SELF-REVELATION FORMULA for specific contrast to the disease-sign element in the promise.

Setting

On setting for the aid and murmuring editions of the story, see the discussion of the redactional framework to the wilderness traditions. The etiology belongs to the locality, Marah. Since there are no other allusions to Marah in the OT (except the itinerary in Num 33:8-9), a more precise definition of setting is not possible.

The Dtr setting is illumined by the shift from third-person reference to God in the introductory conditions to a first-person address from God in the remaining parts of the sentence. The change of subject reflects the speech of a leader in the community announcing conditions to the congregation, with the consequence for obedience or disobedience set in a first-person address from God.

Bibliography

G. W. Coats, *Rebellion in the Wilderness: The Murmuring Motif in the Wilderness Traditions of the Old Testament* (Nashville: Abingdon, 1968); V. Fritz, *Israel in der Wüste: Traditionsgeschichtliche Untersuchung der Wüstenüberlieferung des Jahwisten* (Marburg: Elwert, 1970); E. Gerstenberger, *Der bittende Mensch: Bittritual und Klagelied des Einzelnen im Alten Testament* (WMANT 51; Neukirchen-Vluyn: Neukirchener, 1980); B. O. Long, *The Problem of Etiological Narrative in the Old Testament* (BZAW 108; Berlin: Töpelmann, 1968).

THE LEGEND OF BREAD — AND MEAT — FROM HEAVEN, 16:1-36

Structure

I. Itinerary	1
II. Meat and bread narration	2-12
A. Speech	2-3
1. Introduction: all the people to Moses and Aaron	2-3aα1
2. Speech: murmuring	3aα2-b
a. Death wish	3aα2-aβ
b. Accusation	3b
B. Speech	4-5
1. Introduction: God to Moses	4aα

A single itinerary formula, element I, ties the traditions in Exodus 16 into the overall structure of the wilderness theme (cf. The Framework, Chapter 3). The chapter itself comprises four principal elements of structure (II, III, IV, V), with a conclusion in v. 35 (VI) and a gloss in v. 36 (VII).

In its present state, the chapter stands together as a unit (cf. the transition function of vv. 13-15a). Yet a distinct disunity pervades the entire scope of the chapter. The disunity is partially due to a combination of complex traditions over the course of transmission from one generation to another. Thus element II narrates the appearance of meat and bread, while elements IV and V focus on the bread, name it "manna," and provide for a memorial throughout Israel's generations without clear reference to the meat (see Childs, *Exodus,* 280-81). Vv. 13-15a provide a transition between the two parts.

The chapter's disunity may also be attributed to source complexities. Unfortunately source analysis cannot be developed with certainty, particularly in element III (cf., e.g., v. 22). At best traces of two literary sources can be detected (against Malina, Coppens, see Childs, *Exodus,* 274-76). Thus one can see two speeches with instructions for gathering bread in preparation for the Sabbath (v. 29 would be taken as a continuation of the speech in vv. 25-26), two speeches with instructions for preserving an omer of manna, and two conclusions. The remnants of a second etiology should probably be isolated in vv. 13-15a. V. 8 preserves fragments, perhaps a doublet of v. 5, although its corrupt state makes source identification virtually impossible. The results are: P appears in vv. 1-3, 6-21 (22), 23-24, 27 (28), 33-35a; J appears in vv. 4-5, 22, 25-26, 29-32, 35b. Vv. 4bβ and 28 constitute Dtr expansions. The gloss in v. 36 should probably be attributed to a late commentary on the chapter after the two sources had already been combined.

The structure in P is:

I. Meat and bread narration	16:2-3, 6-12
A. Speech	2-3
1. Introduction: all the people to Moses and Aaron	2-3aα1
2. Speech: murmuring	3aα2-b
a. Death wish	3aα2-aβ
b. Accusation	3b
B. Speech	6-7
1. Introduction: Moses and Aaron to all the people	6a
2. Speech	6b-7
a. Knowledge formula	6b
b. Appearance of *kĕbôd 'ădōnāy*	7a
1) Announcement of the appearance	7aα
2) Reason (murmuring)	7aβ
c. Self-abasement formula	7b
C. Speech	8
1. Introduction: Moses to the people	8aα1
2. Speech	8aα2-b
a. Knowledge formula introduction	8aα2-aβ
b. Self-abasement formula	8b
D. Speech	9
1. Introduction: Moses to Aaron	9aα
2. Speech	9aβ-b
a. Messenger commission formula: Aaron to all the people	9aβ1

Traditio-historical disunity also appears in P. In effect, P combines two distinct units of tradition, related only by a similar subject. The first unit, element I, narrates the appearance of meat and bread together without using more precise designations for the objects. Structure in this unit is dominated by the patterns of the murmuring motif (cf. Coats, *Rebellion*). The first speech, I.A, addressed by all the people to Moses and Aaron, undercuts the exodus tradition and its theology in two ways: First, a death wish ("Would that we had died ... in the land of Egypt") is in fact a wish that the exodus had never occurred. Second, an accusation ("you brought us out into the wilderness to kill this whole assembly with hunger") challenges Moses' and Aaron's role of leadership in executing the exodus (see the crucial verb "to bring out," *yāṣā'*).

The second speech, Moses' and Aaron's response to the accusation (I.B), is a fitting defense for their role in the exodus. The knowledge formula argues that on the basis of the meat and bread miracle the people will know that Yahweh, not Moses and Aaron, held the leadership in the exodus. V. 5a parallels the knowledge formula in construction. But it introduces the "glory of Yahweh" *(kĕbôd 'ǎdōnāy)* as part of the miracle, with the implication that the appearance of the glory of Yahweh will bring punishment for Israel's murmuring (cf. the causative construction in v. 5b). The self-abasement formula in v. 5 carries the same point. It was Yahweh who led Israel out of Egypt, not Moses and Aaron. Thus the murmuring, in fact, challenges Yahweh's leadership. (The fragments in v. 8 make the same points. Thus v. 8a is basically an introduction to a knowledge formula [cf. Malina] and v. 8b repeats the self-abasement formula.)

The speech in v. 9 carries on the implications of punishment from v. 5. Moses commissions Aaron to prepare the people for the glory of Yahweh. Again a causative construction shows that the reason for the procedure lies in Israel's murmuring. The instructions are carried out, the glory appears, and God commissions Moses to address the people. Again the reason for the divine speech to the people lies in the murmuring. One might expect the message itself to contain an oracle of judgment, like the indictment-judgment combination so common in the prophets. But rather than judgment, the message announces the coming miracle of meat and bread. The concluding knowledge formula has no reference to the exodus challenge.

Element I reflects a stage of tradition history when two originally independent traditions, one about bread and one about meat, were combined. The murmuring motif belongs primarily with the meat tradition (cf. Numbers 11). Indeed, there is some tendency to dissociate the bread tradition from the murmuring, particularly when the specific designation, "manna" *(mān)*, appears (against Malina). Thus no influence of the murmuring motif can be seen in the remaining elements of this chapter, and Numbers 11 does not tie the bread tradition with murmuring. Cf. Pss 78:24-25; 105:40; Neh 9:15. The relationship between God and Israel in the manna stories seems to be positive. Indeed, one must ask whether the message God commissions Moses to address to the people (vv. 11-12) does not reflect a stage of the meat-bread traditions that viewed both the miracle of meat and bread and the appearance of the glory as responses to Israel's cry for help, not a rebellion against Yahweh's leadership (so Coats, *Rebellion*). For further stages in the tradition history, see Numbers 11.

Element II builds around a series of speeches containing instructions for gathering the bread, interspersed with narration notices that the instructions were fulfilled or violated. The opening narration in vv. 13-14 (II.A) is somewhat ambiguous. It reports appearance not only of the bread but of meat as well, significantly with two terms not previously used in the chapter. The meat is identified as quail *(haśśĕlāw)*, although it is not mentioned again. The second element is not bread *(leḥem)*, but dew *(ḥaṭṭal)*. V. 14 shows, however, that the dew is not the central element. The unidentified bread remains when the dew disappears in the morning, provoking the first speech, v. 15a (II.B). The people ask what the thing left by the dew might be. Behind the present construction of vv. 13-15a lies a wordplay. The people's question, "What is it?" *(mān hû')*, should elicit a response playing on the word "manna," *(mān;* cf. v. 31). But the play is broken. Moses' response in v. 15b does not name the bread but refers to it simply as the bread God gave to meet the hunger crisis. Vv. 13-15 thus function more sharply as a transition from element I, the meat and bread tradition with its negative stamp, to element II, the manna tradition with its positive relationship between God and people (cf. the double subject, meat and bread, in v. 13).

Moses' response, v. 16, then details instructions for gathering the bread. Significantly, the bread is not named in the series of instructions following this introduction. The note in vv. 17-18 observes that despite the amount gathered by each man, the instructions in v. 16 were carried out to the letter. The next speech, v. 19 (II.E), expands the instructions by prohibiting the people from storing some of a day's portion until the next day. These instructions were not carried out (v. 20). The result was spoiled bread, breeding worms, and an angry Moses. But the point of this notation is not the same as the negative stamp of the murmuring. It functions not to emphasize a bad relationship between the people and God but to anticipate the miraculous double portion on the sixth day, in preparation for the Sabbath (cf. v. 22). Thus v. 20 marks the failure by some to execute the instructions, while v. 21 notes a general execution of the instructions on a day-by-day basis.

A third speech, v. 23 (II.H), then instructs the people for preparing for the Sabbath. The general response is positive (v. 24), although again some fail (v. 27). But the function of the failure is to emphasize not so much the negative response as, in contrast to the regular appearance of the manna from day to day, the failure of the manna to appear on the Sabbath.

A new stage in the history of the bread tradition thus appears. The rhythm of the bread cycle underscores the Sabbath as a day of rest, almost to a point of subordinating the bread itself. Yet, as central as the Sabbath is for the series of instruction speeches, it does not provide the principal structural device. Element II comprises speeches instructing the people for gathering the bread on a day-to-day basis and for the peculiar preparations for the Sabbath. There is no emphasis on the entire week as a structural pattern, as there is, for example, in Genesis 1 (against Malina). The structural device of the element is interaction between instructions for gathering the bread, both daily and in preparation for the Sabbath, and narration notices that the instructions were carried out.

The focal subject of the tradition is emphasized again in element III with a speech of instructions for preserving manna for future generations (cf. v. 32). The conclusion, element IV, marks the manna as a unifying device for the wilderness period and connects with the reference to manna in Josh 5:12.

The structure in J is:

I.	Instructions for gathering bread	16:4-5, 22, 25-26, 29-30
	A. Speech	4-5
	1. Introduction: God to Moses	4aα
	2. Speech	4aβ-5
	a. Announcement of bread	4aβ
	b. Instructions for gathering it	4b-5
	1) Day by day	4b
	2) Preparation for the Sabbath	5
	B. Report of double portion on the sixth day	22
	C. Speech	25-26, 29
	1. Introduction: Moses to the people	25aα1
	2. Speech: instructions for preparing for the Sabbath	25aα2-26, 29
	D. Execution of instructions	30
II.	Naming the manna	31
	A. Narration of naming	31a
	B. Description	31b
III.	Speech	32
	A. Introduction: Moses	32aα1
	B. Speech	32aα2-b
	1. Introduction: "God said"	32aα2
	2. Citation: instructions for preserving an omer of manna	32aβ
IV.	Conclusion: period of time for eating manna	35b

J is much simpler in construction than its P counterpart. In this chapter J shows no trace of the meat/quail tradition, no trace of the murmuring motif. Yet Numbers 11 demonstrates that J knows the meat tradition and ties it closely to murmuring patterns. In Exodus 16 J presents only the bread/manna tradition, preserved in the context of positive relations between God and people. The opening speech announces the coming miracle and then divides instructions for gathering the bread into two parts. The first is the daily routine. The second provides for exceptions in the daily routine when preparation for the Sabbath is in order. V. 22 then reports the double portion of bread on the sixth day, and the second instruction speech, vv. 25-26, 29, emphasizes the proper preparation for the Sabbath. V. 30 notes that the instructions were carried out; the people rested on the Sabbath.

This emphasis on the Sabbath may be the oldest record of Sabbath regulation in the OT (so Noth, *Exodus,* 136). As in P, so in J the rhythm of the bread underscores the unique position of the Sabbath in the working week. Yet the structural patterns here clearly do not play around the seven-day week. The Sabbath stands out vis-à-vis all other days as one requiring special, advanced preparation. Moreover, the Sabbath does not constitute the principal subject of the tradition. One must recognize from the emphasis on the Sabbath in J that at a distinct stage in the history of the manna tradition, the Sabbath forced its stamp onto instructions for gathering the miraculous bread. But the principal subject of the unit is the bread. This point is made clearly by elements II and III.

The naming in v. 31, element II, is problematic. It represents the naming element of an etiology, an element normally built on some previous key (cf. Long). One could expect an antecedent like the question in v. 15a. The sound of the words *mān hû'* would play on the name *mān,* suggesting that the name was deduced from the question. But no key appears. To reconstruct a single etiology from vv. 15a and 31 would be too hypothetical. Despite the problem, the naming in v. 31 draws the focus of J's presentation back to the bread.

V. 32, element III, makes the focal point even clearer. The speech provides for a memorial for the manna throughout Israel's generations. Significantly, the memorial is not intended as a warning to future generations that they should not follow the fathers' wilderness example. It is a sign of God's aid to his people. The manna stands here as a symbol of a positive relationship between God and his people during the wilderness period.

In Deut 8:3 and 16, manna reflects the same positive relationship between God and people; it functions as an instrument for testing the people (see Exod 16:4). But the purpose of the test was to benefit the people. Indeed, the abstraction in Deut 8:3 picks up the aid theme of Exodus 16. God provides for his people, in this case not only with food but also in all other things. The tradition history of manna would not be complete without reference to Numbers 11, Nehemiah 9, and Psalms 78 and 105. Significantly, Psalm 105 does not include manna in its negative scheme, although it makes reference to the patterns of the meat-murmuring tradition. The reference to manna in Psalm 105 thus does not accidentally drop all allusions to the murmuring pattern; it preserves the primary configurations of the tradition (against Malina).

Genre

Exodus 16 cannot be easily categorized under one genre. The final stage in the chapter's development is simply a continuation of the Moses SAGA, a compilation of two earlier stages. P represents a combination of two units. The first, vv. 2-3, 6-12, carries the patterns of the murmuring/aid traditions and could be identified as part of a SAGA about God's aid to his people subsequently altered to highlight the people's rebellion (cf. Exodus 14). Yet the development of plot, even in this section of P, is problematic. The crisis of the plot would be Israel's rebellion, demanding punishment. The resolution would be the gift of God's aid, presupposing a cry for help. A murmuring/aid saga may stand behind this part of P. Even with the double character of the tradition, however, the plot does not develop clearly enough to permit a genre classification (→ The Framework, Chapter 3).

The second part of P, vv. 13-24, 27, is not a (→) narrative but a series of instruction speeches and notes about execution. There is no crisis here, no resolution, no plot. There is only INSTRUCTION developed into a foundational regulation for the Sabbath. Behind the Sabbath emphasis may lie an etiological tradition, with the explanation of the name a primary element of the tradition's scope. In J the same stage of tradition appears, and the same genre observations apply.

Formulas in the chapter include the KNOWLEDGE FORMULA (vv. 6, 8, 12), the SELF-ABASEMENT FORMULA (vv. 7, 8), and the MESSAGE COMMISSION FORMULA (vv. 9, 12). For descriptions of these formulas, → 7:7–10:29. The etiological elements reflect the patterns of the type I ETIOLOGY (cf. Long).

ANNOTATION. Despite the obvious tensions in this narrative, for basic reasons one may still argue plausibly beyond Coats's discussion for ascribing a genre — specifically the genre of LEGEND — to the narrative, rather than denying it. Basically, it is implausible to exempt a developed narrative from the discernment of its genre. The problem of discerning the specific genre of this narrative lies in the tensions within the narrative. These tensions are twofold.

One involves the relationship of the bread and meat traditions and their generic characteristics. The development of this relationship is clear. J speaks only about bread — *from heaven* (v. 4aβ), whereas P speaks about bread and meat. P has expanded the aspect of "God's aid to his people" (Coats, *Rebellion*, 195) to the aspect of "the meat and bread miracle" (Coats, *Rebellion*, 90). For P the combination of bread and meat is nothing else than the gift of God, too, miraculously, "from heaven," as J had said, and even more so.

One may understand that P had reason for not adding another, quite plausible element to this list of miraculous, legendary gifts of Yahweh for Israel's sustenance in the wilderness, of water (through the miraculous effect of a "piece of wood," 15:23-25, and of Moses' "rod," 17:1-7; cf. also 7:9; 14:16; 17:9), and also bread and the meat (of the quails) from heaven, namely, fruits (and vegetables) — also from heaven. They are not produced by human hands as bread and meat, but grow from the ground of the earth directly; see Josh 5:12.

At any rate, the discrepancy between the traditions is dissolved by the integration of the bread and meat traditions under the motif of food "from heaven." This basic motif is typically legendary in nature.

The other tension arises from the more complex relationship of the trajectories of two different motifs through the narrative: the murmuring-punishment and the danger of hunger–gift of food trajectory. The question is whether these two trajectories squarely oppose each other, or whether one appears to be subservient or dominant to the other. The answer can scarcely be in doubt.

The murmuring-punishment trajectory — a long-standing focus in Coats's research — is undeniable. But it does not carry the narrative, neither in J nor in P nor in the combination of both sources. Indeed, it functions within the danger of hunger–gift of food trajectory as yet another, also miraculous but subordinate, aspect: Yahweh's prioritizing the gift of food over his possible judgment for Israel's murmuring.

This prioritizing is already indicated in the legend's beginning. Israel murmurs, but the reason that causes their murmuring is the danger of hunger. Yahweh immediately, and basically, reacts to that reason rather than to Israel's murmuring, namely, to their possible hunger for lack of food — however wrong Israel's rebellion was; cf. vv. 3-5. This prioritizing prevails throughout the narrative. In its conclusion by P in vv. 31-35, especially about the lasting ritual legacy "throughout your generations," it prevails so much that the eating of manna in the wilderness "forty years" is the only aspect left.

By keeping the two trajectories combined rather than eliminating one of them, the narrative portrays the image of the logic of Yahweh, who keeps carrying out his reaction to the root problem while at the same time attending to both the troublesome cause for its outbreak and Israel's equally troublesome reaction to Yahweh's ongoing gift, yet also preventing them from prevailing over the root problem of the hunger–gift of food trajectory. The punishment never happens.

After all, had the logic of the murmuring-punishment trajectory prevailed, even been left in square opposition to the hunger–gift of food trajectory, the problem of food in the wilderness would still have been decisive, but unresolved, and the narrative could not have become as it developed and stands.

Yahweh's gift of food is a reaction to Israel's need, even as it is prompted by their murmuring and considered as a test for Israel following from it. This gift is nowhere based on the condition of Israel's obedience and understanding; it is always independent of that requirement. Indeed, that requirement flows out of the gift, though also of Yahweh's epiphany. Yet even Israel's failure to heed it does not replace the ongoing gift by punishment.

In light of the logical relationship of the two trajectories, one can neither say that the narrative depicts a change in Yahweh's decision and action, from judgment to grace, so to say, as is the case in OT texts of such kind; nor can one say that Yahweh preferred one way of proceeding at the expense of the other. One can only say that Yahweh prioritized his two parallel procedures in such a way that the subordinate one would not interfere with his dominant motif, even if it were, and even as it later was, executed as judgment.

Coats identifies one of two units in P "as part of a saga about God's aid to his people," and the other as influenced by "a murmuring/aid saga." In light of the programmatic and predominant importance of the "bread from heaven" motif, however, without which it would lose its defining aspect, the narrative focuses on the legendary nature of Israel's sustenance in the wilderness. It is a LEGEND. This legend ends: "the manna ceased on the day they ate from the produce of the land, and the Israelites no longer had manna; they ate from the crops of the land of Canaan that year" (Josh 5:12).

Setting

At its latest level the narrative unit belongs to the larger redactional context, particularly the Moses SAGA (→ The Framework, Chapter 3). The setting is thus a literary one. The manna tradition was preserved, at least in part, within a cultic setting. This point seems to be clear in the stipulation of a memorial pre-

135

served "before Yahweh," or "before the testimony." The same setting should also be detected in the stage of the manna tradition interested in founding the Sabbath regulation. Where the tradition might have circulated at earlier levels in its history cannot yet be clearly determined.

The bread-meat tradition, with its emphasis on the murmuring motif, may derive from a similar context (cf. Coats, *Rebellion*). But the evidence for controlling setting in this stage is far more tenuous.

Intention

The murmuring stage of the meat-bread tradition intends to undercut exodus theology by undercutting the exodus event itself. The exodus generation forfeited its rights under exodus election theology by wanting to return to Egypt (see the discussion under Exodus 14). Behind the murmuring patterns, one can still see a positive tradition about Yahweh's aid to his people. The intention here is to confess God's care for his people in the wilderness period and to narrate Moses' role in it. The manna tradition isolated from the meat would derive from the same general theme. With the stamp of the Sabbath foremost in view, God's aid concentrates on the regulations for Sabbath rest and its attendant blessing. But with the emphasis on the manna, the same point of aid can still be seen. Whether by word of instruction, by Sabbath regulation, or by gift of food in the face of hunger, God defends his people, and Moses administers the defense.

Bibliography

G. W. Coats, *Rebellion in the Wilderness: The Murmuring Motif in the Wilderness Traditions of the Old Testament* (Nashville: Abingdon, 1968); J. Coppens, "Les traditions relatives à la manne dans Exode xvi," *Estudios eclesiásticos* 34 (1960) 473-89; B. O. Long, *The Problem of Etiological Narrative in the Old Testament* (BZAW 108; Berlin: Töpelmann, 1968); B. J. Malina, *The Palestinian Manna Tradition* (AGSU 7; Leiden: Brill, 1968).

THE MERIBAH-MASSAH SPRING LEGEND, 17:1-7

Structure

I. Itinerary	1a-bα
II. Narration of God's aid	1bβ-2
A. Exposition	1bβ
B. Speech	2a
1. Introduction: the people to Moses	2aα-aβ1
2. Speech: request/demand for aid	2aβ2

A single itinerary formula, element I, ties the Meribah-Massah tradition into the overall structure of the wilderness theme (→ The Framework, Chapter 3). A major caesura between vv. 2 and 3 marks the division between elements II and III. In element II the narration develops first with an introductory statement of crisis: there is no water to drink (v. 1bβ). Then follows a speech from the people to Moses with a request/demand for water to meet the crisis (v. 2a), and Moses responds to the request (v. 2b). Element III opens in the same manner with an introductory statement of crisis: the people thirst for water (v. 3aα). A speech from the people to Moses follows (v. 3aβ-b), and Moses responds (v. 4). Yet this duplication cannot be explained as a combination of two different sources. Vv. 1bβ-2 and 3-4 are not doublets but two successive stages in the growth of tradition, and both stages have been preserved by a single source (J).

The point can be demonstrated as follows. The exposition of crisis in v. 1b sets the scope of the tradition in a wilderness crisis over water. The people address Moses with a request, or better, a demand for water (a 3rd m. pl. [or s.; cf. Sam Pent] Qal imperative from *nātan,* "give us"). The request is introduced by a 3rd m. s. Qal imperfect *waw* consecutive from the verb *rîb,* commonly translated "to find fault." But the verb is not necessarily negative in character. It can mean simply to process a (legal) demand. Moreover, the choice of the verb is controlled not by an intention to describe the people as faultfinders but by an intention to lay foundations for the Etiology in v. 7. The question must be interpreted, then, from the perspective of a complaint, a request for aid in the face of a wilderness crisis adapted to fit the legal character of the etiology. Moses' response, at least in the first part ("why do you find fault with me?"), also lacks negative connotations. Its impact, as in 14:15, is positive. The request for aid will be granted, the crisis resolved (cf. Coats, *Rebellion*). The second part of Moses' response ("Why do you test Yahweh?") is patterned on the basis of the wordplay with *rîb* in the first half and, like that play, lays a foundation for part of the etiology in v. 7. This formulation is more directly negative in character than the request for aid, however. The object of the verb is Yahweh (not the case with *rîb* in the first half of the response), suggesting that Israel suffers a marked lack of faith (cf. the citation in v. 7). The same point of view about Massah can be seen in Deut 6:16; 9:22; and Ps 95:8-9. But it should not be taken as an original part of the tradition in this unit. Moreover, no firm evidence suggests an independent Massah tradition (so Lehming). Both this statement and the second part of the ETIOLOGY (IV.B.2) derive from Dtr expansions.

In contrast, v. 3aα repeats the exposition of the plot's crisis, but Israel's response is not a legal request for water to meet the crisis. It is open rebellion, cast in the patterns of the murmuring motif. The accusation attacks Moses' role in the exodus ("Why did you bring us up?" [*'ālâ*]). V. 4 then states Moses' response, a petition to God rather than a direct defense to the people. The response has the rebellion of the people, now ready to stone Moses, fully in view. Thus vv. 3-4 do not constitute a doublet for vv. 1bβ-2. They present a new and distinct stage in the history of the Meribah tradition.

The aid patterns introduced in vv. 1bβ-2 might have had a petition, like the one in v. 4, for mediating Israel's request for water to God. It is thus significant that the speech from God to Moses in vv. 5-6a gives instructions not for responding to rebels almost ready to stone their leader but for meeting the crisis over water. V. 6b notes that the crisis was resolved. God met Israel's need, once again miraculously protecting his people in the face of wilderness dangers. The final speech is ambiguous. If it is intended as a response to the rebelling people, it would not recognize the implications of rebellion for Moses' leadership in any way. It seems to the contrary to have the patterns of the aid motif more fully in view. This point is supported by reference to v. 5b. The instrument for effecting the miracle is Moses' rod, defined by an explicit reference to the sign cycle in the exodus theme. In the plague cycle the rod works for the benefit of Israel, not for their punishment. The parallel is perhaps more telling in 14:16. In this verse, Moses' rod also appears in the context of a speech from God to Moses with instruction for resolving a crisis to the benefit of the people. In both cases one can see some clear dependency of the wilderness traditions on the exodus pattern.

Element IV, the ETIOLOGY, is not fully integrated into the narrative. The span of tension moves from the crisis exposition in vv. 1bβ or 3aα to a conclusion in v. 6, with no intrinsic opening for the etiology. Indeed, the etiology depends on the crisis of the narrative (v. 2), not on the resolution. It cannot be totally separated from the narrative since the foundation for the naming lies in v. 2. But it cannot be defined as the primary goal of the narrative. The naming formula itself contains two names, with the explanation for the names breaking into two parts. In both cases the names are deduced by assonance from key words in the explanation, words also found in v. 2. As in v. 2, so here the name Massah and the play on testing God *(nāsâ)* must be deemed a Dtr expansion of a basic Meribah tradition.

The latest stage in the tradition history of this unit is the Dtr expansion with Massah, using the events at the springs as examples for future generations in Israel to avoid. The murmuring stage of the tradition would be responsible for the primary stamp of rebellion against Moses and God associated with the spring at Meribah. Behind this stage lies a tradition about a spring that presupposes a positive relationship between God and his people. In the face of a water crisis in the wilderness, God provides for the needs of his people. Indeed, Deut 8:14ff.; Pss 78:12ff.; 105:37f.; Isa 48:21; Neh 9:9ff. (cf. also Pss 107:35; 114:8) suggest that the tradition of a spring out of the rock was not originally attached to Meribah. The aid tradition would have been grafted onto a local tradition, etiological in character. At this stage it would not be clear that the principals in the event were Israel and their leaders. Indeed, the spring element does not seem to have been part of the original local tradition. The etiology would draw simply from an opening statement that legal cases were resolved at a particular place.

Genre

The murmuring/aid tradition about a spring at Meribah moves from an initial crisis to its resolution in a clear development of plot. There are no subplots, no extraneous characters. The simplicity in describing a crucial event in Israel's past suggests that the story should be considered an episode in the larger exodus SAGA. It would thus belong with a series of murmuring/aid narratives scattered throughout the scope of the wilderness theme (cf. Exodus 14). The ETIOLOGY probably reflects an original ETIOLOGICAL STORY. People present a LAWSUIT *(rîb),* and the legal process founds the name of the locale.

Setting

On the setting of the murmuring/aid traditions, → The Framework, Chapter 3. The local tradition would have been preserved by the circles responsible for the legal procedures at Meribah-Kadesh, and transmitted subsequently by the tribes moving from Kadesh to the southern kingdom in Israel.

Intention

The murmuring stage of the Meribah tradition intends to describe Israel's rebellion against Moses as a rebellion against God and thus a moment when Israel's fathers forfeited the privileges of God's election in the exodus. The

Massah addition builds on the murmuring pattern and the events at Meribah to cast Massah and, by implication, Meribah (cf. Ps 95:8-9) as a warning against further demonstrations of faithlessness. The aid stage casts the events at Meribah as one in a series celebrating God's aid for his people in the face of impossible wilderness crises. The local tradition would explain the name by reference to legal suits processed there.

Bibliography

G. W. Coats, *Rebellion in the Wilderness: The Murmuring Motif in the Wilderness Traditions of the Old Testament* (Nashville: Abingdon, 1968); S. Lehming, "Massa and Meriba," *ZAW* 73 (1961) 71-73.

A MOSES HERO LEGEND: THE ENEMY, 17:8-16

Structure

I. Exposition		8
II. Battle narration		9-13
A. Speech		9
1. Introduction: Moses to Joshua		9aα1
2. Speech: instructions for battle		9aα2-b
B. Execution of instructions		10a
C. Battle narration		10b-13
III. Speech		14
A. Introduction: God to Moses		14aα1
B. Speech		14aα2-b
1. Instructions for writing and reciting tradition		14aα2-aβ
2. Content of the tradition		14b
IV. Etiology		15-16
A. Narration of naming		15
B. Explanation of the naming		16

This unit does not have an itinerary formula to define its place in the wilderness theme (cf. in contrast Exod 17:1). Rather, element I, the exposition in 17:8, places the unit under the structure of the ITINERARY FORMULA in 17:1. The battle occurred at Rephidim. The principal function of the exposition, however, is to define the subject of the unit and to introduce the principals: "Amalek came and fought with Israel at Rephidim."

The major narration of the unit appears in element II. II.A and II.B set the necessary conditions for a battle narration. The leader instructs his lieutenant to enter battle with the foe, and the instructions are carried out. The narration continues without speeches through II.C, vv. 10b-13. Significantly, these verses depend on a portion of the instruction speech and could be understood structurally as a continuation of the execution narration in v. 10a. But the narration describes an act of the instructor, not the one who received the instructions. In the instruction speech, Moses announces his own role in the coming battle: "I will stand on the top of the hill with the rod of God in my hand." Vv. 10b-13, the largest segment of the narration, do not describe the details of two armies clashing. The fate of the battle is tangential to the narration. This most crucial segment of the narration describes the execution of Moses' role. That role stands somewhat removed from the clash. Moses watches from the safety of a hill. Yet his act must be seen as a crucial part of the battle tradition (against Grønbeck). By quasi-magical ritual, he determines the proceedings of the battle. When his hand (not the rod) is raised, the battle favors Israel. When it is lowered, the battle favors Amalek. A problem arises when Moses grows weary and can no longer hold his hand high. The resolution comes when his assistants assume responsibility for securing their leader's crucial stand. The primary focus in the structure of the element, however, lies in the designation of Moses' faithfulness to the task (so Coats, "Moses versus Amalek").

Elements III and IV are not integrated into the narration but stand apart, presupposing the completion of the narration (cf. Grønbeck). The speech from God in element III, v. 14, instructs Moses in the proper preservation of battle tradition. Significantly, both written and oral tradition stand side by side, with equal importance. But of more importance in the history of the battle tradition is the content of the speech. The instructions mention nothing of Moses' heroic efforts to hold his hands high. They refer to Yahweh's intention to wipe out all memory of the Amalekites (cf. Deut 25:17-19; 1 Sam 15:1-33). Future generations will now carry on that opposition. The same theologizing appears in element IV, the etiology of vv. 15-16. Moses names the altar he built "Yahweh is my banner" *(yhwh nissî).* The explanation for the name in v. 16 is obscure. If the Vulg preserves the original text, the verse would read: "A hand on the banner of the Lord" *(solium Domini),* and the tie with the narrative and the name of the altar would be complete. It is nonetheless clear that the etiology, basically extraneous to the narration (against Noth, *Exodus,* 143-44), draws on the same theological foundation reflected in v. 14. Yahweh, not simply Moses, has a war with Amalek. Moreover, the relatively narrow limitations of element II, a particular battle at a particular time and place, are broken by both elements III and IV. Yahweh seeks victory over Amalek not only in the battle of the past but in all coming generations (cf. Deut 25:17-19; 1 Sam 15:1-33).

The disparity of the unit cannot be attributed to different sources. This unit as a whole was preserved perhaps by J (cf. Noth, *Exodus,* 141), although evidence for assigning it to any of the sources is meager. (Element II has more in with the P version of Exodus 14 than with J.) Rather, the disunity reflects different stages in tradition history. The oldest tradition appears in element II, without theological reflection. Moses, not God, instructs Joshua to enter battle. Moses, not God, announces that he will go to the top of the hill. To be sure, he takes the rod of God *(maṭṭēh hā'ĕlōhîm)* with him. But no further reference to the rod appears. The instrument for Moses' quasi-magical role is henceforth his hand. Moreover, no influence of the murmuring motif, so prominent in other wilderness traditions, can be seen here. Its absence can be explained, perhaps, by reference to the close contact between the murmuring motif and the motif of Yahweh's aid for his people. Had this battle tradition been cast, like Exodus 14, as a legend about Yahweh's aid, it might have been recast as a murmuring story.

Elements III and IV belong to a second stage in the tradition's history. Initiative for the action is wrested from Moses and attributed to God. God, not Moses, will have battle with Amalek for all generations. The opposition has become a standing principle. Finally, element IV ties the unit into a position in the organization of the wilderness theme. The battle occurred at Rephidim.

Genre

The narration section has close parallels with the legend of the sea in Exodus 14. Moses plays a decisive role in a battle with enemies. The instrument for his act, as in the legend of the sea and the sign cycle, is the rod (cf. 7:9; 14:16). It is defined in this case as the rod of God rather than Moses' rod as in 14:16. This point can perhaps be understood in terms of the theologizing process of the tradition in its second stage. Cf. 4:20, also a late stage in the history of the vocation tradition. But the rod can also be called on occasion the rod of Aaron (cf. 7:12; 8:13 [*NRSV* 17]). Since designations for the rod vary in widely scattered contexts, the name of the rod here does not support efforts to eliminate the rod from the unit as a secondary, intrusive element. Moreover, as in the story of the sea (14:16, 21), so here Moses stretches out his hand to effect the miracle (no reference to the rod). As in the story of the sea, so here there is a conscious patterning of the tradition on the basis of the sign (cf. 7:19; 8:1, 13 [*NRSV* 8:5, 17]). These points of contact show that the rod need not be eliminated from the unit (against Noth, *Exodus,* 142). They also show that the wilderness theme of traditions cannot be easily separated from the exodus theme. Yet they do not provide sufficient basis for defining genre in 17:8-16. The genre of this unit appears predetermined by the generic character of the oldest stage in its tradition history.

The oldest stage belongs to battle tradition. But the battle itself is not the subject of the narration (so Exodus 14). Neither is the subject Yahweh's intervention, as it is in the legend of the sea. The oldest stage of tradition does not reflect local tradition (against Grønbeck). The subject, the point of crisis and its resolution, center on the heroic stature of Moses, remaining firm with the help of his assistants until the battle is over. This heroic stature is already depicted as legendary in the sense that the hero Moses, performing the quasi-magical ritual of his stretched out hand(s), miraculously effects the outcome of the battle. This is the substance of the HEROIC/HERO LEGEND (cf. de Vries). It is found in II, vv. 9-13, yet without the element of the "rod of God."

The middle stage theologized the hero legend by qualifying Moses' hand by the "rod of God" in his hand (v. 9b), and by expanding it with the stipulation for transmission and an ETIOLOGY. (So in III and IV, vv. 14-16.)

In this stage, the legendary act of the hero Moses has been transferred to the legendary act of Yahweh through the hero Moses on behalf of his people

Israel and its consequences for their history. Cf. Exodus 14. The extent to which this stage is still a Moses hero legend is predicated by this theologized portrait of Moses.

Reference to an altar on the hilltop suggests that the unit at this level may be considered a local STORY (cf. Grønbeck).

In its final, extant stage the unit, including I (v. 8), must be seen as one among those narratives, according to which Moses, representing Yahweh's legendary protection of his people, leads Israel's exodus and their migration from Egypt to the promised land, from one miraculous event to another.

The INSTRUCTIONS for transmission contain a stereotyped expression, with a parallel in Deut 25:17-19. The formula functions to maintain animosity between Israel and Amalek. The ETIOLOGY fits Long's type I, particularly if the Vulg reading is accepted. The foundation narration with a naming REPORT constitutes the first element. Then an explanation, built on assonance with the name — or the name itself — specifies the importance of the name (cf. Long).

Setting

Both the latest stage and the theologizing process of the middle stage belong to the organizational schemes of the wilderness theme (cf. The Framework, Chapter 3). The middle stage also shows contact with the cultic concern for holy war in terms not of a particular battle but of perpetual animosity (cf. the etiology). The earliest stage doubtless belongs to the war machinery as well. But it focuses on one battle, not a perpetual principle. Its setting would be in the context of preparation for succeeding battles (cf. de Vries), thus in the context of the Moses saga (→ The Moses Saga, Chapter 1B).

Intention

The latest stage intended to celebrate Yahweh's victory over an enemy in the wilderness, both as a sign of his presence with his people at a point in the past and as a justification for continuing animosity toward the Amalekites. The etiology connects in some way with an altar, perhaps the sanctuary of a particular locality. The intention of the name cannot be determined with clarity. But at least the impact introduces the justification for perpetual animosity against the enemy, and the justification has a cultic character. Cf. also the institution for the tradition in v. 14. This stage of the tradition is reflected in Deut 25:17-19; 1 Sam 15:1-33 (cf. esp. vv. 2-3). Cf. also 1 Sam 28:18; 30:1-20. This stage may belong to a particular group of tribes or to a particular locality facing long-term hostility with the Amalekites.

Intention in the earliest stage is different. The subject is not a perpetual battle but a single conflict, and the focal point is not Amalekite destruction but heroic faithfulness to the battle. The intention of heroic legend is to demonstrate to subsequent warriors, faced with the demands for faithfulness in battle, how the faithful leader sticks to his task despite his weariness. The example should inspire his successors to similar feats (cf. de Vries). Its position in the Moses saga depicts the hero of Israel's past as a faithful leader, the source of military strength.

Bibliography

G. W. Coats, "Moses versus Amalek: Aetiology and Legend in Exod xvii 8-16," in *Congress Volume, Edinburgh 1974* (VTSup 28; Leiden: Brill, 1975), 29-41; J. H. Grønbeck, "Juda and Amalek: Überlieferungsgeschichtliche Erwägungen in Exodus 17:8-16," *ST* 18 (1964) 26-45; B. O. Long, *The Problem of Etiological Narrative in the Old Testament* (BZAW 108; Berlin: Töpelmann, 1968); J. de Vries, *Heroic Song and Heroic Legend* (London: Oxford Univ. Press, 1963).

ADDENDUM. B. P. Robinson, "Israel and Amalek: The Context of Exodus 17.8-16," *JSOT* 32 (1985) 15-22; H.-C. Schmitt, "Die Geschichte vom Sieg über die Amalekiter Ex 17,8-16 als theologische Lehrerzählung," *ZAW* 102 (1990) 335-44.

ANNOTATION. Schmitt's study is form-critical. It discusses genre (Lehrerzählung), literary form, intention, traditio-historical aspects and an exilic or postexilic setting. Robinson's is rhetorical, investigating the chiastic structure of the unit.

THE STORY OF JETHRO'S VISIT WITH MOSES: PRAISE OF YAHWEH AND JUDICIAL REORGANIZATION, 18:1-27

Structure

The Jethro-Moses traditions in Exodus 18 have no itinerary formula to define their position in the wilderness theme (contrast 17:1; 19:2) and no allusions to tie with a previous formula (contrast 17:8). V. 5, part of the exposition, defines the site for events described here as the wilderness, the mountain of God. The term "mountain of God" refers, at least apparently, to Sinai (cf. 3:1; 4:27; 24:13; 1 Kgs 19:8). Yet the unit is held apart from the events at Sinai in Exodus 19. For example, the itinerary formula in 19:2 notes departure not from the mountain of God but from Rephidim (cf. 17:1), and suggests that the itinerary chain provides no firm context for the traditions of ch. 18. Moreover, even if the itinerary formula is dropped as part of a secondary structural framework, the tradition in ch. 18 does not seem to be well integrated with the Sinai tradition in ch. 19 (so Noth, *Exodus,* 146). It is a peculiar unit.

The unit contains four basic elements of structure: I, an exposition; II, a narration of Jethro's response to the events of the exodus and the wilderness; III, a dialogue between Moses and his father-in-law setting out a new order in administration of justice; and IV, a conclusion. Unity in this structure is nevertheless problematic. Elements II and III stand out as virtually independent units, drawn together into a single body by the coordination of elements I and IV (cf. Noth, *Exodus,* 146; Cody). Yet element II provides a crucial foundation for the legal council in element III (Knierim).

Element I, the exposition, introduces the principals of the unit with a lengthy explanation of Jethro's appearance with the wilderness company. One finds no reference to Jethro as part of the wilderness group other than in Exodus 18 (cf. Num 10:29), indeed, no indication of his presence with the exodus group. Thus vv. 1-4 account for his singular role with Moses in the wilderness. Vv. 2-4 seem to allude to a distinct unit of tradition, an account of Moses sending his wife and two children back to Jethro. Reference to two sons contrasts with the one son presented in 2:22 and recalls the allusion to sons (pl.) in 4:19-23. The references to the two sons assume the structure of a naming etiology. A name is cited, followed by an explanation of the name deduced from a wordplay (cf. Long). The exact parallel between 18:3 and 2:22 suggests at least that the two texts are related as different stages in the same tradition (cf. the late stage of tradition in 4:19-25). The exposition concludes with a description of reunion between Moses and Jethro, not Moses and his family (cf. 2:11-22, where the focus of attention falls on the Moses-Jethro relationship).

Element II describes a cultic event. It begins in v. 8 with a report to Jethro about the events of the exodus and wilderness wandering. Significantly, one can see a clear distinction between the two themes. Jethro's response to the report is expressed in three distinct points. The first, v. 9, describes Jethro's praise (on the verb "to rejoice," *ḥādâ,* see the negative expression in Job 3:6). The reason for his praise is limited in this case to the events of the exodus. Jethro's speech in vv. 10-11 makes the praise more explicit. The first part of the speech is a blessing of God. The second part sets out reasons for the blessing, again limited to God's act in the exodus. The speech does not suggest that Jethro now becomes a devotee of Yahweh (so Brekelmans). Nor does it suggest that Moses learns of Yahweh from Jethro. There is no clear justification for the Kenite hypothesis here (so Brekelmans, Cody). Behind the speech may lie an explanation for contact between Levitical priests and Midian (cf. also v. 12, where only Aaron and the elders of Israel, not Moses, participate with Jethro in the meal). But even this point does not suggest that the Levites receive their priestly instruction from Jethro. If an etiological element is to be seen here, it would justify a traditional meeting between Israelites and Midianites, not the authority of Levites. Rather, the speech suggests that Jethro enters a covenant relationship with the Israelites, like the one described between Abimelech and Isaac in Gen 26:28. The sacrifice and meal in v. 12 would point in the same direction (cf. Cody).

Element III begins with a general statement of setting, in effect, a transition from element II. The initial exchange in the dialogue (vv. 14-16) is constructed as an informal accusation with its necessary response. Jethro accuses Moses of inept administration of juridical procedures, and Moses explains his process. It is important to note that Jethro does not accuse Moses of misappropriation of power; Moses clearly stands in a legal office. Nor does Jethro introduce Moses to legal responsibility. The text presupposes that Moses carries a legitimate juridical position. The instruction speech in vv. 17-23 establishes a new order for juridical procedure, with a hierarchy of assistants to help in the administration of Moses' office. The assistants thus represent a decentralization of Moses' juridical responsibility (so Knierim). The new order is related in some manner to the organization of the military (vv. 21b, 25b), but the military structure is not simply imposed on the process of justice. Rather, the text reflects a distinct juridical order, subsumed into military organization as leaders in the citizenry assumed a juridical role (cf. Knierim). The new order is not directly related to the justice in the gate, effected by every full citizen. Rather, it reflects a new institution of professional judges (so Knierim). This office should not be contrasted with the Mosaic office as if the assistants handle civil cases and Moses handles sacral cases (so Knierim, against Noth, *Exodus,* 150). The office is Mosaic in structure, a decentralization of Moses' judicial responsibility (cf. Deut 16:18-20; 19:18-19). Vv. 24-26 then note that the instructions were carried out.

Element IV stands in parallel with element I. Just as the opening notes Jethro's arrival, so the closing notes his departure (on the parallel with Gen 26:31, cf. Brekelmans).

The unit shows several points of duplication. Cf. especially vv. 9a//9b, 10a//10b. But these points should be considered stylistic elements of structure, associated with cultic repetition of divine events (so Knierim). The unit belongs as a whole to one source, identified by almost all source critics as E. One must ask, however, whether the primary point of unity in this unit does not lie in a special tradition about the mountain of God, rather than an extended narration of the entire tradition. The tradition history would involve at least three stages: (1) The latest stage, including allusions in vv. 21b and 25b, ties juridical organization with military organization and casts both under the authority of Moses. (2) The basic unit presents the origin of the juridical office. (3) The oldest level describes a covenantal relationship between Jethro and the Israelites.

Genre

The unit is an evidently self-contained (→) narrative about an event whose subject is of special importance for and interest to Israel's community. It is narrated for the sake of its content. This content is not legendary or fabulous, nor of the sort in (→) reports, though it seems to imply the function of an (→) account. Its content reflects primarily persons whose identity is distinctly known by tradition, conditions that in Israel's cultic and legal traditions were acute realities, and also etiological combined with genealogical elements.

The content wants to be taken as real. The narrative is a STORY, indeed, a sort of family (reunion, i.e., reencounter) story. This story implicitly functions etiologically. In addition to its self-contained place in its context, the fact of the family story of these specific persons also indicates that the story had its

147

own history from which it was adopted into the larger Moses saga. The basic caesura between vv. 12 and 13 rests on the two distinctive aspects in the development of the one story. Vv. 8-12 constitute a REPORT of cultic activity, recitation of divine deeds, and worship response to the process. The activity may belong to covenant making between two parties of equal status (so Cody). But the covenant process has not decisively influenced the genre of the material. In vv. 13-26 the basic structural device is DIALOGUE. The dialogue itself begins as a legal exchange. But the legal character of the dialogue breaks off in vv. 17-18, and INSTRUCTIONS cast as advice for a new administration take their place. This unit is essentially dependent on vv. 8-12, thus standing as an expansion of the initial report.

Formulas and stereotyped expressions include the ETIOLOGIES in vv. 3 and 4, both type I (Long). The BLESSING FORMULA in v. 11 constitutes a PRAYER conceived as a reaction to God's deeds, not as a contribution to God's power. The DIALOGUE in vv. 14-18 has been stamped with the procedure of preofficial legal process.

Setting

The sophisticated structure of the juridical administration suggests an origin in court, which would be capable of sustaining an intricate organization, rather than in the loose structure of the early confederacy (cf. 2 Chr 19:5-11). It would not be completely divorced from the cult, however (cf. Knierim). The earlier level belongs more directly to the cult. The report of the meeting between Jethro and Moses, leading to a covenantal bond, shows the interest of the cult in overshadowing the heroic element. Deeds recited by the ritual are Yahweh's, not Moses'.

Intention

The latest level of the unit intends to justify the origin of professional judges under the stamp of Mosaic authority, and thereby the decentralization of Mosaic authority. It thus has an etiological function (so Knierim). The earlier level focuses more directly on the cult, intending to express a praise response to recitation of God's deeds. This function is, in all probability, tied with covenant making between two parties of equal status, in this case between Jethro and Moses (cf. Cody). Its intention, then, may also be to justify a compatible relationship between a portion of Israel and the Midianites, Israel's traditional enemy (cf. Exod 2:11-22).

Bibliography

C. Brekelmans, "Exodus xviii and the Origins of Yahwism in Israel," *OTS* 10 (1954) 215-44; A. Cody, "Exodus 18,12: Jethro Accepts a Covenant with the Israelites," *Bib*

49 (1968) 153-66; R. Knierim, "Exodus 18 und die Neuordnung der Mosaischen Gerichtsbarkeit," *ZAW* 73 (1961) 146-71; B. O. Long, *The Problem of Etiological Narrative in the Old Testament* (BZAW 108; Berlin: Töpelmann, 1968).

ADDENDUM. J. Van Seters, "Etiology in the Moses Tradition: The Case of Exodus 18," *HAR* 9 (1985) 355-61. He discusses it as etiology for the establishment of law courts.

GLOSSARY

INTRODUCTORY EXPLANATIONS

Like other volumes of the FOTL series, the current volume is also particularly involved in the aspect of narrative genres.

Speaking of genres in narrative means that narrative as such is not understood as a distinct genre beside others. It may be considered as a macrogenre in the sense that it points to the act of narration and a narrated text as distinguished from those types of expressions that either describe a permanent condition or define an attitude, or in the sense of prose as distinct from poetry. In any case, narrative employs genres that belong to the art of narrative, but it is not another one of those genres. As in past volumes, the words *narrative* and *narration* are also used in the current volume in the sense just stated.

For describing narrative genres it is, then, necessary to focus on those criteria by which genres may be distinguished from each other. In order to discern these criteria, it is first of all inevitable that one distinguishes between those characteristics that are shared by all narratives and by classes and groups of narrative genres, and those that point to the distinctiveness of each genre in comparison to all others. For a description of (→) narrative, see the definition below.

Evidently, the focus on the distinctiveness of a genre does not mean that the characteristics that it shares with the others are ignored. On the contrary, the recognition of its distinctiveness depends on the awareness of those other characteristics in it.

One may have the impression that terms such as *report, story, tale, account,* and even *legend* are sometimes used interchangeably. Such use might mean that they refer to essentially indistinguishable kinds of literature, because what they have in common is central whereas their differences are peripheral or irrelevant. In this case one need not bother about distinct genres. Of course, such use may also mean that what is distinctive for a genre and what it has in common with others has not been clearly pointed out or even recognized.

Three examples, two more specific, one shorter, may be of help.

1. The legend is said to be concerned with the wonderful and miraculous, to aim at edification and belief, but without a distinctive structure of its own and narrating for the sake of enjoyment of telling and listening to stories.

True as these characteristics are, their mere juxtaposition does not go far enough. It does not clarify which of them are decisive for the genre of legend and which belong to more than legend alone.

The aspects of the wonderful and miraculous are also said to belong — more or less — to fairy tale, fable, myth, tale, or even story. Also the aspects of edification and aim at belief are by no means confined to legend alone. Moreover, that it is not concerned with a structure or story line of its own nor with the purpose of narrating for the sake of enjoyment does not mean that the legend, unlike the other genres, would have no structure and story line at all and could not also be enjoyed.

Therefore, the legend shares with other genres the characteristics of structure, plot or story line, a moral point, of entertainment or education as well as the aspects of the miraculous and wonderful and the claims to belief. The legend is unique, however, in focusing on the miraculous and wondrous *in the real world,* unlike myth, fairy tale, or fable, which focus on the wonderful in unreal worlds, and unlike other genres in which this dimension is incidental or irrelevant or intentionally absent altogether. Inasmuch as legend claims belief, it does so because of its unique focus on the wondrous *in the real world,* i.e., the world of humans and their experience, as distinct from the myth's claim to belief in the wondrous but unreal world, i.e., the world outside the space and time of human experience.

What constitutes the distinctiveness of the genre of legend vis-à-vis other genres is, therefore, the focus of its contents on the wondrous and miraculous *in the real world* — the world of humans, even in known historical events or persons. It claims belief specifically because of this focus. All other characteristics also found in legend, of narrative in general and the class and group to which legend belongs, are subservient to this criterion.

2. The tale requires discussion here because it has been referred to in FOTL thus far, especially in FOTL I. The word is often used as a synonym for story. Such use means either that the two words refer to the same genre, or that any kind of difference between them is peripheral to or irrelevant for genre identification. In either case, one might prefer the term *story* to *tale,* not because there is no such thing as tale but because the term *story* appears to be more appropriate, especially regarding the nature of the OT texts.

The assumption of synonymy of the two terms obscures the distinctive difference of each. This difference can be addressed apart from the question of whether there are tales in the OT, and apart from how the term *tale* is typically used. It is said that the tale belongs to folklore, is originally part of oral tradition carried on by storytellers, characterized by a minimum number of characters and a single scene or plot that employs an exposition, a tension, and a resolution, and that it has an entertaining function.

Again, all these characteristics are found in what in English literature has been called tale, and in German literature *Erzählung.* Yet the strung-out list of these characteristics does not reveal the distinctive characteristic of the tale by which it is constituted and those characteristics that it shares with other genres.

Folklore is not confined to tale. It includes all sorts of popular themes and especially other genres such as stories, legends, fables, fairy tales, and sagas. Also, there is the tradition of tales that are original literary productions, i.e., not adaptations from oral tradition and not orally performed but written by storytellers.

Likewise, a minimum number of characters, a single scene, and a plot with exposition, tension, and resolution are certainly characteristics of the narrative class to which the tale belongs, but they are by no means characteristic only of the tale. The same is true for its entertaining and educating function and moral fiber. What then constitutes the tale as a distinctive genre in oral folklore or folklorist literature?

A criterion can be filtered out by which tale can be recognized as a distinctive genre, unlike any other genre for which this criterion is not constitutive. It is the act, or performance, of telling for the enjoyment of such telling itself — orally or in writing — and for the enjoyment of its listeners or readers. It is entertainment for the sake of entertainment.

This aspect has been one of those by which tale especially has been understood. It is neither new nor does it replace the other aspects true for it. It is the criterion that distinguishes the tale from other narrative genres, which belong to the class of essentially short narratives. It refers to the performance, the actual telling, of story. Such stories are tales, not because they share many attributes with other genres and not because of particular kinds of contents, but because before all else they are told for the sake of enjoyment and entertainment. As the telling of stories as such has belonged to folklore, too, it points to the aspect in folklore of telling, of narrating as performance.

In this sense it appears legitimate to speak of tale as a distinct genre, also as distinct from story. Whether this genre occurs in the OT, too, depends on evidence for it in its traditions and literature and, also in this respect, on the study of its corpus. However we define the genre of Isa 5:1-7 (cf. FOTL XVI, 121-31), it could not be what it is without the depiction of the prophet as having started his message as a teller of stories.

In the light of this description as well as an insufficient differentiation between tale and story in ancient biblical and Western literatures, the use of the term *tale* in FOTL I and also in Coats's original manuscript of FOTL IIA has been abandoned. This retraction is explicitly confirmed by Professor Coats, who some time after completing his text for IIA submitted a note for FOTL XXIII that says, with reference to tale: "Replaced, for the purpose of this project, by the category Story."

3. The use of the term *story* is form-critically meaningful only if story stands for a genre as distinct from the other narrative genres. As in the cases of the other narrative genres, the story too contains elements that are common to several genres rather than characteristic only for it. Yet it also shows aspects that belong to its uniqueness. The description of story in the following Glossary, as well as those of other narrative genres, attempts to highlight what is

153

genre-specific in these narratives. They do not invalidate those indicators, especially those discussed in the commentary, which point to the characteristics of narrative in general and to classes of narrative and their groups.

Based on what has been said, we offer some perspectives by which the OT narrative literature may be ordered.

It seems relevant that we distinguish between two *classes* of narratives to which individual genres belong. One may be characterized by *narrative as an art form,* and the other by the *form of objectifying narrative.* Both classes share the basic characteristics of style, structure, plot, function, and intention of narrative by which narrative can be distinguished from types of genres that belong to law, ethos, prophecy, hymns, wisdom sayings. Although the characteristics of each class overlap on occasion or to some extent, the two classes are essentially different.

One class consists of genres that are shaped by the *art form of narrative.* They have in common the artistry of expression and composition, the dynamics of progressing plot, inventive creativity and imagination, various kinds of fictional elaboration and ornamentation, entertaining and educational functions — all for the benefit of what is narrated, the content of the narratives. The art form of the tale is specifically shaped by its focus on the telling for enjoyment and entertainment.

The genres of this class consist of two subgroups: one that includes genres of larger and complex literary works, in which the essential subjects are extensively or fully developed and which are cohesively organized and conceptually coherent. The other includes those genres whose narratives are basically though variously short, confined to a minimum of necessary characters and to elementarily constructed plots. To the first subgroup belong the genres of epic, novel (German: *Roman,* rather than the short *Novelle* = novella or even novelette in English), saga (cf. the ANNOTATION on SAGA in the Glossary), and history writing. To the second subgroup belong the genres of story, anecdote, legend, myth, fable, fairy tale, and also tale. The characteristics of the *class* of narrative, which is called here the *art form of narrative,* belong to both subgroups of this class and also to each genre in this subgroup.

Two qualifications, especially regarding narrative art, are relevant: one concerns the issue of fiction, and the other the issue of truth in narrative. First, in modern narrative art, fiction is or may be taken as a particular genre beside others. This understanding does not lend itself to the distinction of genres in biblical narrative, however, because all genres of biblical narrative art share the characteristics of imaginative creativity. Therefore, the dimension of fiction or the fictional also in OT narrative should not be assumed to be genre-specific — characteristic for only one genre. Except for the reporting genres, fiction pervades more or less all genres of biblical narrative. As a particular attribute of narrative, it is characterized by imaginative creativity. This creativity may be applied to inventing unreal worlds, as in myth, fairy tale, or fable, or to suggesting real and true, especially human, conditions through narrating unreal but for those conditions transparent events, as in fable. It may suggest real events that mean something other than what is told, as in allegory; and it may also be applied to elaborating on known and verifiable historical facts, as in the historical novel. While in this last case the fictional element does not claim to be taken verbatim, it does claim to be true in the sense that it is based on, reflective of, and controlled by what is otherwise held as established fact.

Second, qualifications of narrative art such as "true" or "untrue" are different from characterizations such as "real" or "unreal." While the distinction between the real world and unreal worlds — i.e., between forms that point to the world of human experience, and between those forms from human perception that point to worlds beyond human experience — is inherent in the contents, functions, and purpose of narrative art, the question of the truth of, or in, any narrative is extraneously determined by what is understood to be true, but not by its narrative genre, its content, or the contrast between the real or an unreal world.

Genres that are shaped by what is here called the *class of objectifying narrative* are different. They too rest on characteristics that are basic for all narrative. While one should not say that they are devoid of the influence of artistry, their style, structure, and discernible function and intention betray that what is narrated is, or implies to be, essentially controlled by the factual roots of its contents rather than by the freedom from those roots. To this class belong the genres of list, record, and report, including a form that one may call summary report.

The account, having an apologetic or authenticating function, also claims to be factual and accurate, but it may or may not have been accepted as verifiable.The memoir claims to be factual, accurate, and verifiable in what is said in it. But its tendentiousness controls what is said and what is not said, and how it is said. It stands in the intersection between reporting what is accurate and not reporting what would also be accurate. It is by and large apologetic and similar to the account.

In conclusion, one can say that each genre partakes in the characteristics common to all narrative, in the characteristics of its respective class and of its group in its class. But what distinguishes it from the other genres depends lastly on those criteria that are genre-specific. The following Glossary focuses specifically on those criteria for narrative genres.

GENRES

ACCOUNT (Rechenschaftsbericht). Exod 4:27-31; 5:1–6:1. A particular kind of (→) report, an accounting report.

Characteristic for the account is the element of discharging accountability in reporting. An account may be long or short. It presupposes and answers situations that provoke the need for explaining, justifying, defending, or confessing certain facts or statements about facts. It is related to (→) disputation, (→) trial, (→) memoir, (→) confession of sin, and similar genres.

While presupposing a report or containing the features characteristic for it, an account relates additional factors or viewpoints by which the neutrally reported facts may be elucidated. Specifically, an account may be a narrative that responds to the challenge or rejection of a previously reported statement. (→) disputation. Cf. 1 Kgs 22:19-23; Amos 7:14-15. Or it may be a narrative that as such is structured on the directly or indirectly discernible intention to substantiate certain external aspects that are related to but only presupposed in what is said. Cf. Gen 1:1–2:4a (Israel's Sabbath week, directly discernible); or the apologetic functions of Isaiah 6; Hosea 1 and 3 (indirectly discernible). Cf. also the apologetic function in the dedicatory ancient Near Eastern royal inscriptions. Or it may be a narrative that renders account of an action, event, condition, or history, rather than merely neutrally reporting or describing them. In this sense, all so-called history works in the OT are historical accounts.

This description focuses on what distinguishes an account from other genres such as (→) story, (→) report, etc., and as a genre rather than as another word for narrative. The reason for this distinction is that the OT contains narratives that are characterized as accounting for words or acts, especially in defense of their previous rejection or of accusations, or in disputes. The description presupposes that the account contains those characteristics that belong to narrative language in general, and also those that belong to a class, in which the shape of narratives is controlled by what must or needs to be said rather than by what may fictitiously be created.

→ Memoir (e.g., Nehemiah).
Cf. FOTL IX, 243; X, 291; XI, 426; XIII, 172.

ACCUSATION (Anklage). Exod 1:18; 5:14; 10:3a-bβ; 18:14-23; 32:11, 21-24. A speech alleging that someone has broken the law or otherwise done wrong. This speech form had an official setting in judicial practice, but was adapted by the prophets and could be used in a literary context. It may be addressed directly to the accused or refer to them in the third person. The simplest form of an accusation is a declaratory sentence (cf. 2 Sam 12:9b; Jer 29:21, 23) or accusing question (2 Sam 12:9a; Jer 22:15). A more developed form establishes a causal connection between the offense and its consequence (cf. 1 Sam 15:23).
Cf. FOTL XI, 427; XIV, 243; C. Westermann, *Basic Forms of Prophetic Speech* (tr. H. C. White; Philadelphia: Westminster, 1967) 142-48.

ADMONITION (Ermahnung gegen). An attempt at dissuasion from doing something wrong or not doing what is right; a negative expression, such as "do not forget," by which one party appeals to the mind either of an addressed (2nd person) or a third (3rd person) party in an attempt to dissuade those addressed or implied from wrong action or behavior.

What would be done wrong may consist either of an improper act or behavior or of a failure to act or behave properly. In either case, the nature of the wrong is predetermined by what appears to be disadvantageous, as, e.g., in wisdom reflection, as well as by the violation of established customs, positive ethical standards, laws, commands, prohibitions, and instructions.

While the various kinds of societal standards must, by virtue of their intrinsic authority, not be violated — even unconditionally — the admonition focuses on the danger of their violation that lies in the unsteadiness of the human mind, or psyche, and in its temptation, ability, or unwillingness to avoid doing what is right, necessary, decreed, or even apodictically commanded or prohibited. The admonition aims at deactivating the negative potentials of the mind so as to overcome the obstacles in it by discouraging wrongdoing or not doing what is right. It does so by appealing to persons either directly or indirectly by way of explanatory or empirical argumentation. Like (→) exhortation or (→) parenesis, it is in principle motivating.

It is, however, no more than an attempt. Whether it will succeed is just as open as the aims of exhortation, and as whether laws or directives are obeyed.

Admonition can be discerned by expressions of direct appeals at dissuasion, ad hominem, even in grammatical forms of prohibitives (as especially in the Wisdom literature; cf. Murphy, FOTL XIII, with reference to Bright), but also in additions to laws, prohibitions, commands, prophetic announcements, et al., which function as explanations to otherwise given interdicts.

The grammatical forms may, however, belong to the genre of prohibition or of admonition. The criterion for distinguishing their genre should be whether they focus on discouragement from the negative human attitude in action and behavior, as in admonition, or on the nonnegotiable authority of what is said and regardless of the addressees' general psychological predisposition, as in prohibition.

→ Exhortation; (→) Parenesis; → Prohibition; → Command; → Order.

ADOPTION LEGEND (Adoptionslegende). Exod 1:15–2:10. The adoption legend corresponds closely to the pattern of the *Legend of Sargon*. The pattern includes the narratives of conception, birth, and exposure of a foundling — significantly by leaving the unwanted child in a basket of reeds in a river — then wondrous discovery of the child, adoption, rearing, and the child's subsequent rise to a position of power. It is one of the genres used in the (→) heroic saga.

→ Legend.

ANNALS (Annalen). See Exod 1:15 for NAME LIST. Records for and from the archives of the royal court (Gen 14:1-24). Cf. FOTL IX, 243-44.

APPEAL (Anrufung, Berufung). Exod 5:15; 32:12-13; 33:18. Specifically, a call by one to another, mostly authoritative, party to justify or reconsider a decision or change a situation. → complaint. Generally, an urgent call to incite a certain kind of conduct, but without the assumption of an obligation on the part of the addressee to respond to such a call. → Petition. Cf. FOTL XI, 427; XVI, 515.

BIRTH STORY (Geburtsgeschichte). Exod 2:1-1. A birth narrative based on the characteristics of (→) story. Cf. Genesis 16; 18.

BIRTH-ADOPTION LEGEND OR STORY (Geburts-Adoptions-Legende oder -Geschichte). Exod 1:15–2:10. A narrative about both the paternal/maternal birth of a child and its adoption by a different party. It focuses on these two select aspects in a genre characterized either as (→) story or as (→) legend.

    The element of Moses' birth in Exod 1:15–2:10 is characterized by story, whereas the element of his adoption belongs to legend. Since each of these two elements is part of the whole narrative unit, which emphasizes the miraculous nature of Moses' beginnings, the element of story is part of the legend of Moses' birth, rescue, adoption, and rise. It functions for anchoring the aspects of the wonderful in events of the real world.

CENSUS LIST (Zensusliste). → List. Cf. FOTL I, 318 (List); IX, 245-46 (Catalogue).

COLLECTION (Sammlung). A general term describing any combination of genres. Thus a collection of sayings would be a combination of individual tribal sayings organized according to the traditional list of the twelve tribes.

    → Catalogue, cf. FOTL IX, 245-46; → List, cf. FOTL I, 318; IIA, List.

COMMAND (positiver Befehl). Exod 5:7b, 8-9, 11, 18; 13:2a, 5, 10, 11-12. An authoritative positive expression by one party that directs either an addressed (2nd person) or a third (3rd person) party to what is unconditionally expressed without regard to the psychological disposition of those directed. By directing only positively what must be done, the command alone does not address a possibly or actually prohibited opposite — whether or not such an opposite is implied or presupposed.

    The command may refer to a single act or to an ongoing activity. It may or may not be accompanied by an explanation, and it may stand alone or in a series.

    The authority of the command rests either in the official authority of the person giving it, or in the force of its content by virtue of its custom, or law, or an immediate necessity, represented by the commanding person.

    → Order; → Prohibition; → Parenesis; → Admonition; → Exhortation.

COMMISSION (Beauftragung, Sendung). An authoritative charge given by a superior to a subordinate. In Exod 3:1–4:18; 6:2b-8, 10-11; 7:2-5, the commissioning authority is the deity. Cf. FOTL IX, 246; X, 295-96; XI, 429; XVI, 516-17.

COMMISSION REPORT (Sendungsbericht). A narrative characterized by the genre of (→) report.
→ Account.

COMMISSION SPEECH (Sendungsrede). Exod 3:7-10. The part in a (→) commission report in which the commissioning speech is quoted verbatim.
→ Account.

COMPLAINT (Klage als Beschwerde, Beschwerde-Klage). Exod 2:23aβ-b; 5:22-23. A statement that describes personal or communal distress, often addressed to God with a plea for deliverance (Job 3; Hab 1:2-4; etc.). The description of the distress is characterized by vivid language (cf. the so-called confessions of Jeremiah, 12:1ff., etc.) and by the use of the question "why?" (Gen 41:55; 16:28b). Cf. FOTL XI, 429; XIV, 246 (Complaint Element); XVI, 518. In contrast to (→) lament, the complaint presupposes a reversible calamity or injustice that it desires to be changed.

CONFESSION (Bekenntnis). → Confession of Guilt.

CONFESSION OF GUILT (Schuldgeständnis, -bekenntnis). Exod 9:27-28; 10:16-17. A statement in the midst of juridical proceedings or in situations conceived judicially, in which a defendant formally acknowledges his or her guilt. At its simplest, the confession of guilt consists of a formulaic (→) plea of guilty (expressed mostly as ḥāṭā'tî, "I have transgressed/sinned," Exod 10:16; 1 Sam 15:30; 2 Sam 12:13; 24:10). In more complex examples the speaker refers to the offense (Josh 7:20-21; 1 Sam 15:24; 2 Sam 19:20-21 [NRSV 19-20]; Ezra 10:2) and includes a petition or a pledge that in some way puts the situation right (1 Sam 26:21; 2 Sam 19:21 [NRSV 20]; cf. Exod 9:27-28; 2 Kgs 18:14). Thus the speaker's intention is usually to effect mercy or a turn for the better (e.g., Exod 9:27-28; 10:16-17; 1 Sam 15:30; 2 Kgs 18:14). Proximity to the judicial setting and language associated with trials accounts for the first-person singular style of the confession (but see Ezra 10:2). Cf. FOTL XI, 429.

CULTIC ORDINANCE (Kultische Verordnung). An official order structured according to a system for the practice of cultic customs or rituals. → Ordinance.

DEATH REPORT (Todesbericht). Exod 1:6. A (→) report about the death of a person; cf. Exod 1:6; Deuteronomy 34. Cf. FOTL XI, 429.

DECLARATIVE PRAISE (Ankündigung von Lob). Exod 15:1-19. Focusing on one particular event, the worshiper declares his or her intention to offer praise for God's deliverance (e.g., at the sea). The cohortative introduction (cf. Pss 13:6b [NRSV 6a]; 57:8 [NRSV 7]; 89:2 [NRSV 1]; 101:1;

104:33; 108:2 [*NRSV* 1]; 144:9; as well as Judg 5:3) leads to the principal body of praise in the *kî*-clause (cf. Psalms 117, 148).
→ Hymn of Praise; → Hymn of the Individual; → Personal Hymn. Cf. FOTL XIV, 249.

DEDICATION REPORT (Einweihungsbericht). Exod 32:5-6. → Dedicatory Inscription.
Cf. FOTL IX, 247; X, 298.

DIALOGUE (Dialog, Zwiegespräch). Exod 2:7-8, 18-20; 3:4-6; 4:2; 5:1-5; 8:4-7; 10:29-26; 18:14-18; 32:21-24. A combination of speeches, each in response to the other, with the pattern of response significant for special types of dialogue. This structure determines the genre. Cf. FOTL I, 317.

DISPUTATION (Disputation, Streitgespräch). Exod 1:15-21; 2:13b-14a, 18b-20. A discussion between two or more parties about different points of view on a subject normally involving a complex set of aspects and regardless of the authority or status of those involved. It focuses on the question of the (more) persuasive or convincing and the (more) just and true argument. It may be more or less controversial, legal or nonlegal, and belong to legal or nonlegal societal settings. See especially the book of Job and the disputation speeches in Deutero-Isaiah.
→ Disputation; → Disputation Speech.
Cf. FOTL IX, 248; XI, 429; XVI, 519; XIX, 349.

DISPUTATION SPEECH (Disputationsrede). A particular form of the genre (→) disputation. It is found in texts in which conflicting arguments normally represented by the opposing parties are debated in a speech of only one party about or to the other, who does not answer. Cf. Deutero-Isaiah.

DISPUTE (Streit, Zank, Kontroverse). Exod 1:18-19; 2:13-14. As distinguishable from (→) disputation, the dispute is essentially a controversy between two parties about a specific case. It consists of an accusation and the defense against it or a counteraccusation. Its subject may be legal or nonlegal, and be debated in legal or extralegal settings. More than the disputation, however, it involves quarrel, conflict, and feud.
→ Disputation.

DIVINE SPEECH (Gottesrede). A reference to or quotation of a speech of the deity.
→ Speech.

ETIOLOGICAL SAGA OR STORY (Ätiologische Sage oder Geschichte). → Etiology; → Saga; → Story.

ETIOLOGY (Ätiologie). Exod 2:10b; 4:24-26; 12:26-27a, 39; 15:23; 16:31; 17:7, 15-16; 18:3, 4. A narrative designed in its basic structure to support

160

some kind of explanation for a situation or name that exists at the time of the storyteller. It builds a connection between a saying in the body of the genre and a conclusion that provides the explanation. Sometimes it is a simple wordplay (Gen 32:2-3). Cf. FOTL IX, 248; XI, 430; XIX, 349.

ETYMOLOGICAL ETIOLOGY (Etymologische Ätiologie). Exod 2:10, 22b. → Etiology; → Story.

ETYMOLOGICAL NARRATIVE (Etymologische Erzählung). → Etiology; → Story.

EXHORTATION (Ermutigung). Exod 1:10; 12:13aa, 17. An attempt at persuasion to do something right or to avoid doing what is wrong; a positive expression, such as "remember," by which one party appeals to the mind either of an addressed (2nd person) or a third (3rd person) party in an attempt to persuade those addressed (or those implied) to right action or behavior. What should be done right may consist either of a proper act or behavior or of the avoidance of a wrong act or behavior. In either case, the nature of what is right is predetermined by what appears to be advantageous, as well as by the adherence to established customs, positive ethical standards, laws, commands, prohibitions, and instructions.

While the various kinds of societal standards must by virtue of their intrinsic authority be observed, even unconditionally, the exhortation focuses on the human inability or unwillingness to fulfill those standards. It aims at activating or motivating the positive faculties of the mind so as to overcome the obstacles in it by encouraging the fulfillment of what is right or the avoidance of what is wrong. It does so by appealing to persons either directly, ad hominem, or, indirectly, by way of explanatory or empirical argumentation.

Exhortation is no more than an attempt. Whether it will succeed is just as much open as the attempt of parenesis or admonition, and as whether laws and directives are obeyed.

Exhortation can be discerned by expressions of direct appeals at persuasion to or for persons, even in grammatical forms of imperatives, but also in additions to all sorts of texts, which encourage support and understanding of the statements in those texts.

The grammatical forms of imperatives may reflect the genre of command or exhortation. The criterion for distinguishing their generic nature should be whether they focus on the encouragement of the positive human attitude in action or behavior, as in exhortation, or on submission to the nonnegotiable authority of what is said, as in command.

→ Admonition; → Parenesis; → Prohibition; → Command; → Order.

GENEALOGY (Stammbaum, Genealogie). Exod 6:14-25. Builds on a system of enumeration rather than narration. It is more nearly akin to (→) list, but can incorporate (→) story in its scope. It derives ultimately from tribal circles as a means for the history and validation of tribal units.

Linear Genealogy (Gen 4:1-26; 5:1–9:29; 11:10–25:11; 22:20-24; 25:1-6).

Segmented Genealogy (Gen 10:1-32; 25:12-16; 36:9-14).

Cf. FOTL IX, 249; XI, 430.

HEROIC/HERO LEGEND (Heldenlegende). Exod 17:8-16. A narrative about a heroic figure that basically, rather than only in certain elements, focuses on the legendary in the hero's portrait.

→ Heroic/Hero Saga; → Legend.

HEROIC/HERO SAGA (Heldensage). Exod 1:15–Deut 34:12. A type of (→) saga that focuses on events in the life of one central figure who is significant for the people who remember him or her. Heroic saga typically includes some account of the hero's birth, marriage, vocation, death — along with displays of virtue and heroic deeds. The intention is not simply to describe the hero as he or she really was, but to interpret him or her according to stereotyped, imaginative categories. An example in the OT of heroic saga is that of Moses, Exodus 1–Deuteronomy 34. Cf. FOTL XI, 430-31.

HYMN OF PRAISE (Hymnus, Loblied, Lobgesang). A macrogenre for the praise of one party by another through hymnic poems. The praising party may consist of an individual or a community. The extolled party is in the OT above all Israel's God, Yahweh, but also Yahweh's Zion, his chosen king, his Torah, and wisdom.

The poems consist mostly of two basic parts: a summons by the praising party either to oneself ("I will praise/sing," "let me praise," "let us praise") or to the community ("sing . . . ," "praise Yahweh") — which may be called its declarative part — and the content of the hymn proper, which in the main body of the poem accounts for the summons.

The reasons for the summons, given in the poems' contents, are manifold, and so are their more or less characteristic stylistic forms. Distinctive in the contents are those aspects under which either Yahweh's past actions are recounted or his ever-present actions or attitudes are described (Westermann's *berichtender* and *beschreibender Lobpsalm* [declarative and descriptive psalm of praise, respectively]; see C. Westermann, *Praise and Lament in the Psalms* [tr. K. Crim and R. Soulen; Atlanta: John Knox, 1981]). Furthermore, extolled is either a specific act of Yahweh, as in the hymns of Yahweh's victory in Exod 15:1-18, 20-21, or the history of Yahweh's acts in creation and history.

The settings of the hymns of praise belong to the history of Israel's worship of and meditation about Yahweh. The setting of an individual hymn depends on its particular place in that history.

Cf. FOTL XI, 431; XIV, 249; XVI, 521; XX, 111.

INDICTMENT (Anklage). Exod 7:16aβb. → Indictment Speech.

INDICTMENT SPEECH (Anklagerede, Anklageerhebung). One of the (→) trial genres. The indictment speech is a component of the trial speech. It is a statement formally handed down by a judicial authority charging a person with having committed an act punishable under the provisions of the law. It is presented either on approval of an accusation or in its own right.

Because of the particular structure of Israel's and Judah's judicial system, the judicial authorities who issue an indictment may function as both accuser and judge, such as a king or a tribal judge (cf. 1 Sam 15:17-19; 22:13; 1 Kgs 2:42-43; 18:17; 22:18; 2 Kgs 20:2, 36). Other officials may also bring an indictment against someone before a judicial authority (cf. Jer 36:20; 2 Sam 19:22).

A modified form of the indictment speech can also be employed in prophetic literature as the accusation or the reason for punishment in the (→) prophetic judgment speech (Isa 8:6; Jer 11:9-10; Mic 3:9-11), the (→) prophetic announcement of punishment against an individual (Amos 7:16; Jer 23:1), and the (→) prophetic announcement of punishment against the people (Isa 30:12; Hos 2:7-8).

Cf. FOTL IX, 251; X, 302; XI, 431; XX, 111.

INDIVIDUAL THANKSGIVING (Danklied des Einzelnen). → Thanksgiving Song.

INSTRUCTION (Instruktion, Unterweisung). Exod 4:3aα, 4a, 6aα, 7aα; 12:21a-22; 14:2; 16:4-5, 29-30. A writing or discourse, chiefly in imperative mode, that offers guidance to an individual or group by setting forth particular values or prescribing rules of conduct. Instruction typically tends to deal with universals: broad values, traditional rules for conduct, or aphoristic knowledge drawn from wide experience. The settings and occasions of use for instructions must have been quite diverse. In Israel and Judah, instructions were probably created by persons of some official or aristocratic standing, such as lawgiver, priest, prophet, scribe, wisdom teacher, or even king. In Egypt the best examples derive from scribes who formulated didactic works to summarize accepted knowledge or, in some cases, produced instruction in the guise of an after-the-fact testament from a king to his successor, with propagandistic overtones (*ANET,* 414-19; more generally see M. Lichtheim, *Ancient Egyptian Literature* [3 vols.; Berkeley: Univ. of California Press, 1973-81] 1:58-80). Similarly, the clearest examples from the Hebrew Bible are in the didactic literature (e.g., Prov 1-9; 22:17-24:22). Prophetic examples tend to be employed for persuasive purposes, and they become somewhat more specific by focusing on the wisdom of continued adherence to Yahweh, who promises to defend Zion and the Davidic house, and on the opportunities for national restoration presented to Judah by Yahweh's bringing about catastrophe (e.g., Isa 8:16-9:6 [*NRSV* 7]; 28:1-33:24).

Cf. FOTL IX, 251; XI, 431; XIII, 177; XIV, 251.

ITINERARY (Wegverzeichnis, Itinerar). Exod 15:22, 27; 16:1; 17:1a-bα. A formal structure of (→) accounts or (→) reports, which relate movement by stages. Itinerary often includes special formulas, noting the point of departure ("set out from so-and-so") and/or the point of arrival in a journey ("encamped at so-and-so" or "came to so-and-so"), and thus may serve as a literary skeleton for larger collections of varied material (e.g., Exod 17:1–18:27; 19:1–Num 10:10; 1 Kgs 19:1-18). If the itinerary appears with little or no narrative materials between stages of movement, it should be understood as a type of (→) list, as, e.g., Num 33:5-37, 41-49. Cf. FOTL I, 318.

ITINERARY INSTRUCTION (Itinerarinstruktion). → Itinerary.

JUDGMENT SPEECH (Gerichtswort). Exod 32:9-10. → Trial Genres.

LABOR CONTRACT (Arbeitsvertrag). Exod 2:9a. A party's acceptance of a commission by an employing party for work at promised wages.

LAWSUIT (Prozess). → Trial Genres.

LEGEND (Legende). Exod 7:7–10:29; 11:1–12:36; 14:1-31; 17:8-16; 22:1–24:25. A narrative essentially concerned with the wonderful and miraculous events or persons in the real world. It claims belief in the wonderful dimensions in such events or persons, and aims at edification (Gen 22:1-19; 39–41; Numbers 12). Cf. FOTL I, 318; IX, 252; XI, 432; XIII, 177; XX, 111.

LIST (Liste). Exod 1:1-6; 6:14b-25. A written document that consists of the line, or lines, of collected names of persons or objects. In a rudimentary form, such a collection is not determined by a systematized order of the names within it but by an aspect by which they belong together as a group regardless of their relation to each other. This group aspect may or may not be head- or sublined in a text.

List is a literary macrostructure that is particularly representative of the ancient science of lists *(Listenwissenschaft)*. However, since virtually all known lists are also governed by various types of systematization, the specific genre of any list depends on the specific type of its systematization and its purpose. A series may originally be written or oral. → Name List (Gen 35:22b-26; 36:15-19, 40-43; 46:8-27).

→ Genealogy; → Catalogue; → Register; → Chain.
See FOTL I, 318; IX, 253; X, 305; XI, 432; XIX, 350; XX, 112.

MARRIAGE NARRATIVE (Heiratserzählung). → Marriage Story.

MARRIAGE REPORT (Heiratsbericht). → Marriage Story; → Report.

MARRIAGE STORY (Heirats-, Hochzeitsgeschichte). Exod 2:11-22. A narrative about the development of a marriage. As story, it reflects one of the typical events in a community's life, focusing on those aspects of such events that are considered essential but nevertheless particular. These aspects are: an introduction about the encounter of the principal characters and its circumstances; dialogue between father and daughter(s); the marriage report proper; and the focus on the relationship between the bridegroom/son-in-law and his father-in-law. For parallels of these aspects, cf. FOTL I, 166-71 in the servant of Abraham novella Gen 24, and 209-23 in the Jacob-Laban novella esp. in Gen 29f.

MESSAGE (Botschaft). Exod 3: 16b-22; 7:2bβ; 12:3aβb-11. The content of a communication, typically a speech, sent from one subject to another by a third party, designed to deliver information or instruction for some particular goal. See FOTL I, 318.

MYTH (Mythos, Mythe). Exod 4:24-26. A narrative form set in a fantasy world designed to account for the real world by reference to activities of the gods in the divine world (Gen 6:1-4). Cf. FOTL XIII, 178; XIX, 350; XX, 113.

NAME LIST (Namenliste). Exod 1:2-4. A (→) list of proper names of persons, cities, or countries. It is based on and organized according to a certain unifying aspect that is normally defined in its superscription.

The aspects vary. They may be related to (→) genealogy, (→) lists of heroes or officials, of (→) census for labor, taxes, and particularly the military registration of the adult male population, etc. The lists belong to administrative settings. The book of Chronicles has 61 name lists (cf. Gen 46:8-27). Cf. FOTL XI, 432.

NARRATIVE (Erzählung). Exod 13:17–Deut 34:12. The oral or written text in which any and all sorts of happening, of actions, events, thoughts, speeches, or experiences are narrated.

At least form-critically, narrative includes all texts that are determined by narrative style, i.e., the verbal forms of the sentences and their connectedness throughout a text — as distinguished from those kinds of texts that either describe permanent conditions or define attitudes or express (→) commands, (→) prohibitions, (→) admonitions, (→) exhortations, and even laws and prophetic announcements in which narrative style is also used.

A narrative may therefore consist of one sentence that narrates, e.g., that a person did or does or will or may do something, or that something did, does, will, or may happen. It consists mostly of smaller or larger units whose parts are either also of narrative character or governed by their narrative unit, and narrated sequentially. The sequentially narrated parts are related under the perspective of the forward movement of what is narrated. The forward movement may be seen as a sequence of

165

the narrated events in terms of time or, e.g., of causality. It may be presented in the form of a unilinear sequence, or in a form of two or more sequences that happen simultaneously or at different times.

A narrative may be long or short, refer to past, present, or future events, and to real or imagined things. It may be told for any purpose and with or without much detail. The narrative encompasses classes of narratives and genres of such classes. It is constitutive for the narrative character of all classes of narrative and their genres, but not for the character of those classes themselves and of their genres. What is class- and genre-specific within narrative is determined by the criteria pertinent to class and genre, respectively. The term must therefore not be mixed with terms for particular narrative genres such as (→) story, (→) account, (→) report, and (→) legend. At best, narrative may be called a macro-genre, in distinction from poetry or forms of prescriptive or predictive language.

In German the use of the term *Erzählung* must distinguish between its meanings of narrative (as above), i.e., a narrated text *(das Erzählte),* and the act of narrating *(das Erzählen),* and especially of (→) story (Gunkel's *Sagen der Genesis* are not legends but stories, hence translated as *The Stories of Genesis* [tr. J. J. Scullion; ed. W. R. Scott; Vallejo, Calif.: BIBAL, 1994]), and so are Westermann's *Arten der Erzählung in der Genesis* (cf. the Eng. translation: "Types of Narrative in Genesis," in *The Promises to the Fathers* [tr. D. E. Green; Philadelphia: Fortress, 1980], 1-94).

Cf. FOTL XIII, 179; XVI, 525; XX, 114.

NARRATIVE FRAME A form of inclusion in which some element from the beginning of a (→) narrative is taken up again at the end of a unit to mark it as a completed whole. See pp. 3-20, 50.

NATIONAL SAGA (Völkersage). A (→) saga about a nation or the nations.

NEGOTIATION (Verhandlung). Exod 5:1-5. An exchange of (→) speeches moving toward agreement or disagreement and focused on a particular issue (1 Chr 21:20-25; 2 Chr 2:3-16). Cf. FOTL XI, 432.

ORACLE (Orakel, Gottesrede). Exod 11:4b-8a. A communication from the deity, often through an intermediary such as priest or prophet, especially in response to an inquiry (→ oracular inquiry, see FOTL IX, 254). The OT also describes oracles as unsolicited. In all cases the structure and content vary; oracles have to do with, e.g., salvation, healing, punishment, judgment, promise, encouragement, warning. Some oracles commission a prophet to a lifelong vocation, and frequently the prophet's speeches are presented as God's own words, hence as oracle. Settings and intentions vary, according to content and circumstances. Some clue as to solicited oracles comes from (→) reports that mention dreams, prophets, and priests as involved in procedures for obtaining divine communication (cf. 1 Sam 28:6; Num 22:7-12, 19-20; Josh 7:6-15; 1 Kgs 20:13-14; 22:5-6, 15-17; Ezek 20:1-8). Cf. FOTL I, 319.

ORACLE OF JUDGMENT (Gerichtsorakel). → Trial Genres.

ORACLE OF SALVATION (Heilsorakel, Heilsspruch, Heilsankündigung). Exod 6:1. A divine assurance of grace, expressed formally by a priest or other officiant in Israelite worship. The existence of such a liturgical practice has become a matter of debate in OT scholarship. J. Begrich postulated this form (usually initiated by the formula "do not fear"; → assurance formula, see FOTL XIV, 258; also FOTL XVI, 547), principally on the strength of its occurrences in Second Isaiah (Isa 41:14; 43:1; 44:2; etc.; accepted by Gunkel, Westermann, Kraus, Schoors, et al.). R. Kilian has contested the existence of such a form in the agenda of individual complaint. Frequent usage of the formula, however, would also indicate fixed cultic habits, and individual complaint must be seen in its communal setting, as Kilian himself demands. Consequently, Ps 35:3 asks for a divine response to be articulated in the worship situation (cf. also the different types of salvation oracles in Pss 12:6 [NRSV 5]; 91:2-8, 9-13; 121:3-4). One need not assume, then, that salvation oracles explain a psychological change from distress to exuberant joy; rather, one can regard them as potential ingredients of petitionary liturgy, similar to the "assurance of grace" or "words of assurance" following confession in Christian worship. See FOTL XIV, 253, for references.

ORDER (Anordnung). Exod 5:7; 12:20, 46-47. A particular form of expression in which a (→) command and a (→) prohibition are juxtaposed in antithetical parallelism. This type of expression intends to make certain that what is commanded is clarified and reinforced by the explicit addition of its prohibited opposite. Conversely, it intends to make certain that what is prohibited is clarified and reinforced by the explicit addition of its commanded opposite. This terminological specification for order is used for the sake of differentiating among different types of generic expressions.
→ Command; → Prohibition; → Parenesis; → Admonition; → Exhortation.

ORDINANCE (Verordnung). Exod 12:1-28, 43-51; 13:1-16. A rule prescribing authoritatively what is to be done. As a broad legal category, ordinance includes many specific types and fields of laws (e.g., cultic ordinances, festival ordinances), but an ordaining authority is normally the common element.

PARENESIS (Paränese). Exod 12:20. A particular form of parenetic expression in which an (→) admonition and an (→) exhortation are juxtaposed in antithetical parallelism. This type of expression is designed to make certain that what is admonished is clarified and reinforced by the explicit addition of its exhorted opposite. Conversely, it intends to make certain that what is exhorted is clarified and reinforced by the explicit addition of its admonished opposite. This terminological specification for parenesis is used for the sake of differentiating among different types of generic parenetic expressions.

→ Command; → Prohibition; → Admonition; → Exhortation.

PETITION (Bitte, Bittrede, Bittschrift, Petition). Exod 32:12b-13. A request or plea from one person to another asking for some definite response. The petition may occur in contexts that express ordinary, day-to-day situations. In such cases the structure of the petition includes both the basis for the petition and the petition proper, expressed directly or indirectly (e.g., Gen 18:3-4; 23:4; 1 Kgs 2:15-17; 5:17-20). The petition also occurs as the central element of all (→) complaints, in which the supplicant asks for divine help. It is usually formulated in the imperative, but the jussive, imperfect, and cohortative are also employed to express the supplicant's "wish." Cf. FOTL IX, 255; XI, 433; XIV, 254; XX, 116.

PRAYER (Gebet). Any communication of a person toward his or her God. It is a direct address to God in the second-person singular and encompasses a wide variety of expression, motivation, purpose, and societal setting. Thus prayer may take a number of different literary forms or genres depending on content, intention, and setting, e.g., (→) complaint song of the individual, (→) hymn, (→) prayer of dedication, (→) prayer of petition. Besides the book of Psalms, which contains in effect many cultic prayers, we find mention of prayer in narrative contexts, e.g., Gen 24:10-14; 2 Kgs 20:3; Gen 18:23-32; and even in (→) vision reports, e.g., Amos 7:2, 5. Cf. FOTL XI, 433.

PROHIBITION (Verbot). Exod 5:7a; 12:15b, 16, 19, 43b, 45, 48b; 13:3b, 7b. An authoritative negative expression by one party that directs either an addressed (2nd person) or a third (3rd person) party not to do what is unconditionally expressed, without regard to the psychological disposition of those directed. By directing only negatively what must not be done, the prohibition alone does not address a possibly or actually commanded opposite, whether or not such an opposite is implied or presupposed. The prohibition may refer to a single act or an ongoing activity. It may or may not be accompanied by an explanation, and stand alone or in a series. The authority of the prohibition rests either in the subjective authority of the person giving it, or in the force of its content by virtue of its custom, or law, or an immediate necessity, represented by the prohibiting person.

→ Order; → Command; → Parenesis; → Admonition; → Exhortation.

PROMISE OF SALVATION (Versprechen von Rettung, Heil). Exod 7:3-5. An announcement in which the positive event of salvation and/or its contents are promised.

→ Promise; → Prophecy of Salvation; → Oracle of Salvation; → Prophetic Announcement of Salvation; → Account of Trouble and Salvation.

PROPHECY OF PUNISHMENT (Prophetische Strafankündigung). A prophetic word that announces the divine punishment of an individual or group for an offense against God or God's order in the world or Israel. It is a particular element of the (→) prophetic judgment speech, which amounts to a juridical sentence in which the punishment is pronounced after an accusation or indictment and a verdict of guilt either implied in the accusation or directly expressed. It may occur alone, without a reason.

PROPHETIC JUDGMENT SPEECH (Prophetische Gerichtsrede). A speech in which the prophet as the spokesman for Yahweh announces judgment on an individual, group, or nation or society.

   As a unit the speech consists of two parts: (1) a statement of the reason(s), expressed as accusation, indictment, and also verdict of guilt; and (2) the announcement of the consequences, the punishment, which is the judgment proper or sentence. As the latter part, the announcement of punishment is usually introduced by a logical connective such as "therefore" (lākēn), and the messenger formula, "Thus says Yahweh." Additional elements occur frequently. The reasons for judgment are often, but not always, presented as the prophet's own words, and the announcement as the words of Yahweh (e.g., Mic 3:9-12; Isa 8:6-8; Jer 11:9-12).

   The relationship of the two parts of the one prophetic judgment speech rests on the rational connectedness of a reason and its consequences, regardless of their alternating sequence in texts. It presupposes that a violation has destructive consequences — expressed in terms of Yahweh's direct actions or in terms of his influence on a process of approaching evil — and that judgment proper or punishment is not without reasons.

   Since the word judgment (just like Gericht) may refer to punishment only but also to the unity in judgment of both statement of reason and announcement of punishment, it is important that these two meanings be distinguished when the word is used. Most helpful has been C. Westermann's definition of the prophetic judgment speech in terms of Gerichtsankündigung and Gerichtsbegründung (announcement of judgment [as punishment] and reasons for or substantiation of judgment [as accusation or indictment or verdict], respectively).

   Compare the various descriptions of this genre in FOTL IX, 257; XVI, 533; C. Westermann, Basic Forms of Prophetic Speech (tr. H. C. White; Philadelphia: Westminster, 1967; repr. Louisville: Westminster/ John Knox, 1991) 129-209.

PROPHETIC ORACLE OF JUDGMENT (Prophetische Gerichtsrede). → Prophetic Judgment Speech.

REPORT (Report, Bericht). Exod 4:30; 7:14, 19; 7:26-29 (*NRSV* 8:1-4); 14:5a; 16:22; 18:1. A particular kind or oral or written communication, based on narrative form, through which one party relates to or for another party the content of an event and its course. The report may or may not contain an explicit affirmation by the reporting party — e.g., by a formula of affirmation or even an oath — that the report is factual, accurate, and true, and corresponds in part or as a whole to the course of the reported events. Whether a report actually corresponds to an event is not decided by the use of this genre. As is the case with all rhetoric, the report may be slanted or even be perjury.

   This understanding of a report in the actual setting of a communication event needs to be distinguished from the function of this genre in the larger literary works of the OT such as saga and history writing. In these works the choice of this genre functions as their own device for the portrayal of the nature of a communication by one party to another. The question of such a report's factuality, accuracy, and truth for the readers of those sagas and histories does not depend on the use of this genre for the literary and rhetorical purposes of these works, but on the question of the meaning of these works themselves for their readers.

   Next to reports in historical literature about events such as specific military campaigns, the genre is most ostentatiously employed in narratives of authoritative divine speech, especially about the laws in the Pentateuch and about divine pronouncements in the prophetic literature. Introducing a speech by nothing more than a short report formula, the narrator claims the following speech to be the quotation of a received divine speech that must be taken verbatim and without apology by the speaking authority or its mediator or messenger, as in (→) account.
   Cf. FOTL I, 319; IX, 259; XI, 434; XVI, 536.

RESPONSE (Antwort, Erwiderung). There are various types, including response to accusation (Exod 1:19) and to summons (5:22-23).

RESPONSE OF COMMUNITY (Antwort der Gemeinde). The congregation's affirmative response to words said or sung by officiants or choirs. Group worship in all cultures normally functions responsively, with the officiants or choirs reciting a song and the congregation joining with affirmative responses. For example, Asaph and his kindred sing hymns (1 Chr 16:7-36a), and "all the people respond 'Amen!' and 'Praise be to Yahweh!'." (v. 36b). Other short liturgical shouts attributed to the community include "his mercy lasts forever" (Pss 100:5a; 106:1a; 107:1a; 118:1a, 29; 135:3a; 136:1a). Moreover, all first-person plural refrains may be attributed to the community (e.g., Pss 8:2, 10 [*NRSV* 1, 9]; 46:8, 12 [*NRSV* 7, 11]). This dialogic structure has been continued in Jewish and Christian worship.

RHETORICAL QUESTION (rhetorische Frage). Exod 4:11. A question asked for its rhetorical or telling effect, which does not require a reply. It is found frequently in argument and persuasion, and occurs as a subgenre in all parts of the OT. The supposition is that the answer is clear, usually the only one possible, and a deeper impression is made on the hearer by the question form than by a statement. Cf. FOTL XI, 435.

SAGA (Sage). A long, prose, traditional narrative having an episodic structure developed around stereotyped themes or objects. It may include narratives that represent distinct genres in themselves. The episodes narrate deeds or virtues from the past insofar as they contribute to the composition of the present narrator's world.

Types of sagas are:

(1) PRIMEVAL SAGA (Ursage). A narrative account of the beginning of time, the time that produced the world as it is from an original ideal world. Episodic series. (Yahwist's version, Genesis 1–11.)

(2) FAMILY SAGA (Familiensage). A narrative account of the events that compose the past of a family unit, exemplified primarily by the affairs of the patriarchal head of the family. Episodic series. (Yahwist's version of the Abraham Saga, Genesis 12–26.)

(3) HEROIC SAGA (Heldensage). A narrative account of the events that compose the past of a people's leader who, by virtue of his identification with his people, made it possible for them to endure. Episodic units. (Yahwist's version of the Moses Saga.)

Cf. FOTL I, 319; IX, 260; XI, 435.

ANNOTATION. In OT form criticism the technical use of the word *saga* in English has been controversial, because the word refers originally to the medieval Icelandic/Nordic tradition of prose narratives and only secondarily to any narrative or legend of heroic exploits. It is difficult to exclude the secondary use of the term in English because the subject especially of heroic saga occurs not only in Nordic but also in English literature, e.g., in the heroic poem *Beowulf,* the "highest achievement of Old English literature" (*Encyclopedia Britannica,* 13th ed., Ready Reference I, 989). Cf. also the *Legend of King Arthur,* called "legend" because of the wonders and marvels of the hero Arthur and his heroic band.

These prose narratives or poetic epics rest on oral tradition. They represent historical fiction, imaginative reconstruction of the past. As far as they focus on heroic persons, aspects of other characters, sites, and events may be verified even if the hero her- or himself is historically uncorroborated.

In German the word *Saga* is distinguished from the word *Sage,* but in such a way that the word *Saga* refers to the Nordic sagas specifically, whereas *Sage* is primarily defined by the nature and perspective of its narrated subject and only secondarily by its ethnic or territorial origin. From the eighteenth century on, *Sage* has been the standard term of folklorists for a particular type of prose narratives. Resting on elements of traditional oral folklore, these narratives are told about events and persons of the distant past as a matter of history. They are amplified by fantasy in such a way that the connection to events with known historical data, localities, and general circumstances, and especially the references to the heroic persons may or may not be historically verifiable. Particularly the named heroes may only be otherwise personifications of character types or roles of unverifiable persons.

Although the substantive characteristics of *Sage* are also found in English literature, just as in other ethnic literatures, there has been no adequate translation for it in English. In light of the lack of such a translation, the use of the word *saga* for the Moses narratives seems defensible — for Coats in FOTL I and IIA — as long as it is understood that the portrait of the decisive life of a person of the past, especially when heightened to heroic proportion among and for her or his people and their history, refers to its Israelite rather than a Nordic, Germanic, or any other origin and worldview.

Finally, the long saga, often consisting of sagas combined as a sequence or cycle, needs to be distinguished from the short, local or migratory, saga.

SOLILOQUY (Selbstgespräch). Exod 2:6. An act of conversing with oneself or of uttering one's thoughts without addressing any person.

SONG (Gesang, Lied). Exod 15:1-19, 20-21. A poetic composition performed by an individual or group. → Boast (Gen 4:23-24). Cf. FOTL XIII, 182, 174; I, 67.

SPEECH (Rede). Exod 5:1-5; 6-9; 7:1-5, 9, 14a-18; 16:2-3, 9. A general term describing any oral communication enacted by one of the principals of a pericope. More detailed definition of speech is desirable. For example, a speech may be an (→) oath, an (→) oracle, an (→) accusation, etc.

SPEECH REPORT (Bericht einer Rede). Exod 7:8-9, 14-18, 19; 26-29 (*NRSV* 8:1-4); 9:1-4, 13-19. → Report.

STORY (eine erzählte Geschichte). Exod 1:7-14; 2:1, 2-4, 11-22; 5:1–6:1; 12:43-51; 13:1-16; 15:1-19, 20-21; 18:1-27. A self-contained, relatively short narrative about an event the nature of which is perceived to belong to common experience, and the content of which is of special importance and interest for a community related to it and may even be a part of that community's life. It focuses on its content and its informational, educational, even instructive but also aesthetic relevance. It is in principle not free of questions concerning the specific veracity of its historical and factual origin. But it is free to be shaped by narrative artistry.

→ Account; → Anecdote; → Tale; → Legend; → Fable; → Fairy tale; → Report.

Cf. FOTL IX, 261; XI, 435; XIII, 182; XIX, 357.

SUMMARY STORY OR REPORT (Eine Geschichte oder ein Bericht in summarischer Form). Exod 1:1-14; 2:23-25; 4:19-23; 12:37-42; 13:17-22. A narratological device for condensing potentially fully developed stories or reports into a summary of short, prismatic, and essential elements. The elements can be generically diverse. Characteristic for this kind of summary is the incorporation of the elements into a narrative pattern through which they appear as successive stages of events or conditions.

This form does not represent an independent genre but is a particular form of (→) story or (→) report. It is positioned at certain junctures of larger narrative contexts where it functions as a transition from developed narratives that precede to those that follow it. The purpose of its transitional function is to move the larger narrative effectively forward.

The difference between story and report in such summaries is relative. It depends on whether one or another characteristic in a summary is dominant.

SUMMONS TO TRIAL (Aufforderung zum Prozess). Exod 5:20-21. → Trial Genres.

TALE (ein Erzählen). A distinctive genre of narrating for the sake of entertainment. Cf. "Introductory Explanations" to this Glossary; FOTL I, 320.

THANKSGIVING PSALM (Dankpsalm). → Thanksgiving Song.

THANKSGIVING SONG (Danklied). Jubilant cultic song to celebrate victory, divine help, good harvests, and all sorts of joyful occasions. There is a personal (= small group) and a national or communal (= secondary organizations) variety to thanksgiving psalms. See FOTL XIV, 14-16.

THEOPHANY REPORT (Bericht einer Gotteserscheinung, Theophaniebericht). Exod 3:2-3; 3:1-6; 33:19-34:3. A type of (→) report, occasionally in poetry, which recounts the manifestation of God, as distinct from (→) epiphany, which refers more generally to the appearance of any kind of divine being (e.g., angels, cherubim) or divinely influenced phenomenon. Two elements are characteristic: (1) description of Yahweh's approach, (2) accompanying natural upheavals (wind, fire, storm, etc.), along with reactions of fear and awe (e.g., Judg 5:4-5; Deut 33:2; Amos 1:2; Mic 1:3-4; Ps 68:8-9 [NRSV 7-8]). Cf. 1 Kgs 19:9-14. Either member may be expanded with additional motifs (e.g., Isa 19:1; 26:21; 30:27-33; Nah 1:2-6; Hab 3:3-12). Possibly set originally in celebrations of military victory, and hence aimed at praising the God who gives victory, these reports are now found in various literary contexts, such as (→) hymns (Ps 97:2-5) and (→) prophecy of punishment (Isa 19:1-4; 26:21). Cf. FOTL XI, 436 (Theophany).

TRIAL GENRES (Prozessgattungen). A collective term for generic elements related to legal procedure and the context of the law court. The setting may be the jurisdiction of the civil courts held at the gates of a city (cf. Ruth

4:1-12), the sacral jurisdiction of the sanctuaries (Joshua 7; Jeremiah 26), or the royal court (2 Sam 12:1-6; 1 Kgs 3:16-28). Legal genres and formulas appear in many situations of daily life; they are especially prevalent in the prophets, where they appear to have had some influence on the (→) prophetic announcements of punishment, the (→) prophetic judgment speech, and prophetic forms of (→) instruction.

One characteristic prophetic form of the trial genres is the so-called (→) trial speech, often identified as the "*rîb*-pattern" or the "(covenant) lawsuit" form. Examples appear in Isaiah 1; Jeremiah 2; Hosea 4; Micah 6; and various other texts, especially in Deutero-Isaiah. The term *rîb* means "controversy" and can refer to a legal case brought by one party against another; in the case of the prophets, it typically refers to Yahweh's case against Israel for violation of the terms of the covenant between Yahweh and Israel (cf. Isa 3:13; Jer 2:9; Hos 4:1; Mic 6:1-2). Characteristic elements might include a (→) call to attention (Isa 1:2; Hos 4:1; Mic 6:1-2), an appeal for a legal proceeding (Isa 1:18-20), an (→) accusation (Isa 1:2-20; 3:12-15; Hos 4:4-8; Jer 2:5-34), (→) rhetorical questions (Isa 1:5, 12; 3:15; Jer 2:5, 14, 31-32), and finally an (→) announcement of judgment (Jer 2:35-37; Hos 4:4-10) or some form of (→) instruction in proper behavior (Isa 1:10-17; Mic 6:6-8).

VOCATION ACCOUNT (Berufungsbericht, Rechenschaftsbericht über eine Berufung). Exod 2:23–4:23; 3:1–4:18; 6:2–7:6. A genre in which a prophet or the prophetic tradition refers to an initiatory call, ordination, and commissioning. There are two different types: (a) connected with a vision in which the prophet sees the heavenly court of God (1 Kgs 22:19-23; Isa 6:1-12; Ezek 1:4-28); (b) instead of the visionary element, everything is subordinated to the coming of the word of God (Exodus 3–4; Jer 1:4-10; Ezek 2:1–3:15). The components of type (b) are: a personal encounter between Yahweh and the appointee, a word of initiation and commissioning, objection and answer, call-sign or ordination procedure. Cf. FOTL XI, 436; XVI, 542.

VOCATION DIALOGUE (Berufungsdialog). Exod 3:7–4:17; 6:10-12. A dialogue in a (→) vocation account.

VOCATION NARRATIVE (Berufungserzählung). → Vocation Account.

FORMULAE

ACCUSATION FORMULA (Anklage-). Exod 1:18; 2:13b. Typically begins with the interrogative particle *lāmmâ*, "Why have you done this thing?" or *mahzō't 'āśît*, "What have you done?" The formula is constructed in the second person as a direct challenge to some previous act (Gen 3:13; 4:6,

10; 12:18-19a; 16:5a; 20:9; 26:9a, 10; 31:26-28a; 31:30, 36b-37aα;
29:25b; 42:1b; 43:6; 44:4-5, 15).

ADOPTION FORMULA (Adoptions-). Exod 2:10a. "I will be your father and
you shall be my son," with variations (1 Chr 17:13; 28:6).

AGE FORMULA (Alters-). Exod 6:16b, 18. Establishes the statistic in relationship to a particular event of seminal importance for the subject's life. Cf.
FOTL I, 320.

ASSISTANCE FORMULA (Beistands-). Exod 3:12a; 4:12. The formula affirming
Yahweh's presence with his people or an individual. The basic form is
cast as divine speech, "I am with you," with appropriate variations for
human speakers and situations (Gen 26:3aβ-b; 26:24; 28:15; 31:3; 39:2-
3, 21; 48:22). Three main usages are found: (1) in an oracle as a part of a
divine promise; in such cases the assistance formula ordinarily is introduced by the reassurance formula, "fear not" (cf. Isa 43:5; Jer 30:11;
46:28; Judg 6:12, 16); (2) spoken by people as a promise, wish, or question (in slightly different form; cf. Gen 28:20; 48:21; Exod 10:10; 18:19;
Num 14:43; Deut 20:1); (3) as an assertion or confession (cf. Gen 39:23;
Num 23:21; Deut 2:7; Josh 6:27; 1 Sam 16:18; 2 Chr 13:12; Ps 46:8, 12
[NRSV 7, 11]). Cf. FOTL I, 320; XI, 437.

BLESSING FORMULA (Segens-). Exod 18:10. Introduced with the verb "bless"
(bārak) and constructed with imperatives (Gen 1:28; 8:17b; 9:1-2; 9:26-
27; 10:8a; 12:2-3; 27:29; 28:3-4; 28:24b; 32:30b [NRSV 29b]; 43:14, 29;
48:15, 16, 20), an utterance that expresses the wish for goodwill or (divine) favor toward another. In some cases, as in the blessings formally
given to one's children, the words are believed to set into motion what
they call for. A very old blessing of the congregation is preserved in
Num 6:24, "Yahweh may keep you" (yĕbārekkā yhwh wĕyišmĕrekā; cf.
Gen 28:3; Ps 121:7). This formula was originally used in greetings but
then came to be used in cultic proceedings. Later, the passive form
"blessed be you" (bārûk 'attâ; cf. Deut 7:14; 28:3-6; 1 Sam 15:13; Ps
115:15) apparently became more frequent. In the Psalms the bārûk wish
is mostly used as an expression of praise directed to Yahweh (Pss 18:47
[NRSV 46]; 28:6; 31:22 [NRSV 21]; 41:14 [NRSV 13]; 66:20; 68:20-36
[NRSV 19-35]; 72:18-19; 89:53 [NRSV 52]; 106:48; 119:12; 124:6;
135:21; 144:1). Cf. FOTL I, 320; XI, 437.

CALL TO ATTENTION FORMULA (Lehreröffnungs-, Aufforderung zum Hören-).
Exod 3:4. This formula was developed from the short invitation, "Listen"
(Gen 37:6; 1 Sam 22:7), which could be used by anyone who wished to
open a conversation. It is also a formula that opens a public presentation or
address and intends to attract the attention of the hearers to the speech that
follows. The constituent elements include: (a) an invitation to listen — "listen," "hearken," "hear me" (1 Chr 28:2; 2 Chr 13:4; 15:2; 20:20; 29:15);

(b) mention of the addressee(s) (Gen 46:2a); and (c) an indication of what is to be heard. This call would be used by, e.g., a singer (Judg 5:3), a wisdom teacher (Prov 7:24), or an official envoy (2 Kgs 18:28-29). It is frequently found in the prophetic literature in various forms, and is often expanded by relative clauses (Amos 3:1; Hos 4:1; Mic 6:1; Isa 1:10; Ezek 6:3; cf. 2 Kgs 7:1ab). It is also found in cultic (→) parenesis and (→) instruction (Pss 34:3, 12 [*NRSV* 2, 11]; 49:2 [*NRSV* 1]; 50:7; 81:9 [*NRSV* 8]). Cf. FOTL I, 320; X, 319; XI, 437; XIV, 259; XIX, 359.

COVENANT FORMULA (Bundes-). Exod 6:7a. A two-part encapsulation of the relationship between Yahweh and his people, perhaps originally simply: "I am Yahweh your God; you are my people." This would have been essentially a description. In this simple form it does not appear in the OT. In a future-oriented formulation, "I will be your God, and you shall be my people" (Gen 9:9-11; 9:12-16; 17:10a; 1 Chr 17:22; 2 Chr 15:12-13; 23:16; 34:17), it is familiar in both prophets (Jer 7:23; 11:4; Ezek 36:28) and legal materials (Lev 26:12; Deut 29:12-13). In many instances this future-oriented formulation appears with the third person, "they shall be my people," rather than the second (Jer 24:7; 31:33; Ezek 11:20; 14:11; 37:23, 27). All of this future-oriented usage constitutes, however, a development from a purely descriptive intent to a promissory or hortatory one.

The elaboration of the formula in Deut 26:16-19 suggests that its basic setting was as an element within a covenant-making or renewing ceremony. The naturally close connection to marriage, adoption, and other legal formulas is apparent, as is the modification of the covenant formula in Hos 1:9 into an annulment. Cf. FOTL I, 320; XI, 438.

ENTHRONEMENT FORMULA (Inthronisations-). Exod 15:18. A third-person ascription of praise to Yahweh for being/having become king and reigning. It belongs to the formulaic repertoire of the Yahweh/kingship texts. Cf. FOTL XIV, 258.

ETIOLOGICAL FORMULA (Ätiologische-). Gen 2:24; 4:25; 16:13-14; 19:22, 37, 38; 21:31; 26:20b, 21b, 22aβ-b, 33; 28:16-17; 31:48-49; 32:3b; 32:31, 32-33 (*NRSV* 30, 31-32); 38:29b, 30; 50:11; Exod 2:10b; 15:23b. → Etiology.

INSULT FORMULA (Beleidigungs-, Beschimpfungs-). Exod 5:2; 1 Sam 17:26; 25:10. A patterned expression by which someone insults someone else by degrading that person's position and worth. It belongs to a wider range of stereotypical formulae by which speakers abase not only others but also themselves, as, e.g., in Exod 3:11; 16:8; Gen 37:26. Its twofold basic form consists of a question (who am I/who is the other) and a statement about one's own or the other's action or qualitative position. See Coats, *Self-Abasement and Insult Formulas.*

INTRODUCTION FORMULA (Einleitungs-). Functions to introduce a new narrative unit, e.g., "It was in those days . . ." (Exod 2:11, 23; Judg 19:1; 1 Sam 28:1). Cf. FOTL I, 321 (Introductory Formula).

ITINERARY FORMULA (Itinerar-). The formula is composed of two parts: a notice of departure from one site and a notice of arrival at another (Exod 12:37a; 13:20; 15:22a, 27; 16:1; 17:1aba; 19:2; Num 11:35; 12:16; 20:1, 22; 21:4a, 10, 11, 12, 13, 16, 18b, 19, 20; 22:1; cf. Gen 12:8-9; 13:1; 13:18; 13:3; 20:1; 26:17; 26:22aa; 26:23; 28:10; 33:18; 35:16a; 35:21; 46:la; 46:5-7. → Itinerary.

KNOWLEDGE FORMULA (Kenntnis-). Exod 6:7b-8; 7:5, 17; 8:10, 18b (*NRSV* 22b); 9:14, 15, 29; 10:2; 11:7b; 14:4aβ, 18; 16:6b, 8b, 12. → RECOGNITION FORMULA in FOTL IX, 265; X, 323; XIX, 362: A formula which expresses that humans will recognize the identity of Yahweh in their own expreience of divine actions. Its main elements are: You/they shall know — that I am Yahweh.

MESSENGER FORMULA (Boten-). Exod 4:22ba; 5:1ba; 7:2aba, 15-16aa, 18, 19, 26; 8:5, 12, 16; 9:1, 13; 11:2, 3aa; 16:9, 12; 19:3. Part of the speech commissioned by the sender for delivery to the recipient. It is an introduction to the message and functions to identify the sender for the recipient, if not also to claim the authority of the sender for the message (Gen 32:5bβ-6 [*NRSV* 4bβ-5]; 45:9; 24:30). This introduction is a stereotyped second-person expression marking the message's commission (Gen 50:17; 1 Sam 18:25; 2 Sam 7:8; 11:25; 1 Kgs 12:10; 2 Kgs 22:18; Jer 23:35, 37; 27:4; 37:7; 45:4; Ezek 33:27; 1 Chr 17:1; 2 Chr 10:10). Cf. FOTL I, 321.

MESSENGER COMMISSION FORMULA (Botensendungs-, Botenbeauftragungs-). Exod 3:14ba, 15aa, 16a. Addresses the messenger directly with the commission to act for the sender as bearer of a message (Gen 32:4-5bα [*NRSV* 3-4bα]; 44:4; 45:17, 18; 46:34; 50:4).

RESPONSE FORMULA (Antwort-). Exod 1:19; 2:14a. Narrative introduction to an answer.

SELF-ABASEMENT FORMULA (Selbsterniedrigungs-, Selbstdemütigungs-). Exod 3:11; 16:7, 8. A formula that makes the speaker less significant or worthy because the speaker measures him- or herself over against some greater or more notable person or being (Gen 18:27; 1 Chr 17:16).

SELF-INTRODUCTION FORMULA (Selbstvorstellungs-). Exod 6:2. A formula by which a speaker reveals his or her identity to an addressee by announcing his or her name. While individuals occasionally use this pattern of speech in the OT, e.g., Joseph in Gen 45:4, a major interest centers on Yahweh's use of this formula in the expression "I am Yahweh" or "I am Yahweh your God."

In theophanies the formula serves to reveal the otherwise uncertain identity of the deity speaking, and thus inherently expresses an element of gracious freedom, but a variety of other aspects can also be involved. Since "I am Yahweh your God" can function as the first half of a (→) covenant formula, its use at the beginning or end of paragraphs of laws can function to identify the role of these commandments as marks of Israel's peoplehood, i.e., as being a way of expressing what "you are my people" means. This usage is particularly common in Leviticus 17–26, but cf. also Pss 50:7; 81:11 (*NRSV* 10). In Isaiah 40–55 it functions as part of messages of reassurance (e.g., Isa 48:17), and in Ezekiel it plays a role in the (→) recognition formula.

SELF-REVELATION FORMULA (IDENTIFICATION) (Selbstoffenbarungs-, Selbstenthüllungs-). Exod 3:6a; 6:2bβ. Constructed with the first-person pronoun "I" (*'ānî*) plus a proper noun, especially a name (Gen 15:1b; 15:7; 17:1ba; 24:24; 26:24; 27:19; 28:13aβ; 31:13a; 35:11-12; 45:39; 45:3, 4; 46:3-4).

TRANSITION FORMULA (Überleitungs-). Exod 1:6, 8; 2:11, 23aα, 24. A variety of temporal or circumstantial phrases employed to introduce a new phase or episode in narration (1 Chr 2:22; 20:1, 44; 21:28; 29:21; 2 Chr 1:7; 7:8; 16:7; 18:2; 20:1, 35; 21:8, 18-19; 24:17, 23; 25:14, 27; 28:16; 32:1; 33:14; 35:14). Cf. FOTL XI, 439.